MY LIFE AS A DAME

MY LIFE AS A DAME

The PERSONAL and the POLITICAL in the WRITINGS of

CHRISTINA McCALL

edited by **STEPHEN CLARKSON**
foreword by **ELEANOR WACHTEL**

ANANSI

This edition published in 2008 by
House of Anansi Press Inc.
110 Spadina Avenue, Suite 801
Toronto, ON, M5V 2K4
Tel. 416-363-4343
Fax 416-363-1017
www.anansi.ca

Distributed in Canada by
HarperCollins Canada Ltd.
1995 Markham Road
Scarborough, ON, M1B 5M8
Toll free tel. 1-800-387-0117

Distributed in the United States by
Publishers Group West
1700 Fourth Street
Berkeley, CA 94710
Toll free tel. 1-800-788-3123

House of Anansi Press is committed to protecting our natural environment.
As part of our efforts, this book is printed on paper that contains 100%
post-consumer recycled fibres, is acid-free, and is processed chlorine-free.

12 11 10 09 08   1 2 3 4 5

Library and Archives Canada Cataloguing in Publication Data
McCall, Christina, 1936–2005
My life as a dame : the personal and the political in the writings of Christina McCall /
by Christina McCall ; edited by Stephen Clarkson.

ISBN 978-0-88784-221-4 (bound)

1. Canada—Politics and government—1945–. 2. Canada—Social conditions — 1945–.
3. McCall, Christina, 1936–2005. 4. Journalists — Canada — Biography.
I. Clarkson, Stephen, 1937– II. Title.

FC600.M35 2008   971.064   C2007-907241-0

Jacket design: Ingrid Paulson
Jacket photo: Courtesy of Stephen Clarkson
Text design and typesetting: Ingrid Paulson

 Canada Council   Conseil des Arts    ONTARIO ARTS COUNCIL
for the Arts   du Canada   CONSEIL DES ARTS DE L'ONTARIO

*We acknowledge for their financial support of our publishing program
the Canada Council for the Arts, the Ontario Arts Council, and the Government of Canada
through the Book Publishing Industry Development Program (BPIDP).*

Printed and bound in Canada

Contents

Foreword by Eleanor Wachtel 1

Introduction 5

PART I THE JOURNALIST'S JOURNEY 11

1 My Life as a Dame: Chapter 1 15
2 My Life as a Dame: Chapter 2 37
3 The Prospector in the Pink Penthouse 44
4 The New Machismo 54
5 Mag Cult: The Opiate of the Faddists 62
6 Lapping It Up 66

PART II CANADIAN SOCIETY: THE LOW AND THE HIGH 75

7   Springhill: The Town That Won't Give Up 81
8   The New Power in the New West 89
9   The Long Ordeal of William Wilder 101
10 Canadian Cities: Let's Cherish Their Safety While We May 114
11 Politics and Pornography: The Yonge Street Cleanup 120
12 Requiem for the High Life 129
13 Cathedral of Chic 136

PART III FEMINIST IN ARMS 151

14 Strong Women Who Could Endure 155

15 Some Awkward Truths the Royal Commission Missed..........162

16 Down with Alimony...167

17 The Split Syndrome...172

18 In Ottawa, Women Are Either Babes or Blobs...................176

19 Women and Political Power: What's Holding Us Back? 182

PART IV **THE DRAMA OF POLITICS** **193**

20 The Unlikely Gladiators:
    Pearson and Diefenbaker Remembered...........................201

21 The End of an Era...215

22 What Was Important About the Gordon Commission..........222

23 How Mel Watkins Brought Socialism to the NDP...............228

24 Growing Up Reluctantly...238

25 The 10 Percent Solution: Canada's Colonial Neurosis..........249

26 The Unquiet American..253

27 De Gaulle's Gaffe Was a Pivotal Point for Canada..............261

28 Learning French Is No Longer a Courtesy in Ottawa..........266

29 Ten Years: From the Quiet Revolution
    to the Apprehended Insurrection.................................271

30 Bridging the Great Canadian Divide 276

31 Our Heroes on the Russian Front.................................280

32 The Exotic Mindscape of Pierre Trudeau........................294

33 Bowing Out: John Turner's Resignation 308

34 Jim Coutts and the Politics of Manipulation 313

ENDPIECE **341**

35 What Won't Appear in My Next Paradise.........................345

    After Words...349
    Index..363

Foreword

IN HOWARD HAWKS'S 1940 classic, *His Girl Friday*, Rosalind Russell plays the feisty, fast-talking reporter Hildy Johnson, the only woman covering the story, who can write better than anyone, including her boss (and ex-husband), played by Cary Grant. How unusual it was to find a woman in that role is borne out by the fact that in *The Front Page*, the Broadway hit that the movie was based on, Hildy was a man. (Apparently Hildebrand became Hildegard when Hawks's secretary was reading the script to him and he realized the comic potential.) But here was Rosalind Russell, wisecracking, witty, and brilliant, and looking great in a tailored suit and matching hat. It's an image that not only fits Christina McCall but inspired her, "a part," she says, "that fuelled the fantasy I never really got over." With her own beauty, smarts, and dedication—and the fact that she was often the only woman on the scene—Christina was in many ways the star woman journalist of her time. A gifted dame in a man's world.

"Euphoric and a little defiant" is how she described herself at twenty-one, fresh out of university and loving her job at *Maclean's* as an editorial secretary. Within a year, she had a feature story published in the magazine. But as she later acknowledged, she started out as a young writer "in a field that was poisonously misogynist." By choosing to call her planned memoir *My Life as a Dame*, she subverts and empowers in one stroke, a Rosalind Russell for the twenty-first century.

The first chapter of the book you hold in your hands is the memoir, which vividly captures Christina's ambitions and dreams during her final year at college. For me, it's heartbreaking to read because, quite simply, I want more; she was overtaken by illness and intolerable pain before she could finish it. But she left us with a selection of her writings that reveals the richness and acuity of her observations and intelligence — and even glimpses of what might have become part of that autobiography; for instance, her letter to her much-admired friend, Madeleine Gobeil ["Strong Women Who Could Endure," 1975].

Christina McCall was born in Toronto in 1935, the third of four children, and the first in her family to attend university. Her father was an Ulsterman who had emigrated to Canada on his own as a teenager and — as she puts it —"involved himself in the Presbyterian Church and the Conservative Party." He was a firefighter and, later, a municipal building inspector. Her mother, attractive, dramatic, had been a nurse. Christina alludes to her difficult relationship with them, as she wrote to me once in response to my interview with the American, sometime "dirty realist" novelist, Russell Banks. Banks had talked about how tragic his father's life had been, how he didn't want to be like him, that at the centre of his life "lay a great and terrible mystery, and if I could only somehow solve it, I could go on." Solving it meant neither sentimentalizing nor judging either of them. "So much of what Banks said had resonance with me," she wrote, "when he spoke of the mystery of our relationship with our parents."

Christina describes here how long it took her to learn to enjoy life, a pleasure "heightened by memories of my childhood — which you could almost see gave me the fortitude to appreciate the very real rigours of joy."

I had the opportunity to understand that appreciation about ten years ago, when we became friends, soon after she returned from a year's sabbatical in Florence. Not surprisingly, for someone who appreciated style and beauty, she loved Italy. But she was also engaged by the politics and feminism she encountered there; she wanted to write a book about Italy. (Canada, or rather Toronto, she viewed with a certain detachment, wariness, even disappointment.) A couple of years later, she made a brief return trip and came back with a present. I had already been struck by her impressive good taste, but this was my first experience of her impeccable eye. She brought me an exquisite pair of cashmere-lined leather gloves from the famous Madova factory: the precise shade of brown of a new coat I had bought, and, moreover, exactly the correct size. When I expressed amazement that she would know my glove size (after all, *I* don't), she dismissed it as nothing special; she had noticed my hands.

Christina's discerning eye is evident throughout this book, whether she is writing about social trends or fledgling nationalists. In a rather acerbic essay in the late 1970s, about fads and how marriage was suddenly deemed out of fashion (although she herself had just remarried), she writes: "A few weeks before the [wedding] ceremony, I was standing waiting to hear a lecture on 'Sexual Equality in Scandinavia and other Utopian Tales,' when a woman came up to greet me, having only lately learned my news. After an exchange of small civilities, she widened her eyes, which were rimmed with a pale and luminous liner, laid her manicured hand on mine, and whispered so that no one else could hear, 'But my dear, don't you feel funny about it — just a little bit *quaint*? I mean — and the bracelets jangled on her wrist to emphasize her concern — 'nobody's getting married any more.'"

Of course, the great thing about Christina was that she flawlessly translated that astute eye and ear into writing of unique perception and psychological depth. *Maclean's* editor Ken Whyte called her "the best political writer in Canada." Political adviser and analyst John Duffy recently wrote that "No work in the Canadian political library can truly compare with Christina McCall's *Grits: An Intimate Portrait of the Liberal Party* (1982)." So the bold, insightful political pieces here will come as no surprise. More, Christina had talent as a social historian. See the way she writes about not just Pearson and Diefenbaker but also their wives. Or her incisive, deadpan account of Trudeau's honeymoon in the U.S.S.R., her evocation of the nascent nationalism of Walter Gordon, the socialism of Mel Watkins.

Initially, Christina viewed her literary (as opposed to social-science) education as a disadvantage in her career, but I think she came to value it. Certainly she read widely and responded enthusiastically in notes and phone calls to many of the writers I interviewed, though I remember one instance when she read Muriel Spark's memoir. "I read *Curriculum Vitae*," she wrote me, "and didn't like it or her — but learned a lot about what I don't want to do in my book and why."

To me, as to all her friends, Christina was very generous in her interest, encouragement, and support. She was a superb editor as well as writer. Editing is an invisible, even selfless craft, the obverse of the necessary egotism of the writer. Yet Christina embodied both sides of that divide, in keeping with the fascinating and complex "dame" that is revealed in this book.

— *Eleanor Wachtel*
December 2007

Introduction

"**WHEN DID MS. MCCALL** write that piece?" the woman from *Maclean's* asked over the phone. She was checking a few details about "What Won't Appear in My Next Paradise," which the magazine's editor, Ken Whyte, had agreed to publish as a memorial to his colleague, who had died the week before. When I answered "1969," I could hear her gasp in astonishment. The essay's feminist edge and stylistic brio had clearly spoken to this young journalist, who was not even born when the text was penned. This exchange made me think it might be worth bringing Christina's exceptional opus to twenty-first century women and men.

It doesn't much matter whether Christina McCall was the best political writer of her generation, as the then editor of *Saturday Night,* Robert Fulford, once called her. I have brought together this selection from her writings for two different, though related, reasons. First, I wanted to make it easy for readers to savour the sheer brilliance of her writing. One contemporary recalled recently how she used to await Christina's monthly column, "Ottawa Letter," the way she now longs for the next Hendrik Hertzberg editorial in *The New Yorker.* They were engaging, humorous, intelligent articles — elegant and stylish, feminist and nationalist, authoritative but wry. "There was a thrill to it; her work had a quality you didn't see in other writers. She saw through things, while still being funny and irreverent. It was so liberating — something fresh which broadened the way we thought about politics."

Her writing's past glory is one thing; its quality is justification enough to republish her best journalism, and, indeed, she was a role model for a number of younger writers. Its relevance is quite another, and pertinence in the present is the second raison d'être for this volume. Nurtured under the mentorship of her much-admired editors — Ralph Allen at *Maclean's*, then Doris Anderson at *Chatelaine*, Dic Doyle at the *Globe and Mail*, Bob Fulford at *Saturday Night* — Christina's self-declared mission was to write for the general Canadian reader. She distilled information about the world — theories from academe, happenings in the hinterland, trends in the city — into pithy, penetrating, lively, touching essays that helped her readers understand the society they lived in; the cultural forces that were transforming it; and most of all its politics, whether at the local, provincial, federal, or sometimes international level.

As I pored through the selections a year after her death to see how they might make a coherent volume, I started to worry that their context might not be obvious to younger audiences. So it occurred to me that each article's significance might be highlighted more effectively if it were commented on by someone who could interpret it for the new reader. There ensued much e-mail traffic as I approached more than fifty people, asking them to write a paragraph or two of commentary. Their reflections on each piece, which are assembled in the final "After Words" section, offer a dialogue between Christina's lively brain at the time of writing and those who are still engaged in the same issues with which she was engrossed.

Some of these commentaries were written by her closest friends

(Libby Burnham), some by fellow feminists (Chaviva Hošek), some by journalistic colleagues (Martin Knelman). Others were composed by writers who knew her only by her publications (Anne Kingston), still others by the person she profiled (Mel Watkins). I was enormously gratified by the enthusiasm with which these people responded to my invitation and hugely grateful for both their prompt responses and their patience as we polished their texts.

. . .

Honourable Senators, I rise to pay tribute to the late Christina McCall.

If I had a favourite saint, it would be the Apostle St. Thomas, the eternal sceptic, who questioned and doubted the conventional wisdom of his peers and raised questions about the very nature of the human condition.

For me, it could not have been more appropriate that Christina McCall's funeral service be held at Saint Thomas's Anglican Church in the heart of old Toronto, for she was, as all great journalists are, a creative sceptic.

Great writers, like candles, illuminate the darkness enveloping the human condition. The writer's art is to pull together disparate threads and weave them into an authentic, vibrant story, making sense of what apparently is senseless. So it was with Christina McCall.

To those who treasure the written word, Christina was herself a treasure. Breathtakingly beautiful, she carried herself with effortless grace and looked the part of the elegant Rosedale matron that she was. Yet beneath this elegant veneer was a vulnerable, restless, energetic, insightfully brilliant writer. She had a deep, velvety, smoky voice and dark melancholy eyes. Christina spoke purposely, quietly, and slowly. It was always difficult to concentrate on the subject at hand because of the charm she exuded. She was admired by women and men alike, and entranced and enchanted all who came to know her. My mother taught me that a lady wore a hat and gloves. Christina did, and she was. She wrote as beautifully as she looked. Because of her own complex personal experiences, she could parse the complex passions and contradictions at play and that were displayed within the body politic. For her, there was never a glass ceiling.

Christina became a leading political chronicler of her time, and at times she outshone all her peers with her luminous prose and exquisite insights.

As a writer and journalist, she was meticulous in her preparations. She always came prepared with research and notes that she took copiously. She would pause to reread her notes and relaunch her enquiries. Christina could penetrate to the essence with soft, rapier-like questions, always touching the inner core of any subject she was exploring under the prism of her own personal microscope.

She was the very model of journalist and writer, and we will not likely meet her equal again. While she wrote of the foibles and the failures of politics, she never ever tarnished its noble purpose.

To adapt the metaphor she wrote of Pierre Trudeau, her beauty and brilliance "haunts us still." With her passing, the still unlimned political anatomy of our country is darker and dimmer because her bright light was so prematurely extinguished.

To her three beautiful, loving daughters and her husband, Stephen, we can only share a portion of their pain of her passage and the marvellous remembrance of glowing moments passed. Her own words, lustrous words, will forever carve a lasting memorial to her memory.

—*Honourable Jerahmiel S. Grafstein*

. . .

I hope the four parts of this anthology will provide the "lustrous words" of my late partner — eulogized so movingly by Jerahmiel Grafstein in the Senate on May 3, 2005 — with the lasting memorial they deserve.

Part I, "The Journalist's Journey," begins with the last pages she wrote before her death, when she was drafting a memoir about her life in publishing. They depict her literary aspirations as a university undergraduate and recount how she became a magazine writer. Other articles present her critiques of journalism and journalists, machismo and the media. The second section, "Canadian Society: The Low and the High," samples her writings about small towns and provinces across the country as well as her insights into city life. Part III, "Feminist in Arms," then gives a taste of her powerful opus on the plight of Canadian women, and Part IV, "The Drama of Politics," offers selections from the work for which she is best remembered, her writings on federal politics.

Long hours were spent in the university library by my friend Toby Zanin, who tracked down and read through every article Christina had written, critiqued and photocopied the most promising, and put together a proposed selection that I've reworked and reordered. Toby Zanin's complete bibliography of her writings will be found on the House of Anansi web site. Zahra Habib patiently created an electronic text by dictating and proofing every article. My next debt of gratitude goes to Meg Taylor, who took a 600-page manuscript and cut it back to 400. Last, I want to thank those whose commentaries are printed at the end of the book and another dozen who wrote introductions to articles that were subsequently cut when the manuscript had to be slimmed down to publishable size.

Readers will come upon occasional words and phrases that may now appear archaic or politically incorrect. "Indian" was the mainstream adjective applied to Canada's Native peoples. Even though Oxford's Canadian dictionary lists "bugger all" as British coarse slang, the prevailing professional code only let Christina write "b— all."

My Life as a Dame is the title she had chosen for the autobiographical reflections on which she was working when she fell ill. For her, the "dame" was ironic, a play on the pejorative connotation with which North American male journalists still infused it in the 1950s when dismissing women as "dumb broads." In retrospect, the phrase has a double entendre since, in the British lexicon, "Dame" is a title conferred by the Crown to ennoble a woman for her great achievements. Christina McCall's achievement was in surmounting the obstacles to "dames" in journalism, in providing a model to many women who also aspired to do great writing. Her claim to nobility is her printed legacy.

Nothing gave Christina greater pleasure than to receive a letter from a secretary or a carpenter thanking her for helping them understand the contradictions of British Columbia's politics or a federal cabinet minister's mixed motivations. She overworked relentlessly as she strove to understand her subjects, then wrote and rewrote her drafts till they had been purged of jargon and the research had been kneaded until her text became a seamless whole. Nothing would give our daughters and me greater pleasure than to learn that, even beyond the grave, Christina's writings can still enlighten, inspire, delight, and thrill her readers.

— SC

PART I

The Journalist's Journey

THIS SECTION STARTS with the first and only completed chapter for the memoir Christina was writing as debilitating illnesses were invading her body. Her self-portrait starts in her last year at University of Toronto's Victoria College, where, as a student of Northrop Frye, she experienced the epiphany of intellectual liberation, which turned her toward writing.

We continue with the last pages Christina managed to write when chronic pain resulting from breast cancer surgery had disabled her left arm and the stealthily spreading ravages of Parkinson's disease were making her right hand's once-elegant handwriting increasingly illegible. She describes how she apprenticed in what was then Canada's only successful commercial magazine. *Maclean's*, of course, was a bastion of male power in which the writing of serious articles was done by men and only the fluff pieces were assigned to the "dames." Although she started by doing the typical Jane-jobs — making coffee, cleaning up the men's messes — her talent soon prevailed. The editorial staff was astonished when she handed in her first assignment: a brilliant profile of Viola MacMillan, who, far ahead of the women's movement, headed up the mining industry's lobby association. "The Prospector in the Pink Penthouse" was accepted without revision.

After that come three pieces that span her whole career and engage with the foibles and fantasies of her professional culture. "The New Machismo" takes off from the CBC television soap star Bruno Gerussi to explore the manners of the "new masculinity" — a foretaste of Harvey

Mansfield's recent *Manliness*. Already we can see how she places the realm of lived experience within the larger terrain of the media matrix. Long before Naomi Wolf's *The Beauty Myth* and Naomi Klein's *No Logo*, "Mag Cult: The Opiate of the Faddists" elaborates on the way that the magazine industry tyrannizes popular attitudes by addicting readers to the latest trend that it creates. This selection of Christina's writing about Canadian journalism ends with the last article she published in *Saturday Night*. "Lapping It Up" discusses one of the most serious issues with which political journalists have to deal — how close can they get to the politicians they are covering without compromising their objectivity?

— SC

ONE

My Life as a Dame: Chapter 1

IN SEPTEMBER OF 1955, when I enrolled in my fourth and final year as an undergraduate at the University of Toronto, I was twenty years old, only a few months away from the freedom of adult life beyond the university's sheltering walls. Just before the term began, I copied on the inside cover of a new notebook a quote from Milton: "Thy years are ripe and overripe."[i]

I meant this to be a witty epigraph in the ironic style of the English writers I admired. But however much I still revelled in the affectations of academe, the conviction that it was time to get on with my life engrossed me as I moved around the campus that September, my brain teeming with anxieties of various kinds.

Not the least of these was my need to distance myself from my classmates, all those good girls with shiny hair and diamond engagement rings, taking careful notes around me in the lecture rooms, preparing themselves for worthy careers as school teachers or librarians who would mutate before long into stay-at-home wives and mothers in the prosperous Ontario towns from which most of them had sprung.

I was in a state of silent rebellion against what I saw as their unbearably boring fate, an attitude made manifest by the black turtleneck sweaters and thick mascara I had taken to wearing and the cigarettes I chain-smoked when I met my friends for coffee to exchange ideas about literature, love, sex, what constituted exciting work, and how to have a future that involved all four.

Fifteen years later, when the second-wave feminist movement was under way, I described those conversations to a psychiatrist I was consulting about my problems with juggling marriage, motherhood, and work. A magpie of a woman who was discarding the dicta of Sigmund Freud for the theories of Fritz Perls, she broke into my description of the faintly pleasurable melancholia I had felt that last undergraduate autumn by saying that I was talking nonsense.

"You must have been depressed," she said in her thick Hungarian accent. "You didn't know what to do with your life and you were unable to say you were afraid."

She was right about one thing: my fear of showing fear, particularly in the presence of my parents. Any expression of concern about my future evoked one of my mother's standard exhortations, "Just think of how lucky you are!" followed by one of her favourite quotations, "Be good, sweet maid, and let who can be clever; / Do lovely things, not dream them, all day long."[ii]

My father, a Presbyterian of dour demeanour, was of a different cast of mind. He frequently expressed the firm opinion that I already had more education than any woman needed. It was time I found a job.

On this, if on few other subjects, he and I were in total agreement. But just what kind of job was feasible — given the contrast between the narrow opportunities for women in the provincial city in which I had grown up and the extravagant ambitions engendered by my rarefied education and overheated imagination — was the main source of my anxieties.

Three years earlier, when I entered the university fresh from a venerable Toronto collegiate with high academic standards, I had the makings of a good girl/worthy woman myself. Outwardly calm and compliant, I wanted to study literature because I loved to read. Just how a career could be made out of an intoxication with books was far from clear, though I was certain that my life would turn out well.

Subtly, almost imperceptibly at first, the university had changed me, made me dissatisfied with my society, my family, my peers, and, most of all, myself, by demanding that I learn to think. And that I demonstrate this capacity by regularly writing essays on subjects that were mostly arcane for professors who were mostly august and by voicing my views in tutorials led by their teaching assistants, who were often withering in response to undergraduates' inchoate opinions.

My first two years in the rigorous honours course in English Language and Literature were like an apprenticeship ordeal. It didn't occur to me then how odd it was that my classmates — most of whom were women — and I were being trained as critics in a country with virtually no literary tradition of its own and very few indigenous journals in which the literature of our borrowed British culture was discussed, and in a university where the faculty's widespread disdain for women's brains was barely disguised.

Honours English students were expected to encompass our subject in its magnificent entirety by the end of our fourth year in order to pass a notoriously difficult comprehensive examination. In our freshman and sophomore years we were introduced to our task through courses in Anglo-Saxon; Chaucer; Shakespeare; the prose and poetry of the sixteenth and early seventeenth century; and the dramatists, poets, and elegant essayists of the Restoration and eighteenth century. So we could understand the context of the literature we were studying, this heavy load was supplemented by courses in British, European, and Greek and Roman history; ancient and early modern philosophy; Greek and Latin literature; and French poetry and drama.

Docile in manner, honoured to be thought capable of mastering so formidable a curriculum, we tottered home on weekends under the weight of the books we borrowed from the university's libraries. Plato, Bede, Donne, Bacon, Racine, Corneille, Montaigne, Johnson, Pope, Voltaire, Addison, Pepys, Chesterfield, and dozens of others of what was later called the Western canon, as well as their explicators and detractors, were absorbed or at least paged through carefully. Our heads spun. Our stomachs churned. How would we remember all this when the annual examinations rolled around in April, let alone when the time came for the dreaded comprehensive?

Our insecurities, occasionally discussed among ourselves, were rarely stilled by contact with our professors, who seemed as impervious to our feelings as they were inexpressive of their own.

"This seems harmless enough, apart from the fact that on the second page, you've mistaken Sophocles for Socrates," a young philosophy instructor drawled, while handing back one of my early efforts at essay writing, 2,000 tortured words on Plato's theory of the soul.

I was too intimidated to respond that the mistake, though a dumb one, was a typing error. Harried by a workload beyond anything my high school had prepared me for, I had been writing a second essay for a course in Greek drama that was due the same day as the philosophy paper and had typed both of them very late the night before their deadlines. The instructor's condescension had causes I didn't understand for years. He was an Englishman and an Oxonian. I was a woman and a Canadian.

His kind of supercilious attitude had been endemic in the university before, during, and immediately after the Second World War, when most of the important professors were either Brits enticed by better positions than they could command at home to teach in this outpost of the fading Empire, or Canadians who had won graduate scholarships to English or Scottish universities and had returned from their years abroad as pseudo-Brits with mid-Atlantic accents and mannerisms.

By 1953, when my philosophy instructor was belittling me and my classmates with his sarcasms, he was already an anachronism, at least among the younger academics who had done graduate work in the United States and were affecting a breezier, more democratic — though scarcely less misogynist — style.

Women were still barely tolerated in the loftier reaches of academe, though they had gained the right to higher education nearly seventy years before. It was acceptable for them to study Household Science or Physical and Occupational Therapy or to enrol in Pass Arts, a three-year general course that led, as a stale joke had it, to twin degrees, a B.A. and an MRS.

The male students automatically took on the professors' attitudes. The annual song dance and satire show at my college staged a skit one year featuring Patsy Pass Arts, the Headless Girl. At the college orientation weekend, freshman women were told that when they sang the college song, which began with the line, "My father sent me to Victoria and vowed that I should *be* a man," they should remember to change the last phrase to "vowed that I should *get* a man." Nobody objected. Almost everybody laughed.

Women in honours courses who survived those first two undergraduate years became, if not exactly inured to the humiliations some of the dons dished out, at least better able to cope with their effect through hard work and occasional bursts of self-affirmative rhetoric. My own cohort knew that our third and fourth years would be given over almost entirely to the study of literature and that at Victoria College these were also the years when students in Honours English came under the tutelage of Northrop Frye, who had a reputation for being just and straightforward with his students.

In its college system and a myriad other ways, the University of Toronto in the 1950s reflected its roots in the British colonial Canada of the previous century. The professional schools and the teaching of the physical and social sciences came directly under the university's control. But students in the arts were enrolled in (and were mostly taught at) autonomous colleges that reflected the hierarchical and sectarian nature of Ontario society. Anglicans went to Trinity, the establishment college; nonconformist Protestants to Victoria; Roman Catholics to St. Michael's; and everybody else to University College, which had no religious affiliation and attracted Jewish students and other "ethnics" as a consequence. [iii]

That I had chosen Victoria without even considering the other colleges was appropriate to my upbringing and my temperament. Vic had been founded in the eastern Ontario town of Cobourg more than a hundred years before by radical Methodists, dissenters from Anglicanism who eventually made common cause with a breakaway group of Presbyterians to form the United Church of Canada. They were people who had "set their faces against any establishment . . . ecclesiastical, political, or social," [iv] as Kathleen Coburn, one of our professors, described them. Many of them were farmers or small businessmen. A few waxed rich, and the college benefited from the largesse of these Methodist millionaires (the Masseys, the Flavelles, and later the Jackmans) and their descendants, although the custom in Canada at the time was for rich and/or ambitious Protestants to move up the social scale by defecting to the Anglican Church.

All I knew about Victoria's rich history before I enrolled there was that one of my high school teachers had told me that the great Canadian scholar in the field of English literature was Northrop Frye and that Victoria was where he held sway.

When I encountered him first, Frye was in his early forties, just settling in as chairman of Vic's English department, already acclaimed for

Fearful Symmetry, his study of William Blake, writing his famous book, *Anatomy of Criticism*, attracting invitations to lecture at Princeton and Harvard and to publish in important learned journals in the U.S. and the U.K., early indications of his brilliant international reputation as a literary theorist that was to grow more luminous as he aged. At Victoria even then, his fame as a lecturer was harped on by older students so insistently that my cohort grew impatient with the hyperbole.

Frye can't be that good, we told each other with sophomoric cynicism. They're making him out to be a demigod. We were wrong, of course. He was that good, as we were to find out in the first hour of the first course he taught us in the fall of our third year.

Years later I described my response to that lecture in a magazine article about university life in the 1950s:

"[Frye] came into a classroom one September afternoon, wearing an academic gown that was rusty with age, stood behind the lecturer's podium, looked out at us through his rimless glasses, and began to talk about John Milton in a voice devoid of passion. By the time he had finished speaking fifty minutes later, almost everybody in the room was in the grip of an intellectual excitement of a kind we had never known, and that night I wrote in a Commonplace Book I was pretentiously keeping, 'I think my head is coming off.'" [v]

When John Ayre quoted this paragraph in his 1989 biography of Frye, he preceded it with a couple of sentences that first made me laugh and then made me fume. "[Frye's] effect, particularly on girls, was legendary," Ayre wrote. "Christina McCall confessed to virtual intellectual rape in her first classes with Frye in 1954." [vi]

Ayre apparently didn't understand what I intended to convey and, on the evidence of comments elsewhere in his generally admirable book, he never would. He ridiculed women students by suggesting they were groupies who hung around the great man's office, the implication being that Frye's appeal was not scholarly but sexual. If young women were particularly responsive to Frye's clarity of mind, it had to do with the fact that in the 1950s they constituted a majority of his undergraduate students. Nobody I knew thought Frye was sexy. Marlon Brando was sexy. Frye was Olympian.

What we experienced in his presence was the luxury of being part of a community of learning where men and women were treated as equals.

As if to underline his egalitarian attitude to teaching, Frye drew our attention to a quotation inscribed in the college chapel from Thomas Carlyle to the effect that after a lifetime of learning, Carlyle still felt himself to be like a child playing in the sand by the sea of knowledge. Frye elaborated on Carlyle's maxim by saying that by the time you reach middle age, you know what you know and that it isn't very much. The student of necessity stands below the teacher. But they both stand under the discipline.

What Frye had to say about literature over the next several university terms, we copied into our notebooks. What he had to say — glancingly, it seemed at the time, purposefully, it seems in retrospect — about work, God, Satan, modernism, the true purpose of a university, the British colonial world in which he and we had been raised, and the place of Victoria College in that world, we absorbed by osmosis. In my case, his ideas affected how I viewed literature and politics for the next several decades.

FRYE REMARKED ONCE that the university's purpose was to rattle students out of their middle-class complacency, and rattled (rather than depressed) is what I felt in the early weeks of my last undergraduate September as I tried to figure out my future. The easy career choices (teachers' college, library school, early marriage) I had disdained long since. The hard ones (graduate school, theatre criticism, world travel) seemed too fanciful to contemplate.

But as the autumn term sped on, I decided that, come what may, I would *not* be stuck for the rest of my life in the Southern Ontario fatlands, waiting for the region's endemic self-satisfaction to overtake me. I wanted to be a worldly somebody. I intended to have an interesting life.

Once I concocted this vague escape plan, everything that followed in the next few months seemed to help me on my way.

I had written during the previous summer a long essay for a prize that the college bestowed annually on a senior student in the name of an alumnus who had died in France, fighting for the Empire during the Great War.

Though I didn't know it, my choice of subject was a bold one: Morley Callaghan, a Canadian novelist and short-story writer much published in the United States, a familiar of Hemingway, Fitzgerald, and Edmund Wilson, and an outspoken, cantankerous, decidedly not cautiously Canadian panellist on the CBC talk show, *Fighting Words*.

I spent many a hot night in libraries that summer after my day job in a publishing house was done, reading everything Callaghan had written and everything I could find written about him. I even overcame the shyness that had seized me in pubescence and still had me by the throat, and approached Callaghan's editors at Macmillan of Canada to see if I might look through their Callaghan files. Callaghan's fiction, his letters, his reviews in American magazines and newspapers all seemed to me vibrant and real. Under their influence, I wrote the essay in a transcendent state of excitement, convinced I was going to win.

But in early October, when the notice announcing the prize was pinned on the college bulletin board, the student named was a close friend who had written a paper using unassailable scholarly secondary sources on the English playwright Christopher Fry, whose name was on the fourth-year reading list, as Callaghan's was not.

"Bugger, bugger, bugger," I muttered to myself as I turned away from the notice board, fighting tears. (Help! My mascara will run.) Minutes later, I met a professor who had served on the prize committee.

"Ahh, Mith McCall," he lisped in greeting. "Fel-ith-itations on your eth-ay. It was well argued and well written. *Such* a pity you chose a subject that was merely folkloric."

I smiled demurely while thinking furiously: This time, it's not just me who's being patronized. It's Callaghan and Canada. I cannot let this prith-ath get away with it. I *must* write and say what I think.

What's the Matter with Callaghan?

Sometimes I feel like screaming that question at people when I hear them talking about Morley Callaghan. I never can, though. The discussions I get involved in about Callaghan always seem to be carried on calmly, urbanely, unemotionally, dully — they're about as remote from screaming as they are from living. So, instead of screaming, I collect silly statements about Callaghan. Within the last six months I heard these three comments about *the* Canadian novelist.

At the Royal Alex one night last fall, a very learned woman, for whose opinions both about literature and living I usually have a great deal of respect, heard Callaghan's name mentioned and said, in her beautiful voice, that a friend of hers knew "Morley" and was "very amused by his garageman manner." The phrase sounded something like this — "gare-awge man mannah." All I have ever seen of garagemen is their feet sticking out from under cars but if their "mannah" is like Callaghan's, I wish I knew a few of them.

About two weeks later, in an English seminar, we were discussing which Canadian novelist should be studied on a modern novel course. Callaghan's name was brought up for discussion and it had a rather strange effect. A shudder shook the scholarly soul of the presiding professor and he murmured in horror, "Oh God, no — not that dreadful book, *The Loved and the Lost*." It was decided we should study Ethel Wilson's *The Education of Love* and Hugh MacLennan's *Barometer Rising*, both of which are good Canadian novels. *The Loved and the Lost* is a better one.

There's also the comment I heard from an Honours English graduate who makes her living buying short stories for a large magazine. She had been talking to Callaghan and, after a discussion with him, she made this brilliant statement: "Why, Callaghan was raving about how gorgeous Ava Gardner is. That just shows what kind of mind he has." Ernest Hemingway also has been quoted as saying that Ava Gardner is gorgeous and is known to have called Marlene Dietrich "that fabulous Kraut," but neither opinion seems to have prevented him from winning the Nobel Prize.

Callaghan himself complained recently in a magazine article about the kind of criticism he receives from the native book reviewers. He quotes a newspaper critic who stoutly stated that he knew many Montrealers and none of them was as fond of liquor as the characters in *The Loved and the Lost*. This is the kind of criticism Callaghan's work inspires all too often. He is accused of writing about cheap, inarticulate, unimaginative people in a sensational manner. Scorn is heaped upon his head because he has failed to learn anything from his acquaintance with James Joyce. They call him "dead-end-facing Callaghan" or a brittle, technically smart writer, imitating an American fashion.

I like Callaghan. In coming to his defence, I don't want to overpraise him. I just want him to be given a fair reading and a fair judgement as a novelist and short-story writer.

I often think we are too close to Callaghan the person to judge him impartially. He lives in Toronto and he often speaks at various meetings around the city. He can be heard on the radio and seen on TV discussion panels. Once in a while he writes excited articles in national magazines. His novels are set in Toronto or Montreal. He is a part of our lives and people don't bother to place him in the context of American fiction in which he belongs.

There is another problem in making a judgement of Callaghan. He has written hundreds of excellent short stories and is known in the United States as one of the very best of living short-story writers. But in his eight novels, which employ the same style, express the same ideas, he has not achieved a great deal. His novels are never mediocre but they invariably fail perhaps because they aim so high.

His chief virtue, in both the novels and the short stories, is his prose style. His style is controlled and economical, yet his language is never tight or strained. He writes with casual clarity about casual peo-ple, yet he manages to give his prose and his people a depth of feeling.

He specializes in flashes of insight, and in such moments his language is particularly effective. Frequently, a single sentence will contain the core meaning for a story or a chapter of a novel. His method is to give a concise picture of life, and in one sentence to illuminate it at the precise moment when it has its fullest meaning. This technique is brilliant when used in the short stories, but in the novels it tends to fall flat. The situations are too thin, the characters too unreal.

If Callaghan's greatest virtue is his style, his greatest fault is his moral flabbiness. His characters suffer from the inequalities and cruelties attached to living and from their own personal weaknesses. Callaghan lashes out at the forces that make the plight of man so ugly. However, the only remedies he can offer for such huge evils as racial prejudice and selfish egocentricity are vague things like tenderness and compassion. He has never established a firm set of values or a clear, philosophical basis on which to build his reading of life.

It might be said that Callaghan has a dominant theme — a belief in the integrity of every individual — and a dominant response to life — compassion for his fellow man.

These are random judgements of Callaghan; they should be tied
to specific examples from his work. This is not complete or competent criticism. It is intended merely to show that Callaghan deserves
a reading. He has been praised by the best Canadian critics — sometimes lightly, sometimes lavishly. Northrop Frye has called him "a
highly trained and experienced novelist." Desmond Pacey said that
"no other Canadian novelist aims so high nor comes so close." William
Arthur Deacon wrote about Callaghan's "integrity and command of
craftsmanship."

Callaghan is a good writer of fiction. Read the collections of his
short stories, *Now That April's Here* and *Native Argosy*, and you'll recognize the truth of that statement.

— *Acta Victoriana*, March 1956

My ideas positioned me, I decided, on the side of the advocates of
the life force as illuminated by Christopher Fry in *The Lady's Not for
Burning*. (After three years of indoctrination, I was unable even to
express outrage without a literary reference attached.) It was a small
moment but an important one, a first stirring of nationalistic/feminist
feeling akin to the click of recognition feminists cited twenty-five
years later to describe epiphanies that alerted them to the ordinary
ways in which inequities presented themselves.

I began to look for people I could imagine as empathetic. First among
them was Frye himself. He was lecturing us that year on nineteenth-
century thought (Arnold, Mill, Newman, Burke, and Ruskin, with
some brief, carefully considered references to Marx), with the stated
purpose of teaching us how major ideas from the nineteenth century
affected our lives in the twentieth. In another course on modern
poetry and drama, Frye fitted into the political and social context of
our times the great poets Yeats, Eliot, Pound, Hopkins, Auden, Sand-
burg, and Frost. His lucid descriptions of what was happening in the

political world, his remarks about writers who were still alive in fact or memory, whose work was influential and widely discussed even in the general magazines I was absorbing in the Student Union reading room (*The Reporter*, *The New Yorker*, and *The Saturday Review*) turned me into a modernist.

Listening to Frye's lectures in the overheated classrooms of Victoria's main building, largely unaltered since it was built when the college moved to Toronto in 1895 (the steam-heat radiators hissed, the smell of the waxed floorboards permeated the air), we were unmistakably at that "dark and bloody crossroads" described by the American critic Lionel Trilling as "the place where literature and politics meet."[vii]

During that same academic year, two other professors had an impact on me, if not equal to Frye's, at least powerful enough to affect the way I understood the contemporary world. One was Kathleen Coburn, a Coleridge scholar who was gossiped about by college misogynists, male and female, as a spinster and a suffragette, conditions thought to be risible and more important than her international renown.

None of us, even those who admired Coburn, had any way of knowing that conditions for women academics, while hardly ideal, were better at Victoria than at any of the other colleges. Coburn was a full professor, as was Laura Riese in the French department; both were important scholars who had done graduate work at great universities abroad and then returned to teach at their alma mater. Riese saw her mission as straightforward: she intended to enlighten the bumpkins under her aegis. Learning the French language would discipline, perhaps even civilize, the barbarians slouching in their seats in front of her.

Coburn was kinder, though no less rigorous. Her father had been a Methodist country parson; he and his progeny had been educated at Vic and felt a deep obligation to it. While Riese taught by rote, Coburn taught by example. She invited her fourth-year students to dinner at La Chaumière, a French restaurant that seemed daring to kids who thought the Royal York Hotel's main dining room the height of elegance, and afterward to a performance at the Eaton Auditorium by Ruth Draper, a sophisticated monologuist from New York. Later in the term she conducted a seminar on Byron in her coach-house apartment on Lowther Avenue, giving us sherry and playing Vivaldi on the phonograph afterwards, subtle ways of trying to help us struggle with our timidity and our provincialism.

She had taught a memorable course on the origins and development of the English novel from a feminist point of view in our third year and now, in her fourth-year course on the Romantic poets, she continued to coax us into a deeper understanding of how our lives as educated women were likely to evolve.

The class was small and the students were all women; most of us still described ourselves as "girls" even though we had read, or at least read about, Simone de Beauvoir's *The Second Sex*, which had recently been published in English.

"Women are like the Negro and the Jew," Coburn said one memorable day, exasperated by the blandness of class discussions. "We are deemed inferior on sight, and it's up to us to refuse to be diminished by men and to affirm ourselves through excellence in our work." (These remarks so astounded me I wrote them into my course notes.)

The other academic whose ideas excited me that remarkable season was a young social scientist named Margaret Pirie, who had recently come to teach at Toronto after graduate work in the United States; among her colleagues in the Anthropology department was Edmund Carpenter, who had a reputation as an intellectual daredevil. Pirie was giving a one-hour-a-week Anthropology course that could be substituted for Religious Knowledge, a course that had been taught in the individual colleges ever since the university was founded and whose dreariness I had endured in order to please my father. (I never did hear Frye give his renowned RK course on the Bible, the basis for his 1982 book, *The Great Code*; my cohort missed it because Frye was on leave when we were in the academic year in which it was normally taught.)

Pirie was smart, she was slangy, she treated her students as though they were adults, and her subject was electrifying: a comparison of social customs in primitive and contemporary societies. She described in fulsome terms the social structure of Ivy League universities, talked openly about the class system in Canada, said unequivocally that anatomy was destiny and that the women in the class would be exceptionally lucky if we had more than one acceptable marriage proposal.

Emboldened by the very different styles of Coburn and Pirie, I began to speak out in class more often, expressing opinions that went against the conformist norm. I published two audacious (by my own reckoning) articles in the college magazine, *Acta Victoriana*, one on Morley Callaghan, and another on postwar American writers under the title "The New Novelists and the Era of the Naked Zero." Both caused comment among the students and staff. They were "vivid" in argument and style, said one professor, who had given me A's on essays in the past but had warned against "a certain roughness in your prose that if it goes too far could be considered *journalistic*."

A couple of days after the piece on the American novelists was published, Frye raised in one of his classes the subject of nihilism. "I am not perturbed when my students write in a nihilistic vein," he said, looking in my direction. "My hope is that they are getting ready to say something better."

A few days later, we met while walking toward the college from Bloor Street and he talked to me about both articles succinctly, gently. I wrote in my diary that night, "I'm mortified. How *could* I have published such stuff where he could read it?"

Mortified or not, I pressed womanfully on, writing a bold paper for presentation at two seminars on James Joyce I had been assigned to lead in the modern novel course; going to plays joyously every week and writing short, sharp, mainly celebratory comments to read aloud at tutorials on twentieth-century theatre; memorizing reams of poetry, especially Eliot and Yeats, and declaiming them aloud in my room when I would have been better off boning up for the comprehensive.

The New Novelists and the Era of the Naked Zero

We've been waiting for the Third World War for ten years now. It has been a strange decade, a decade in which the futile forties drifted aimlessly into the even more futile fifties. These ten years have produced a new generation of authors. It's not a "lost" generation or anything so charmingly romantic. It's a hopeless generation, a generation of thoughtless cynics, weak-kneed gutless wonders who mourn their imperfect lot in an imperfect world. They sit drearily waiting to be annihilated by the Atomic War, and while they wait, they moan. They have produced depressing literature and the most depressing thing about it for me is that when I read, I am struck with the feeling that this is our generation they are writing about; this is the world into which we are graduating.

In the last fifty years the traditional values, the public truths that upheld the smug self-satisfaction of the Victorians, have slowly crumbled. They have disintegrated under the impact of two forces: the fierce white searchlight of science and the dark distrust of absolutes engendered by two hideous wars.

This loss of values became evident in the twenties, in that era of exiles, of lost and cynical young men, but even before the twenties, writers began to grasp substitutes for the old values, the old religions. Writers were full of life because they were rebelling, because they had new causes to uphold, new religions to put forth. D. H. Lawrence developed the religion of sex; Hemingway championed the religion of violence; Fitzgerald espoused the religion of razzle-dazzle and thoughtless, tragic gaiety; Steinbeck worshipped at the feet of the poor. This new generation of this time between wars has a religion too. It's the religion of despair. They aren't championing this religion loudly, with harsh, exhilarated voices. They are muttering it in dreary depression or disguising it in ugly, terrifying confusion.

It's hard to pick out a single writer and point to him as being typical of this trend. There are many men who belong to the school of despair and their novels have many differences. But they all have this in common: by the time you read the last page you realize that the author believes in nothing. Vance Bourjailhy, J. D. Salinger, John Horne Burns, Truman Capote, Tennessee Williams, Gore Vidal, Norman Mailer — there are many others, but these are the men who most brilliantly express this dreadful nothingness. Many of them wrote disillusioned novels about the war they fought and are writing even more disillusioned ones about the peace they won.

The world of their novels is a kind of nightmare world and, as in nightmares, the degree of proximity to reality varies. Irwin Shaw and Vance Bourjailhy write as though they are having the kind of dreams that horrify because they are so vividly detailed, so close to the conscious world, but Capote and Williams have captured the crazy dreams of drunken and perverted maniacs.

The characters of these novels are involved in a search for something they never find or in a retreat from something they can never escape. Joel in Truman Capote's *Other Voices, Other Rooms* is looking for a father he has never known. Allerd Pennington in Bourjaily's *The Hound of Earth* is running from the horror of having had a part in the destruction of Hiroshima. Mrs. Stone in Williams's *The Roman Spring of Mrs. Stone* is trying to escape the ugliness of middle age.

The people in these novels move through strange worlds. They live in cities surrounded by artificiality, and their cities are distorted by black clouds of depression. Some settings are full of garish colours

and screaming symbolism. The action of *The Hound of Earth* centres
on the toy department in a huge store. It's Christmastime and this
adds to the whole effect of mocking horror. The strains of "Silent
Night" compete with the whirr of sewing machines, the ring of cash
registers, the loud laugh of a Santa Claus in whom not even the children believe. It's as though the commercial world has gone mad, and
Christmas has been transformed from the celebration of the birthday of the Messiah into the chief rite of the worship of the great god,
the dollar. *The Roman Spring of Mrs. Stone* is set in the depraved
atmosphere of a Rome that is peopled by parasitic, impoverished
Italian nobles, idiotic rich American tourists, and perverts of both
nationalities.

The impression of nightmarish despair is conveyed most vividly
in almost all of the postwar novels by a frankness of expression that
pushes the actions and speech of the characters over the borderline
into abnormality. It isn't just the shock value of sex, which was
exploited so widely by the novelists of the twenties and thirties. The
characters are not so innocently normal as Hemingway's Lady Brett
Ashley in *The Sun Also Rises*, who tortured her unhappy soul by sleeping with every man she met. We've come a long way from those
happy days. It has been a fetish of this century to leave nothing
unsaid. With these novelists there is nothing they cannot say but
there also seems to be nothing they cannot think. The characters in
The Hound of Earth range in type from the deranged, sadistic forelady
who dresses up in expensive clothes and drinks milk from a baby
bottle to an equally unbelievable sales clerk who has achieved twenty-
two years and an engagement ring without knowing anything at all
about sex. Mrs. Stone, a true product of Tennessee Williams's disturbed
imagination, is followed through a decadent Rome by a beautiful
though shabby young man who makes obscene gestures when he
catches her eye. Joel Knox in *Other Voices, Other Rooms* is forced

through his despair to turn to the warm arms of his cousin, Randolph, who has a penchant for dressing up in lavender dresses and a white, curly wig. In Paul Bowles's *The Sheltering Sky* the heroine, having left her husband dead in a desert outpost, becomes part of the harem of a savagely passionate, though somewhat smelly, Arab.

This is just a part of the tendency to exaggeration, of the need to assert something that is positive. These authors take a single problem, a single symptom of the sickness of our society, and blow it up into the cause of all their confusion and despair. They involve their persecuted characters in sexual abnormality, anti-Semitism, Jim Crowism, McCarthyism. They come to the conclusion that nothing can be done about these problems since they don't mean anything anyway.

It is generally believed that the novelists of this century have expressed the values of the society and the era about which they are writing. If we are to believe that these novelists are expressing the despair of the 1950s, it seems almost as though there is one final and unavoidable conclusion to which we can come.

It is the conclusion reached by Skinner Galt, the hero of Vance Bourjaily's *The End of My Life*, and it expresses the feelings aroused by all of these postwar novelists. "For me, suicide is an intellectual position, the inevitable result of thinking things through to an end. It is the final stink, in a way, the only way of finally proving to myself that I don't actually care."

Unfortunately, suicide as an intellectual position or a physical reality fails for Skinner Galt and he reaches the state of utmost meaninglessness in which he cannot even kill himself.

This is the literature of our time: this is the way the young, the sensitive, the talented feel about our world. It is not a confident cynicism, a weary worldliness. It's a dead futility, a self-destructive horror. I don't know how you feel about it, but it makes me want to vomit.

— *Acta Victoriana*, December 1955

In early February, exhilarated by my small successes, I made a fateful decision: no more shilly-shallying. I would take a job that would open up after graduation in the editorial offices of *Maclean's: Canada's National Magazine*, the flagship publication of the Maclean-Hunter Publishing Company, where I had worked for several summers to earn my university fees.

"It's temporary," I told a friend who was urging me to come to Europe with her. "When I've saved enough money, I'll quit and come to London too."

In launching myself determinedly into what I thought of as the real world, I was heedless of a quotation from William Blake that Frye had used as an epigraph for a lecture: "They became what they beheld."[viii]

It would take me a quarter of a century to understand fully what I had beheld at the university. And almost that long to decide what it was I was trying to become.

---

i John Milton, *Paradise Regain'd: A Poem* (London: John Starkey, 1671), Book III, line 31.

ii Charles Kingsley, "A Farewell to C.E.G.," revised version in *Poems* (London: Macmillan, 1889), p. 284.

iii See Martin Friedland, *The University of Toronto: A History* (Toronto: University of Toronto Press, 2002).

iv Kathleen Coburn, *In Pursuit of Coleridge* (Toronto: Clarke, Irwin, 1977), p. 9.

v Christina Newman, "The Best Years of My Life and Other Lies," *Maclean's*, January 1972, pp. 31, 56–58.

vi John Ayre, *Northrop Frye: A Biography* (Toronto: Random House, 1989), p. 74. Other books on Frye: Joseph Adamson, *Northrop Frye: A Visionary Life* (Toronto: ECW Press, 1993); David Cayley, *Northrop Frye in Conversation* (Toronto: House of Anansi, 1992); Robert D. Denham, ed., *The Correspondence of Northrop Frye and Helen Kemp: 1932–1939* (Toronto: University of Toronto Press, 1996); Alvin A.

Lee and Robert D. Denham, *The Legacy of Northrop Frye* (Toronto: University of Toronto Press, 1995).

vii Lionel Trilling, *The Liberal Imagination* (New York: Viking, 1951), as quoted in "The Last Great Critic," by Nathan Glick, *The Atlantic Monthly*, July 2000, pp. 86–90.

viii William Blake, *Jerusalem*, Chapter 2, line 54.

TWO

My Life as a Dame: Chapter 2

I DON'T REMEMBER the exact date in the late spring of 1956 when I began my working life as an editorial secretary on the old bimonthly *Maclean's* magazine. I know I travelled by subway from my parents' house in North Toronto to the Maclean-Hunter building at University and Dundas in time to punch the time clock by 8:30 in the morning.

And I do remember how I felt (in a state of intense excitement, on the cusp of the best of times) and what I was wearing (a wonderful dress by an American designer called Anne Fogarty, in black, oh blessed black, and slingback high-heeled shoes I'd bought myself a few days before.)

The clothes had cost more than a week's as-yet-unearned salary. But along with an expensive Italian-boy haircut and a whiff of my newfound bravura, they were meant to signal my transformation from the tongue-tied student who had held summer jobs as a gofer on the magazine for four years into a young woman to be reckoned with.

Never mind that I was full of secret doubts. A ten-minute walk — I realized with a pang as I pulled open the heavy entrance door of the Maclean-Hunter building on Dundas Street — would land me on the university's green lawns, where just a week before, carrying a dozen long-stemmed red roses and wearing a rented academic gown, a mortar-board and a tatty ermine hood, I had looked enough like a prototypical girl graduate to be photographed by the *Toronto Star*. Maybe I should have applied to graduate school? Maybe I wasn't ready to be an adult? I quickly shook off these apprehensions for the umpteenth time. The point was, I needed a job.

Never mind that at $45 a week I would be earning only $5 more than I had as a student temp and couldn't afford even to think about an apartment of my own. Never mind that editorial secretaries were the lowliest wage slaves on the magazine and that you had to be promoted to editorial assistant just to get your name on the masthead. This igno-miny would not, could not, last. I had an honours B.A. in English literature, after all. I had read James Joyce and J.S. Mill. I had cast off my timidity and stood up to old Oxonians and young Yalies. I intended to be a successful woman, substantial and stylish to boot.

AN HOUR AFTER I stepped out of the elevator into the *Maclean's* edito-rial offices that late-spring morning, I realized it was not going to be as easy to realize my ambitions as I had imagined for the past six months. For one thing, nobody on the staff seemed to understand that I had been transformed.

When the copy chief asked the front-desk receptionist, "Who's that new girl?" he may have been inadvertently acknowledging that I looked different than I had as a college kid. But his secretary was sick, and what he wanted was to palm off on me a revised schedule for an upcoming issue of the magazine, to be typed with six carbon copies and distrib-uted *immediately* to the editors whose initials were scribbled at the top.

Before I got going on that — the editor's secretary reminded me starchily — the previous day's sticky mess on the coffee-room table had to be cleaned up and the electric kettle filled at the washroom sink in case any of the men needed reviving before the coffee wagon arrived at 9:45.

By the time the wagon rattled off the elevator and its attendant dinged her come-hither bell, I'd cleaned up the mess and typed the schedules, and was sitting at my desk in the front office, filling in forms for the personnel department while watching the men — oh! the lucky men — come sauntering out of their offices, gossiping, joking, complaining about their deadlines and their hangovers while they bought jam danishes and double-cream-no-sugar coffees in cardboard cups.

Phones rang; manual typewriters clanged; freelance photographers, illustrators, and writers trooped in to see the art director or the articles editor. It was as though I'd stepped into a bit part in a drama I already knew by heart from the scores of summer days I'd spent working at the same joe jobs in this same space.

How was I going to impress on these people that I wasn't just another new girl but a woman who knew how to think and write, who had talents and ambitions like theirs? Kathleen Coburn's dictum sprang into my consciousness ("We women . . . are deemed inferior on sight . . . and it's up to us to . . . affirm ourselves through excellence in our work.") That's it, I thought. I'll have to impress them with how hard I can work. Diligence will get me everything.

Some time that first week, I began to develop an office persona. On the inside I was the real me (sceptical, amusable, critical, and scared). On the outside I wore the mask of an improbably self-contained young woman with a manner that was not exactly eager (what my mother called "the pig-headed Irish" in me precluded that) but willing and capable nevertheless.

Need material from the law school library that would illuminate the parliamentary debate on the TransCanada pipeline then raging in Ottawa? I'd run right down to Osgoode Hall on my lunch hour and bring back the relevant references, carefully copied in my backhand script.

Need airline tickets to be fetched before five o'clock and delivered early next day to the magazine's political columnist when he stepped off the overnight train from Ottawa on his way to Europe and Asia? I'd be glad to get up early and greet him at sunrise with the tickets clutched in my hand.

Did the managing editor with the ego as big as his libido roar from his office door that he had a cold and needed to stave it off with a bottle of aspirin and a quart of orange juice from Sunday's Lunch across the road and then barely grunt when both palliatives were delivered to his cluttered desk in twelve minutes flat? Never mind, one of these times I'd accidentally pour the juice down his bloody neck.

Did the associate editor, who was weeks behind his deadline — as usual — keep dumping successive drafts on my desk to be typed and retyped ad nauseam in order to answer the criticisms written in his manuscript's margins by the über-editors? Never mind, I was editing him myself, surreptitiously softening the solipsisms, doing away with the spelling mistakes, and learning how to structure a magazine article as I typed.

Did the business editor need me to stay late to transcribe the material he had read into his dictaphone from myriad interviews with tycoons (his favourite word for the grey Canadian businessmen who were getting rich in the American boom)? I'd be glad to stay. No trouble at all.

On those long summer evenings, when the office was deserted after six o'clock except for the cleaning staff, I would take periodic breaks from these marathon typing jobs to stretch my legs and expand my understanding. Standing upright at shoulder-high metal cabinets, I read straight through the editorial files at the rate of four or five a night.

They contained a mine of material on how the magazine worked, how the editor got on with the company management, responded to the caterwauling of the advertising, circulation, and subscription departments, and reacted to the peccadillos of his staff. Occasionally, when I was sure I wouldn't be caught, I would riffle through the editors' in-baskets in order to read their comments on manuscripts-in-progress. My hope was to learn how to work in this *genre*, as I disdainfully called popular magazine writing, rolling the "r" on my tongue. (I was trying to keep up my French and learn more about the contemporary European world by reading Simone de Beauvoir and Françoise Sagan.)

My determined industry brought me ever more work, mainly fill-in jobs in the copy and research departments when the editorial assistants went on holidays or fell ill with flu, a widely recognized euphemism for PMS. I began to learn about line-editing and fact-checking, how blurbs, cutlines and heads were written by the male copy editor who cursed a lot while he typed, and to understand production schedules and the mysteries of the art department.

I was like a sponge soaking up everything I read, heard, or observed out of the corner of my eye. Though I didn't know it, I was serving an apprenticeship that scores of young women of my age and sensibilities, fresh out of university with English degrees, would have been happy to take on, right down to the lowliest errand or the longest, back-breaking ten-hours-at-a-manual-typewriter day.

This was the big time. These writers and artists were famous, I was reminded by former classmates, who had landed lesser jobs at Bell Telephone or in the book department at Eaton's, when we talked over egg-salad sandwiches and butter tarts at Mary John's, a cheap lunch place in the Gerrard Street bohemia nearby. At least it's not bor-ring, I'd reply. As we all knew from reading Oscar Wilde, suffering boredom was the worst thing that could happen to anybody.

AS THE AUTUMN wore on, my close involvement with the everyday workings of the magazine intensified while my sophomoric scorn for its editorial content began to wane. I had loved the place when I first worked there as a naïf of seventeen, before the attitudes I absorbed during four years as an undergraduate made it seem irredeemably bourgeois and predictable in its content and style. Now I was beginning to experience a grudging respect for what the editors were trying to achieve. The summer before, at the time of *Maclean's* fiftieth anniversary, the editor had been quoted as saying that he wanted to put out a magazine that would be "both respected and read." It seemed to me that with some articles in some issues he was beginning to achieve that goal.

It was the autumn of Suez and the Hungarian uprising, a politically exciting time that broke the somnolence of the Eisenhower and St. Laurent years. In the office, the men could be heard discussing both events with brio and a far greater knowledge of their impact on world affairs and Canadian life than I had realized they possessed. Political refugees from Budapest, some of them engineering students, flooded into Toronto, and I volunteered to teach English after work at the nearby University Settlement House, where a relief centre had been set up.

I remember the days as sunny, crisp, and perfect. You could smell the hops from a nearby brewery wafting in on the breeze from the lake. When I left the office at dusk to walk over to the settlement house, I'd breathe in the city air contentedly and, as the office towers on University Avenue lit up, tell myself, well, it isn't Manhattan, kid, but it's a start. Walking to the subway, I'd imagine myself as part of the New York of the 1930s and 1940s, when Katharine White was editing fiction at *The New Yorker* and Mary McCarthy was writing for *The Partisan Review.*

I didn't know that this habit of defining life according to American standards and in terms of American dreams was endemic in my society and my newly chosen trade, or that it was a tendency that the editor of

Maclean's, Ralph Allen, and his managing editor, Pierre Berton (he of the loud bellow and the low grunt), viewed with a peculiar mix of suppressed envy and energetic determination. They were Canadian nationalists. They had a mission absorbed from Arthur Irwin, Allen's predecessor as editor, who had hired them both. It was to interpret Canada to Canadians, to make the obvious significant, to show that they could publish a magazine good enough to rival on home ground the American slicks, *Life*, *Saturday Evening Post*, *Reader's Digest*, and the rest.

I took to reading back issues in the Maclean-Hunter library in an attempt to figure out what interested the editorial grandees and why. Pieces on the trivia of everyday Canadian life (a super-duper ice cream parlour in suburban Ontario, a lighthouse in Nova Scotia, small-town bingo across the country, Fuller Brush salesmen hustling brooms in urbania) seemed to me silly. (Read again forty years later, I realized that most of them had something to say about what was happening to Canada as the country expanded economically and struggled socially to slither out from under the British Empire in its decline and to fasten on to the American empire in its spectacular rise.)

The articles that interested me were, predictably, profiles of artists (Emily Carr, Glenn Gould, W.O. Mitchell) and, unpredictably, political analyses (Blair Fraser on Mackenzie King's spiritualism or Lester Pearson's international effectiveness) or social comment disguised as reportage (Fred Bodsworth on the war between the big department stores, Eaton's and Simpsons; June Callwood on the young Queen Elizabeth's first visit to Canada). Serious subjects were assigned to men, the softer stuff to women writers. ("This is the kind of piece they should get a dame to do," I heard a writer say, on his way out of an idea meeting where he'd been fingered to write a piece on teenagers going steady.)

THREE

The Prospector in
the Pink Penthouse[1]

Maclean's, July 20, 1957

CANADA'S SPRAWLING $2-billion mining industry owes its boom to a motley army of men: slick brokers in big-city offices, lonely prospectors and frontier camps, geologists and bush pilots, road builders, professional engineers. But their spokesman is a woman who lives in a pink penthouse, wears a mink coat, and buys size-ten dresses from Sophie of Saks.

For fourteen years Viola Rita MacMillan has been president of the Prospectors and Developers Association, the largest organization of mining men on the continent, and in that time she has made scores of biting speeches that lash out at anything and everything impeding the development of mining. The sophisticated apartment and the soigné clothes are really only trappings. As she says herself, "I'm a miner. I love this business and I want to stay in it until I die."

She doesn't much look like the miner she so proudly calls herself. A small woman, she stands just over five feet tall and weighs little more than a hundred pounds. She has alert cobalt blue eyes and short dark hair. The most striking thing about Viola MacMillan is the agility and speed of her movements. She darts about so quickly that bigger people sometimes feel almost cumbersome when they are in her presence.

Mrs. MacMillan often says with a firm conviction that Canada's future greatness depends to a large extent on the growth of the mineral industry. For more than thirty years she has dedicated her unusual energy and persistence to that industry. In return she has gained both money and prestige.

When Viola MacMillan first caught prospector's fever in 1922 she was a stenographer in a Windsor, Ontario, law office. Before her climb to the tense and involved life of a prominent mining executive, she also worked at one time or another as a switchboard operator, real estate agent, boarding-house proprietor, door-to-door Christmas-card saleswoman, and prospector. Now, at fifty-four, she controls uranium, lithium, and base-metal mining interests with an estimated value of $10 million. She has an uptown mansion as well as the penthouse in downtown Toronto and a winter apartment at the Surf Club in Miami.

Businessmen, government officials, and men in every phase of mine-making respect her keen business sense and her aptitude for organizing. John S. Proctor, vice president and general manager of the Imperial Bank of Canada, calls her "the most remarkable woman in Canada." Mining papers credit her with building the Prospectors and Developers Association from a loosely knit agglomeration of fieldmen and promoters into a powerful organization representing one of the most important segments of the mining industry.

Outside her own world, attempts are constantly made to analyze her success. Financial pages carry colourful stories of her doings. She is tagged with such clearly sentimental titles as "the angel of the sourdoughs," "the Queen Bee," and "sweetheart of the mining men." Feature writers on the women's pages of newspapers use her success as a weapon in their one-sided battle to prove the natural superiority of the female.

Mrs. MacMillan herself has developed two different, but equally definite, theories on how to do well in mining or anything else. In the late 1930s and 1940s she used to say that everything she had she owed to good luck. "It was in the books for me" was the sentiment she repeated often. In the 1950s she has tended to attribute her success to hard work. Now one of her favourite maxims is this: "Anybody, regardless of sex or circumstance, can do anything they want to do. All you need is the guts to stick to things."

Whether you attribute her accomplishments to her luck or to her labour, they make an impressive listing. She is president of six companies and is the director of three others. Her interests include ViolaMac Mines Ltd., a producing base-metal mine in British Columbia; a Saskatchewan uranium property at Lake Cinch; and a lithium property in the Cat Lake district of Manitoba. She also holds promising oil, copper, and gold prospects in various parts of Canada.

Mrs. MacMillan has a broad, if rudimentary, knowledge of all phases of mine-making, from the technique of sinking a shaft to the translation of a geologist's report into the terminology of the ordinary prospector, and everything she knows she learned by practical experience.

Until the last two or three years she spent about eight months of every year in the field, living in bunkhouses, and eating with the men from her mines. Now she, or her husband, George MacMillan, who has mining interests of his own and is a director of some of her companies, visits their properties every two or three weeks.

Viola MacMillan's mines and her leadership of the mining association keep her hopping. Last March she came home from a holiday in Florida and was immediately involved in last-minute preparations for the association's annual convention at the Royal York Hotel in Toronto. The change was so abrupt that when she woke up the morning after

her return it took her a few minutes to realize the bright light streaming through the skylight in her penthouse wasn't Florida sunshine.

That same day, in two hours, early in the afternoon, she had a hasty
lunch; showed a legman from the CBC-TV program *Graphic* through
the penthouse (she was interviewed by emcee Joe McCulley on *Graphic*
last April); talked to me about everything from uranium holdings and
mining legislation to seamless stockings and interior decoration; and
sat in on an association executive meeting to discuss, clause by clause,
a bill going through the provincial legislature.

She kept at this pace during the four-day convention, attending all
the business meetings and technical lectures. She also went to most of
the social functions, from a roof-garden tea for the members' wives to a
square dance for which prospectors were urged to recapture "that old-
time mining spirit" by bringing their sweethearts and leaving their ties
at home. Nobody was surprised when she was re-elected president for
the fourteenth time. The day after the convention Mrs. MacMillan was
back in Miami. As George MacMillan remarks, "If you want to see
Viola, you've got to get up early and catch her on the run."

Viola MacMillan seems to have been in a hurry ever since she was
born on an Ontario farm in 1903. She was one of the youngest of the
twelve children of Thomas Huggard, of Windermere. In spite of her
small stature, she could always cope with jobs usually labelled "a
man's work."

During the First World War three of her five brothers were in the
army, so Viola had to help in the fields and haul gravel down to scows at
the lakefront. She took a commercial course in North Bay and at seventeen went to Windsor to work as a clerk, then a telephone operator, and
finally a legal stenographer with Rodd, Wigle, McHugh, and Whiteside.
After she'd been in Windsor two years she met George MacMillan at a
dance. He was working in the express department of the Canadian
National Railway (CNR). They were married in the fall of 1923.

Before she met her husband, Mrs. MacMillan can't remember having any particular interest in mining. But George's father, "Black Jack" MacMillan, had several claims in northern Ontario. The summer before their marriage the MacMillans went north to visit George's relatives and to "look over some of his old sweethearts." On that trip Mrs. MacMillan caught a feeling of excitement around the mining camp at Cobalt that she had never known before. Next year she was eager to go north again when an uncle of George's asked the couple to do the work required by law to maintain some claims he'd acquired.

For the next five or six years she and her husband prospected without profit in northern Ontario and western Canada. In the winters in Windsor, Mrs. MacMillan ran her own real estate office until business fell off; then she sold Christmas cards and took in boarders. In the meantime she was reading everything she could find about mining. George MacMillan was out of work for a while and just after he got a job as a customer's man with a brokerage house, his wife decided that full-time prospecting was in the books for her. One Tuesday in 1929, she recalls, "I told George I was leaving for the north Friday morning. If he wanted to come along, it would be okay. If he didn't, I'd be all right alone." George decided to go along.

The MacMillans weathered some hard years at the beginning, and George still hates to think about one summer when they were forced to supplement their diet of beans with large quantities of the onions that grew around their shack.

Their first big success came in the early 1930s. They had come out of the bush into Kirkland Lake, Ontario, to take a sick prospector to a doctor. Mrs. MacMillan went into a store for supplies, and the grocer told her about rumours of a gold rush in nearby Hislop Township. As quickly as possible she and her husband set out in their old car for the gold field. They got there at four o'clock in the morning and began immediately to drive in claim sticks by the light of a flashlight. They didn't stop staking even to sleep for the next twenty-four hours and ended up with 2,000 acres of claims recorded in the MacMillan name. Mrs. MacMillan swapped some of their claims for others and, by organizing syndicates of prospectors, acquired an interest in the prosperous Hallnor Gold Mines.

For the next fifteen years the MacMillans prospected right across Canada. They worked in northwestern Quebec, New Brunswick, northern Ontario, the Yukon, and the Northwest Territories. At first they were looking mainly for gold but in 1946 switched their search to base metals.

They didn't really make big money until 1949, when, by borrowing $40,000, they acquired a group of old lead-silver-zinc claims in British Columbia. The first truckload of ore paid a whopping $3,500, and after the excitement subsided Mrs. MacMillan spent part of the money for dynamite for further blasting. This was typical. It is also typical that she goes after whatever metal is most in demand. In 1957 it's uranium; the big thing on her schedule this year is the development of the uranium claims she owns at Lake Cinch, Saskatchewan.

She says the other main interest in her life "besides keeping the wolf from the door" has always been the Prospectors and Developers Association. The organization was formed twenty-five years ago and the membership covers a wide field, including prospectors, muckers, promoters, engineers, and mining stock holders. John Carrington, a mining engineer and editor of the *Northern Miner*, states flatly, "If it hadn't been for Viola MacMillan, it would have bumbled along casually. But after she took hold of it, the association became a power in the mining world."

The MacMillans joined the association in 1933. George was president from 1941 to 1943. During these years his wife was secretary. The next year they traded offices and Viola MacMillan has been president ever since.

During the Second World War she was a member of the government's War Metals Advisory Committee. She stormed across Canada with four geologists, organizing meetings of prospectors as part of the government's education program. Canada needed metals, and Mrs. MacMillan felt sure that the only quick way to get them was to teach prospectors how to go out after them. Classes were held in big towns and small mining camps; the fee for the course was only a dollar but some of the Depression-stricken prospectors couldn't afford even that. Since the war the Prospectors and Developers Association has continued to foster educational programs for prospectors.

Mrs. MacMillan's influence has also been reflected in provincial and federal mining legislation during the last ten years. People in the mining industry like to talk about her remarkable facility for opening the ears of cabinet ministers. One of her projects was the early wartime tax-law amendment granting deductions for exploration expenses, a measure that encouraged expenditure on prospecting.

She often complains about the regulations and restrictions governments have imposed on mining, and punctuates her speeches to the prospectors' association with such dramatic statement, as, "We must rise and cast off our shackles," and, "A free market for gold is the industry's only hope of survival."

She is just as outspoken in her dealings with individuals. When she phoned John Proctor, vice-president of the Imperial Bank, last year to ask him to speak to her association, she gave him explicit instructions: "Make it short, make it snappy, and make them like it."

At an association dinner last March, Joe Rankin, representing the executive, presented a silver tea service to Viola and summed up her activities in his presentation speech: "To our president: a fine lady, a hard worker, and a hell of an organizer."

Easygoing, slow-spoken George MacMillan has encouraged his wife in everything she has attempted. Among mining people he is given credit for being a competent businessman, but it is often said that he likes to hide behind the vivacity and drive of his energetic wife. At the March dinner Mrs. MacMillan presided over a head table that seated more than a hundred government officials and mining men and their wives, all wearing evening clothes. George, in a business suit, sat in the body of the convention hall with two secretaries from the MacMillans' office.

One of his favourite stories about his wife concerns an incident in the late 1930s when they were prospecting in Quebec. This is the way he tells it:

"As everybody knows, Viola likes to look after her own business. We were both out staking claims and had recorded some in each name. Within a couple of hours, Viola was smart enough to find a buyer for her share. It was a big deal — she was going to get $15,000 or $20,000. She took the buyer to the records office but the clerk refused transfer claims because, as he explained, under Quebec law everything she had belonged to her husband. Mad as she was, all Viola could do was go and fetch me to sign over her share."

After a pause George MacMillan adds, "That was really the only time I ever had her over a barrel."

The MacMillans have adapted their way of life to their business interests. Two years ago, when they moved into their new office on the fourth floor of the Knight Building in Toronto, they leased the thirteenth-floor office and turned it into a penthouse apartment. They lunch there and hold evening business conferences in the dining room. When her husband is out of town, Mrs. MacMillan spends the night in the apartment rather than in their large home on Toronto's Oriole Parkway.

Almost everything in the penthouse, from the broadloom to the ice bucket and the paper napkins, is pink — the pretty pink that is used often in the scented interiors of expensive beauty salons or the frilly nurseries of suburban bungalows but is rarely associated with the harsh technical world of mine-making. Ceiling-high mirrors and bleached furniture add to the general impression of lightness conveyed by all the pinks. There is a small piano in the living room — Mrs. MacMillan plays hymns on it — a television set, and a hi-fi phonograph. The only book to be seen is a hardcover pamphlet put out by the federal Department of Mines called *Out of the Earth*.

The MacMillans are proud of the penthouse but Mrs. MacMillan says she has kept it impersonal deliberately so that if she ever had to leave it, she could do so without a qualm.

She maintains that striking it rich hasn't changed her much. "I'm just the same as I always was. I'd be every bit as happy in a tent." She'd sooner talk about the garrulous old prospector who shared tea and sandwiches with her, then explained that he never had to wash dishes because his dog licked them clean, than discuss the dinner dance she gave at the Surf Club in Miami last winter, when her guests included the wife and two daughters of Louis St. Laurent.

During the last few years she has lost about twenty pounds and has acquired chic gowns that are very different from the dungarees and tailored suits she used to wear. But she still prefers to talk business and she's willing to add special precepts for women to her formula on how to get ahead. Last spring four girls, geology students from the University of Toronto, were looking for summer jobs and Mrs. Mac-Millan gave them this advice: "Be prepared to carry your own load and don't expect any favours because of your sex."

She's proved her theory. John Carrington of the *Northern Miner* claims that, except for some old die-hard prospectors whose feeling is the natural resentment of the male for the intrusion of a woman into a strictly masculine world, mining men give her due credit for her accomplishments. "Most people respect her for what she is," says Carrington, "a smart, tremendously energetic woman."

Mrs. MacMillan says herself that she never regrets not having been born a man except when she's feeling left out of stag parties, because "that's when men are at their ease and talking shop. It's probably the very best time to do business."

FOUR

The New Machismo[2]

Maclean's, March 1972

A COUPLE OF DAYS before the picture of Bruno Gerussi, which appears on the cover of this *Maclean's*, was taken — at a time when I was worrying the idea of the new machismo around in my mind — I saw a man who by his very presence brought the whole subject into focus. It was after a children's concert at my daughter's school in midtown Toronto, and among all the mamas in their fur coats standing around outside in the snow waiting for their offspring to emerge triumphant was this guy in the prime of his young middle age, a junior partner in an important law firm, maybe, or a stockbroker from one of the big downtown houses, wearing an expensive navy blue overcoat and a rep tie. He was lean in the manner of somebody who plays a lot of squash and he had this great Celtic colouring, thick black hair going silver around the ears, and grey-green eyes, and he looked as though, in another time, he might have gone to Royal Military College (RMC) and ended up as a lieutenant-colonel in the Queen's Own, which is probably what his grandfather was. I kept staring at him until he nodded in a civilized manner in case we might know each other, but what I was thinking would not have pleased him.

I was trying hard to figure out why it was that ten years ago I would have considered him the handsomest man I'd seen all week and now the way he looked was somehow quaint. He was just too handsome, too barbered, too controlled. I mean, you couldn't imagine him swearing or sweating (except in the confines of the Badminton & Racquet Club) or . . . well, you get the idea. He just didn't have it.

Before I go on, I'd better explain that I don't think my response was particularly unusual, even in that careful crowd. I'll wager if I'd been crazy enough to climb the school steps and holler, "Hey, I'm running a contest and the first prize is your choice of Bruno Gerussi or this sterling-silver citizen," most of the young matrons in the assembly would have mentally picked Gerussi (though what they'd do apart from mentally picking, I'm not sure; years of worrying about good day camps, better orthodontists, and enrichment-versus-acceleration tend to make you cautious).

What the ladies would have been responding to is the new machismo, what an academic friend of mine disdainfully calls "roosterism," the current style in what looks good in and on men. And if they didn't know the word then, before the year is out they will, because it's one of those conceits that take hold in the media every once in a while — words that start out saying something important about an era and become catch-alls, beaten into absurdity by overuse. ("Charisma" was a word like that; it gained currency in the politically ambiguous climate of the late 1950s as a mystical quality of magnetic leadership, as defined by the German sociologist Max Weber, but it ended up being applied to everything from the hold John Diefenbaker had over small-town audiences on the Prairies to tacky boutiques pushing cheap incense and Hong Kong silks.) "Machismo"— which is derived from the Spanish *macho*, meaning male, and is an integral part of the argot of Mexico — is still in its media infancy, but in the past few months I've seen or heard it used to describe two-toned Cuban-heeled shoes worn by dudes in Denver, Derek Sanderson's stickhandling, and any number of overt statements, subliminal attitudes, and sideways glances indulged in by the kind of chauvinistic males that the Women of Liberation despise.

The old authentic machismo, the Mexican kind, comes out of the heart of that country's lifestyle, which is what the sociologists call matrifocal and patriarchal — i.e., the woman of the family keeps everybody going by providing love and tortillas, but the man's word is law. Within this culture, a man's worth is reckoned in terms of his maleness rather than his possessions. To the lower-class Mexican, to be *macho* or show *machismo* (bravery/virility/pride) is more important than anything else. (And this is true to a lesser degree in most of the other countries of Latin America.) A man can prove he's macho in many ways: by physical prowess in defending his honour against all slights; by fighting bulls while dressed up magnificently in tight trousers before a roaring crowd (and at the kill, shouts of "macho, macho" are heard in the roar); by the sexual conquest of many women (the truly macho man figures he can melt the resolve of the most virtuous woman with an eye flash at 50 feet); or by a reckless disregard for money, sobriety, and good sense.

What machismo means to the men who live by it (and the women who suffer under it, for at its worst it breeds brutality and proliferates poverty through its denial of the work ethic) is illustrated in the culture's aphorisms — *Tiene pantalones!* or He has pants! is a good thing to say about any hombre — and in proverbs like, "Never lend your gun, your horse, or your woman." (And whoever made that one up ought to be sentenced to thirty days in a small cell with Valerie Solanis and Betty Friedan.) Just what the new machismo, the North American pop culture version, portends is something a little more complicated. By other names and in other guises, it's always been part of the working-class culture; truck drivers, cowboys, mechanics, miners, guys like that, are all natural macho males. And there have been intellectual manifestations of it for forty years in the blood-and-guts aesthetics of Ernest Hemingway, James T. Farrell, and Norman Mailer and their glorification of bullfights, prize rings, battlefield heroics, barroom brawling, and sexual athleticism. ("The earth moved. And it was good.") But since the late 1960s, and particularly in the last year, the machismo myth has gone beyond the literature into the contrived life-style of the middle class.

There are at least three interconnected reasons for this. Machismo is part of the urban guerrilla mystique of the New Left and militant black movements in the U.S. and such related movements as the FLQ in Canada, with their revolutionary heroes (Che Guevara, Régis Debray); their costumes of work shirts, gun belts, boots; their ugly manners, rough talk, and ceaseless need to show how really tough ("out front") they are. In true macho style, the men of the movement from the beginning reduced women to the role of camp followers, and their leaders — Stokely Carmichael, Eldridge Cleaver, Abbie Hoffman — made statements about women so ugly they were enough to turn the stomach of the most accommodating Aunt Tom. Some of the movement women were too turned on to the egalitarian ideal to put up with this oppression, and the radical feminist groups were the result. A small but noisy group of women began to trespass brazenly on the old masculine preserves, strong language, aggressive politics, free love, the independent life.

Now to go further with this merry theorizing. Already social scientists are saying that feminine aggression as manifested in the women's lib movement, both here and in the U.S., means to a certain kind of masculine mind an usurping of the male's rightful role, and their response is to clamp down, to display their own supremacy, to become as Margaret Mead has described it, "provoked into a display of male fascism." In other words, at a time when sexual roles are becoming more ambiguous, certain men lean harder on their machismo. And this is what we're seeing now on the streets of North America among those who believe that you are what you wear: costumes proclaiming that men are more than merely masculine, they're supermale.

For any woman who wants to go macho-measuring while the machistas are out girl-ogling on the coming afternoons of spring, the following guidelines may help:

- The middle-class male with pretensions to machismo may never get himself in a total macho costume but he'll add macho touches to his everyday wear: brigade boots, wristwatches with big wide black leather bands, denim with metal studs, leather jeans with front lacings, red cotton bandanas knotted around the neck, officers' greatcoats turned up at the collar, and, in the summer, a safari suit in khaki.

- In the movies now there are disappointingly few macho heroes; most of the new stars (Dustin Hoffman, Richard Benjamin) belong to the perennial adolescent or groping gentle misfit category, but actors like Robert Redford and Jack Nicholson (in *Five Easy Pieces* but not *Carnal Knowledge*) are trying. Clark Gable, Humphrey Bogart, and Robert Mitchum were prototype machistas, but the greatest macho star of all time was probably Marlon Brando playing Stanley Kowalski in *A Streetcar Named Desire*.

- Macho males often have friends called Buck or Lefty who are not as macho as their hero but who laugh a lot at his jokes and envy him his style. The sidekick, in fact, is an important part of macho mythology — Don Quixote was a rarefied mad macho hero and he had Sancho Panza; Hopalong Cassidy was a cowboy macho hero, and he had California. There are even sidekicks for macho politicians, and they tend to take the blame for the hero's failings, as Ted Sorensen did for John Kennedy and Marc Lalonde does for Pierre Trudeau.

- Rock singers are macho and so, in careful emulation, are rock fans. Think of Jimi Hendrix, the Grateful Dead, the Rolling Stones, Country Joe & the Fish, and the Beatles in their heyday. The Beatles stopped being macho — and stopped being a group — when a couple of strong-minded women came into their lives, which bears out Lionel Tiger's theory, as expounded in *Men in Groups*, that males don't bond so readily when women gain importance to them as anything more than sexual objects.

- Most folk singers are not macho but Gordon Lightfoot writes some macho songs. (Think of the lines in "That's What You Get for Loving Me": "I ain't the kind to hang around / With any new love that I've found / I've got a hundred more like you / I'll have a thousand 'fore I'm through.") The macho man tends to marry a quiet, accepting, admiring, erstwhile pretty girl who shortly becomes old and resigned, with lines in her forehead and a tight look about the mouth that's more pronounced when she's referred to as "my old lady" and left at home to look after the kids and the dogs while the hero is out drinking beer and seeking easygoing broads who aren't going to become anybody's old lady — not if they can help it.

- The machismo hero tends to call an intelligent girl saying intelligent things "a chick who's into heavy talk." In fact, he is usually put off by any intelligent and/or strong-minded women (unless she happens to be his mother), and he divides women into two groups: the dumb and silly and the shrewd, conniving, and malicious.

The trouble with the new machismo is that it's hard to be sure it's authentic, no matter how many audio/visual aids to macho-watching you may have to go by. Midnight cowboys, bikers, and the devotees of Gay Liberation have picked up on the macho style to make a point about their existence that may be clearer to social psychiatrists than it is to anybody else. The old machismo came out of a culture where sexual roles were clearly defined; we live in a time and place where people put on costumes to hide their insecurities and to remind themselves of who they think they are.

You have to remember, too, that in even the most sympathetic, apparently un-chauvinistic, un-macho male, there lurks something of the machista, and in all but the truly liberated woman there is some terrible atavistic admiration for this attitude.

Not very long ago, in the company of an intelligent, self-sufficient, resolutely enlightened friend of mine, I was embroidering on the feminist thesis that machismo, or the masculinity myth, is an anachronism in the second half of the twentieth century, that it ought to be possible, as Gloria Steinem says, for the so-called masculine and feminine virtues to lose their gender so that we could have courage, daring, and resourcefulness acceptable in women and charity, mercy, and tenderness acceptable in men, and nobody would have to play at being aggressive/dominant or dependent/passive in order to prove their sexuality.

She nodded in furious agreement all the time I was talking, but half an hour later, when we'd moved on to a discussion of great kitsch poetry we had known, she said in dreamy seriousness, "You know, I've always liked that really terrible poem by Richard Lovelace or, anyway, one of the Cavalier poets that is about a soldier coming back to his lady from a war and ends with the fabulous line, 'And he pleasured her with his boots on.'" She caught me laughing and, with a valiant attempt at rue, we agreed that it's going to take more than 5,000 women's libbers objecting and 300 sociologists dissecting to kill the macho myth. It seems, alas and hurrah, to be programmed into the race.

FIVE

Mag Cult: The Opiate of the Faddists[3]

Saturday Night, October 1978

A FUNNY THING HAPPENED to me this autumn. I got married again. Now, you may not find this funny. I certainly didn't. I found it joyful, a reaffirmation of love and hope and laughter.

But a few weeks before the ceremony, I was standing waiting to hear a lecture on Sexual Equality in Scandinavia and other utopian tales, when a woman came up to greet me, having only lately learned my news. After an exchange of small civilities, she widened her eyes, which were rimmed with a pale and luminous liner, laid her manicured hand on mine, and whispered so no one else could hear, "But my dear, don't you feel funny about it — just a little bit *quaint*? I mean" — and the bracelets jangled on her wrist to emphasize her concern — "nobody's getting married any more."

Oh Lord, I thought, it's mag cult. And mag cult's decided that marriage is funny, passé, definitely not what People Are Talking About or expected to Watch Out For.

"Mag cult" is a phrase I have been using for years to encompass the whole range of fashionable attitudes that wash over the magazine world like tidal waves through the Florida Keys and are similarly regarded by the people who believe in them as irresistible manifestations of a Larger Reality.

In the world of mag cult right now, John Travolta is ready to peak; Fran Lebowitz is approaching her prime; art deco sofas are seen as divine; Saarinen tables are being wrapped in gauze to hide their once revered and now reviled severity; Quaalude is referred to wittily if unwisely; and living alone and loving it is the only way to be.

In mag cult, living alone means being free to spend languorous evenings divested of your Maud Frizon ankle boots, sipping Perrier with a zest of lime, reading Andy Warhol's *Interview*, and summoning your lover on the phone should your libido get off its leash. It has nothing whatever to do with spending your evenings trying to decide whether to wash your hair or your smalls, eating a pint of frozen yogurt while standing bolt upright in front of the fridge, or writing a letter to your mother in Manitoba because she's called three times in the last three weeks to find out if you're still alive.

Not all magazines perpetrate mag cult, of course. This one doesn't and neither does *The New Yorker*, and when they were in their heyday *Esquire* and the *Reporter* and *Maclean's* could be said to be anti–mag cult in their sensibilities. In truth, most of the mag-cult magazines are aimed at women, though the city magazines that have flourished in the wake of the success of the old *New York* are mag cult of a bisexual sort and often display quite breathtaking virtuosity in their extensions of the mag-cult style.

Still, since mag cult has its roots in insecurity, mag cult is mainly for women and its history is rich if unvaried. The *grande dame* of the genre is *Vogue*, which has been handing down its mag-cult rulings to women for more than half a century. *Vogue* has always been for upper-class or would-be rich women in their thirties and beyond, and a whole slew of other magazines look after the younger and poorer.

All of them, whatever the income or age range of their readers, run on twin premises. They recognize the fears so many women are prey to that they have not, do not, may never measure up to an undefined "ideal" of sexuality, femininity, acceptability; and they exploit those fears brilliantly by promising women that if only they'll follow mag cult's dictates everything will turn out fine. (Are your thighs too fat? Too fat for what? To wear $300 black leather jeans, that's what. Buy this jogging suit, book into this spa in the Hamptons, try this recipe for *truite au bleu*, swallow this theory about cellulite. Mag cult will save you if only you'll believe.)

It almost looked in the early 1970s as though mag cult was going to be challenged by the energies and realities unleashed by the women's movement. In fact, *Ms.* magazine was established six years ago to counter the whole phenomenon. But the genius of mag cult is its adaptability. It has been able to swallow the women's movement whole, to make it fashionable, to turn its tenets about independence and equality into prescriptions for what women on the rise should wear in order to tone down the glitz (save that for little evenings!) and hasten the split with their pasts. There is no revolution, Sartre once wrote, that capitalism can't corrupt.

Mag cult has no place for subtleties. It's unable to recognize that women can be self-supporting and self-actualizing (that's a mag-cult word) and still want the intimacy and stability of marriage. The ideal woman this year — as my fashionable friend at the lecture was pointing out in mag-cult code — would never think of getting married. She means to remain forever single, childless, about thirty, tough-minded, career-centred, a tigress with her lovers, and hard at work on her thighs so she can buy the leather jeans.

Still, when you've been watching mag cult for as long as I have, you know that its absolutes change. Recently, I saw an issue of *Cosmo* on a newsstand with a cover line that read, "Seven New Ways of Relating to Men — Including, Are You Ready, Marriage!!!" I was going to send it off to my friend, with a note about being in the avant-garde, but I figured she wouldn't think it was funny. Mag cultists rarely laugh.

SIX

Lapping It Up[4]

Saturday Night, October 1995

A MONDAY AFTERNOON in May of 1979, when the federal Liberals were in the thick of losing the election they had been afraid to call for over a year, I boarded their leader's campaign plane in Ottawa as part of the media contingent bent on covering the penultimate week of what was then widely thought to be Pierre Trudeau's last hurrah on the hustings. Already ensconced in the front of the aircraft, in a section reserved for the prime minister's party and divided by a curtain from the area assigned to the journalists, was none other than Trudeau himself, tie loosened, sleeves rolled, briefing notes spread out on the table before him. As the journalists filed silently past his seat, he looked up briefly, caught sight of me in the throng, and called out in mock amazement, "Christina! Are *you* consorting with the working press?"

It was *le vrai Trudeau* talking: the teasing tone that was part of his way of relating to women when he was playing the Gallic gallant; the obvious insult he was offering the media men whose detested presence on his plane he acceded to only because his staff insisted he must; his obliviousness to the possibility that singling me out might cause me problems in the loutish culture of the media pack in its campaign formation — a culture that most serious male political commentators loathed and that the very few women who worked within it then treated warily or emulated awkwardly in an attempt to survive by acting like one of the guys. Under the circumstances, I knew as soon as Trudeau spoke that the best response would be something like, "Prime Minister, I'm not *consorting*. I *am* the working press." But before that easy answer rolled off my tongue, I realized it was a lie.

It was obvious to my confreres that I knew Trudeau outside the antagonistic ambience that prevailed on his campaign planes. I had met him before his ascent to the Liberal leadership and watched his political progress from a seat in the third or fourth row. He had granted me interviews on occasion and answered my questions with care. Allies of his were friends of mine. His ideas about government had been debated in my hearing over a period of fifteen years. I had dined at the same tables, consulted the same soothsayers, seen him operating as a statesman in London, Moscow, and Rome. Plainly, I was not a member of the working press, in the sense that Trudeau was using the phrase.

Although I worked prodigiously hard in the manner of the disadvantaged (my disadvantages being my gender and a literary rather than a social-scientific education), I was not a telejournalist hoping to make the top item on *The National* or an exhausted reporter harried by a contemptuous desk man to produce a destructive headline that the Liberal media managers were striving to ensure wouldn't be there. As a magazine editor on leave to write a book, my anxieties and ambitions were of a different kind.

So instead of tossing off a smart answer in response to Trudeau's mockery, I smiled and shrugged and moved on to take my seat among the boys in the back of the plane, wondering as I went what my unease meant. Could it be that I — who had been trained as a writer under the aegis of three remarkable anti-establishmentarian editors from the West — was becoming uncomfortably like the gentlemen journalists I had joked about in my youth, those chroniclers of Canadian prime ministers of the past whose familiarity with the powerful rendered them unwilling to cast a cold eye on the governing elites?

That small incident — and the heightened awareness of larger dilemmas it created — came forcefully to mind a few months ago when *The New Yorker* published "Read All About It," a piece about American political journalism by the eclectic and talented young writer Adam Gopnik. In it, Gopnik discussed the notion that in the decades since Richard Nixon's political career was destroyed by tenacious reporters, American political commentary has been transformed from what he calls an "access" journalistic culture into an adversarial or "aggression" one.

For Gopnik, the difference between the era of the great American columnists/savants, Walter Lippman and Arthur Krock, who had the ear and the confidence of the mighty, and the current age of malicious talk-show populists and two-bit journalists gleefully harassing politicians off the public stage, marks a change "not only in tone...but in worlds."

"The tradition...in which a journalist's advancement depended on his intimacy with power," he wrote, "has mutated into one in which his success can also depend on a willingness to stage visible, ritualized displays of aggression [against the powerful]...[Those] who used to gain status by dining with [their] subjects...[now gain it] by dining on them."

Gopnik's elaboration on these themes was arresting in part because, although he came of age professionally in the aggression era, he expressed a certain regret about the passing of "the old collusion": that symbiosis between political practitioners and political writers which produced a worldly public discourse quite unlike the "thought-free vacuum" that marks much current American comment, with its sanctimonious cynicism and murderous intent.

Predictably, the piece triggered in me — besides evocations of unresolved and perhaps unresolvable dilemmas — a series of questions comparing Canadian and American political writing of the past and present. Questions about whether our old-style access journalists were as influential as the American titans. John Dafoe of the *Free Press* probably had as much sway over Laurier and King, I decided, as Lippmann had in Washington, though his demeanour was much less august than Lippmann's and his prose style much less Augustan. Dafoe, and the important insider journalists who followed in his wake, notably Bruce Hutchison of the *Free Press* newspaper chain and Blair Fraser of *Maclean's,* saw themselves as nation builders in much the same way Lippmann did, exchanging discretion for inside information and the chance to wield influence over politicians they regarded as their peers.

The obverse questions, of course, had to do with whether our own new-style adversarial journalists are as destructive of public confidence in the democratic process as their American counterparts have been. (On balance, I thought not. Stevie Cameron and Linda McQuaig, for instance, in hugely popular recent books attacking the venality of Mulroney Conservatives, destroyed what was left of the former prime minister's reputation and may have done significant further long-term damage to the once great party he left in disarray. But their ferocious criticisms were mounted from considered positions; they weren't nasty for nastiness' sake in the manner of a Limbaugh or a Liddy.)

A question that's more problematic is whether old-style access journalism has fallen into disfavour in Canada as *The New Yorker* analysis implied it has in the U.S. An early look at Canadian publishers' lists for the upcoming season would seem to indicate otherwise. In the usual slew of political books, those by journalists with access prevail.

Lawrence Martin, who once worked for the *Globe and Mail* as a foreign correspondent, has written the first of a two-volume biography of

Jean Chrétien, for which he is said to have been granted many interviews with the prime minister, his family, and the friends of his youth. And three veteran columnists who might be described as the Canadian Krocks — Dalton Camp, Richard Gwyn, and Peter Newman — are publishing insider books about The Crisis, the one that seized Canada in the 1960s when they began practising punditry and whose fiscal and constitutional fallout they have been viewing with alarm ever since.

Even more promising in terms of the author's insider credentials (or so I thought when I read the book's blurbs) was Ron Graham's *All the King's Horses: Politics among the Ruins*. Graham is a writer now in early middle age whose political pieces published in this magazine in the 1980s — and *One-Eyed Kings*, the book he folded them into — seemed at the time to constitute a one-man revival of insider journalism, as practised in its glory days by Hutchison and Fraser, but with greater stylistic brio and a decidedly sharper edge. Where Hutchison was sentimental and Fraser coolly cerebral in their devotion to the liberal Canadian state — and the Liberal politicians they saw as its best hope — Graham was hip, a practitioner of sceptical chic, open about his close connections with the powerful, and astonishingly self-assured for a man in his thirties who had only recently begun to work at his craft.

Gossip in journalistic circles had it that he wasn't just a chronicler of the Canadian establishment; he had grown up in it, the son of a bicultural Montreal family of means. The confidence he showed was class confidence, the ease in high places inbred. He hadn't been educated rigorously at great universities abroad in the style of the liberal elites. Instead, he had flirted briefly with Quebec nationalist ideas as an undergraduate at McGill in the 1960s, before turning to graduate work in Canadian Studies at Carleton and to travelling extensively to find himself in the style of his affluent times. But as an admirer and intimate of Frank Scott, the McGill law professor and the old elite's conscience and scourge, he had learned their lingo and ingested their paradigm.

As his writing career unfolded, Graham began to display Olympian feats of access. When he went to interview Jean Chrétien at his cottage near Shawinigan after the 1984 election, he stayed several days and ended up helping to write the p'tit gars's memoir, *Straight from the Heart*. John Turner was so incensed by Graham's insider reporting on his political weaknesses that he intemperately berated one of Graham's younger brothers, whom he mistook for Graham himself, at a cocktail party. ("Didn't think much of your fucking article," Turner is supposed to have said. "It's my fucking brother you don't think much of," replied the kid brother in kind.)

Perhaps the most significant of Graham's many accomplishments was the easy rapport he achieved with Pierre Trudeau after he quit politics, a rapport said to be based on their several commonalities: the rich and indulgent families; the mixed French-English heritage; the long quests before deciding on their métiers; the admiration for Scott and his romantic crusades; the familiarity with the mores of the liberal elites, coupled with the pretence of rebelling against them. Graham was among the crowd of old allies and younger admirers who were spotted leaving tête-à-tête lunches with Trudeau in his Montreal redoubt. And it was Graham who was chosen as the chief English-language interviewer for Trudeau's television biography, though even he was unable to wring much that was new or revelatory out of the obdurate Trudeau. ("No regrets," was the old seer's main message. "I have no regrets.")

Bearing Graham's reputation in mind — along with the fact that the Liberal government run by his friend Jean Chrétien has been so cagey with information that its close observers profess not to know what's going on inside Ottawa now — it was with a notable eagerness that I began to read *All the King's Horses*. (It was billed in advance publicity as a book about the election of the Chrétien Liberals in 1993 and their attempts in the nearly two years since to deal with Canada's political and economic problems, the eagerly awaited sequel to *One-*

Eyed Kings.) Alas, the book is a disappointment, at least for those of us holding out hope for a revived and effective access journalism, as the Canadian crisis deepens and cries of "Apocalypse now!" grow shrill.

It has few of the strengths of Graham's earlier work. The self-assured voice has turned arrogant, the mixture of potted socio-political theory and energetic reportage gone wrong. Even the striking details and vivid insights that marked *One-Eyed Kings* are absent or discordant here. Where they are deployed, as in the opening sections on Kim Campbell, the effect is marred by an adolescent smart-assery epitomized in the chapter's main title, "The Taming of the Shrew."

The main problem with *Horses*, though, isn't stylistic; it's substantial. It's as though in deciding to write his "eagerly awaited sequel," Graham found himself caught in a conundrum. He's an access journalist in an aggression era, an elitist in a populist time. The world he was born into, rebelled against briefly, then returned to as a participant observer, the comfortable world of the old homogeneous elites who ran Canada in the decades after the war — that interlocking network of politicians, bureaucrats, and businessmen who were centred on the Montreal/Ottawa/Toronto triangle and were liberal in orientation no matter what their party label — has been disintegrating for decades. And Graham doesn't quite know how to get a handle on what's happening as it transmutes at an accelerated rate.

What he attempts is a new lament for a nation modelled on the philosopher George Grant's seminal polemic of 1965, although the nation he's lamenting is not Grant's conservative, British, and colonial country but the liberal, internationalist, and federalist society of Trudeau's dreams. Instead of being knowing and worldly, imbued with gravitas and good sense, Graham's lament is peevish and pretentious, derivative and contradictory.

In his distress about what's happened to the Canada of his salad days, Graham tries to lay the blame for the decline of the Canadian nation-state on a cliquish political class — to which by his own broad definition he himself clearly belongs — and to empathize instead with "the people," whose recent rightward turn he views as sadly misguided, the product not of the democratic process but of the political class's inadequacies and failure to communicate a countervailing vision. These ambivalent attitudes lead him into many a muddle, both structural and analytical. When an attempt is made to disentangle his main arguments from the byways of his narrative and the thickets of his prose, what he seems to be saying is that a great chasm now divides the governing elite from the people, who are apathetic and frustrated with the political system: an analysis that might be more appropriate to — and perhaps is borrowed from — what's going on in the U.S.

At no time does it explain why, if they're so apathetic, the people in Canada vote in such large numbers; if they are so turned off by politics why vigorous populist parties of the left and right have sprung up; if the political class is so unpopular, why Jean Chrétien — who as the leader at the apex of the system must surely belong to that class — is running a government whose popularity with the electorate continues to astonish, despite the illiberal turns it's taken in response to the problem of the federal deficit.

(One of the several curiosities of this curious book is the near absence from its pages of Jean Chrétien in his current incarnation. Chrétien's governmental style is discussed only cursorily, his referendum strategy in mostly nonspecific terms. Most of the quotations attributed to the prime minister are drawn from *Straight from the Heart*, which means they're ten years old and may have been written by Graham himself. Is the author being circumspect about embarrassing his old friend with praise or blame, or has he been frozen out?)

In his generalized scorn for those who've failed the people — the real culprits are not actually named — Graham also displays a surprisingly superficial knowledge about how real politics works. At one point he suggests airily that the battle against free trade could have been won in 1988 if the country's nationalists had only ousted John Turner from the Liberal leadership, replaced him with Jean Chrétien, and then formed a coalition with the NDP. This is a scenario that goes beyond naivety into the realm of fantasy, given that the Liberal Party would hardly have lent itself to a putsch by outsiders, that John Turner was passionately opposed to the Free Trade Agreement (FTA) while Jean Chrétien was not, and that the NDP of the period vehemently rejected both the notion of coalition and the view that opposition to the FTA should be a priority in its platform.

This same sort of facile fantasizing marks Graham's prescription for a new alliance between the people and a revived pan-Canadian consociational elite, with universal electronic mail as the agent of a revitalized democracy. What Canadians need, he has decided — besides a lobster in every pot and a modem on every laptop — is a new National Purpose, with improved health care as its Holy Grail, and the PM — whom he chides gently for being too pragmatic and too pedestrian in his goals — as its town-hall Galahad.

The chief problem with this grand vision is a reality that Graham avoids throughout his long lament: the hemispheric context within which Canada operates as the millennium approaches. It's not a lack of will that's keeping our political class from putting the shattered Canada together again; it's a lack of power.

When Canada was a nation-state stretching from sea to sea, an interlocking network of elites could afford to dream some national dreams. Now that it's a peripheral region of a super-state seeking to extend its reach from pole to pole, the best its politicians seem able to do is to manage the shattered remnants' survival — a reality that the pragmatic Chrétien understands and that his one-eyed scribe does not.

PART II

Canadian Society:
The Low and the High

CHRISTINA CAME TO know the country in its furthest reaches when she was sent on assignment in her twenties by Doris Anderson, the great editor/publisher of *Chatelaine*. In her first year at the magazine, she reported to her readers that she had travelled 12,000 miles from coast to coast by a variety of conveyances — bush plane and speed boat, first-class train and even a 1933 McLaughlin-Buick. She interviewed "all kinds of people, from provincial premiers to fishermen, TV stars to Ph.D.s," writing ten stories and ghosting or rewriting six others.

When the *Globe and Mail* created a position for her as National Reporter in 1975, she prided herself on her familiarity with the whole country. Before we married in 1978, she almost got killed driving a rented car along an ice-covered highway in northern Alberta, where she was doing a story on life in the northern oil town of Grande Cache. "Springhill: The Town That Won't Give Up" portrays the human and financial pain suffered after a horrific mining disaster by the residents of this Nova Scotia community where the future singer Anne Murray was just fourteen years old.

I have included two articles that engage with her favourite province, Alberta. When we were courting, Christina spent a week with the premier, Peter Lougheed, when he was heading a mission to Europe in 1975 — a tour that I followed by dispatching flowers to her various hotels. Day after day, the *Globe and Mail* carried her front-page reports of the Albertans' encounters with the pomp of the British, the directness of the Scots, the steely seriousness of the Germans, and the dazzling elegance of the French. With petroleum prices and energy supplies again in the headlines, I felt it worth reprinting two insightful essays focusing on Alberta. "The New Power in the New West" is about how Premier Lougheed's "aggressive conservatism" was rooted in the pride and insecurity generated by the province's new oil wealth and how this affected a chronically prickly relationship between Edmonton and Ottawa. "The Long Ordeal of William Wilder" is about the Mackenzie River pipeline, another eternal bone of contention in Canada's political economy in which the forces of continental integration (then fronted by a Harvard-trained Toronto businessman with impeccable social credentials) came up against a newly assertive political culture that had lost its deference to Bay Street and was recognizing Native peoples' claims to primacy in the North. These articles contextualize Albertans' continuing demand for greater respect and more power within confederation, correcting the cornball residue of Ralph Klein's premiership by recalling Lougheed's sophisticated, more modern style as leading apostle of the New West.

Born and bred in Toronto, Christina had a particularly sensitive feel for her hometown's cultural pulse. The 1970 piece on Jane Jacobs's view of Canada's urban agenda, "Canadian Cities: Let's Cherish Their Safety While We May," seems especially prescient. Christina's generally upbeat, but still cautious, report from the urban front contrasts with the late urban guru's far grimmer assessment of future trouble approaching in her last book, *Dark Age Ahead*. "Politics and Pornography: The Yonge Street Cleanup" explores the 1975 attempt to regulate the massage parlours then dominating Toronto's main drag. The initial stages of this cleanup campaign were the product of an urban-minded combo made up of the reform mayor, David Crombie; a respectable downtown business lobby; and the provincial premier, William Davis, who was anxious to find a symbolic issue on which to run his next election. Her report nicely anticipates how the very same cultural fears played themselves out in the sensationalist aftermath of the "shoe-shine boy" murder (August 1977), the gay bathhouse raids (February 1981), and various efforts to expel Toronto's homeless and alienated youth from the city's streets during the 1990s.

Christina was a woman of breathtaking beauty — as you will have seen from the portrait on the cover, which suggests both her elegance and her flair for dramatic hats. Nevertheless, she wrote about style not as a maven of fashion but as a sociologist who could understand its symptomatic value as a signal of a culture's ever-changing mores. In "Requiem for the High Life" you can see how she had learned from such masters as Morley Callaghan to extract significance from a scene, a gesture, or a phrase — in this case the terror that passed over the face of a perfectly coiffed lady who panicked at the glimpse of a natural young beauty passing by outside the hair salon. The tableau is not sketched for the sake of a bon mot — though the brilliance of her writing is breathtaking — but to give us a riff on the North American middle class's futile search for rules that would give entree to the nirvana of a sophisticated life. "Requiem" is not just about social values changing. It's about life in the shifting urban environment of the early 1970s, evoking Susan Sontag's famous essay "On Camp."

Christina was a contemporary of Tom Wolfe, whom she found condescending and imperial when he was invited to bestow his pearls of journalistic wisdom on the staff at *Maclean's*. Like him, she had a portraitist's capacity to single out the telling gesture and an anthropologist's ability to identify how it signified an emerging social trend. Less in-your-face and phrase-coining, more elegant and subtler, her writing reveals a similar fascination with the seismic cultural shifts that were reshaping the commercial and political values of North America. "Cathedral of Chic" catches the search for validation by an increasingly influential and newly rich social stratum that was asserting its claim for status through the pursuit of expensive, imported goods.

"Cathedral" precedes Tom Wolfe's autopsy of dyspeptic 1970s popular culture in the "Me Decade and the Third Great Awakening" and links the emerging super-consumerism with female weight obsessions: "To buy in these shops, you not only have to be rich, you have to be thin." It also prefigures such social critics as Christopher Lasch, whose *Culture of Narcissism* described the manipulative marketplace that had corrupted post-industrial society's ethos, leaving in its place a pathological individualism.

— SC

SEVEN

Springhill: The Town That Won't Give Up[5]

Chatelaine, October 1959

LATE LAST JUNE, exactly eight months to the day after the worst mining disaster in the history of the Maritimes, I returned to Springhill, Nova Scotia. I had first seen the town in November, shortly after the "bump" in the No. 2 mine, which claimed the lives of seventy-five men and threw 800 others out of work. The contrast between that dreary time and the town as it looked in early summer was startling.

The frame houses that in the fall had seemed depressingly grey were pretty now because it was June and the trees were green. The streets that had been drearily empty in the aftermath of an incessant rain were now full of children shouting with that particular joy that comes the day after school closes for the season. At the edge of town where the Dominion Steel and Coal Corporation (DOSCO) buildings loom, the mine rescue station that had figured so often in last fall's stark pictures of the tragedy had been painted egg-yolk yellow and turned into a tourist bureau by the local Lions Club.

But it didn't take long to discover that the changes were mostly external. The town's future was not much brighter than it had been in November, when DOSCO announced its decision to abandon the mine. Now, eight months later, barely 30 of the 800 unemployed had found jobs near home, and as the pinch of bad times was felt throughout town, men not directly connected with mining, from store clerks to garage mechanics, had also lost their jobs. In front of the Miners' Memorial on Main Street, a dozen able-bodied men sat along a stone wall in the sun, trading gossip about job prospects and looking slightly sheepish, as though so much idleness was unfamiliar to them.

Only one new industry — a woodworking company that presently employs about ten men — had actually been started in the town. Plans to build a provincial prison and a new hospital were definite but nobody yet knew exactly when construction would start, or how many men would be employed. It was rumoured that an American firm wanted to open a battery plant, and a group of Springhillers were trying to raise money to start their own coal mine.

But for men like Hugh Guthro, who hasn't worked a day since last October and is trying to support four people on $25 a week, such prospects aren't much more than vague promises. When I went to see Guthro, he and his wife, Margaret, were painting the shingled walls of their small house bright delphinium blue. They went inside to sit on the chesterfield in the spotless living room and talk about last year's bump and the problems the mine shutdown has caused them.

For the Guthros the closing of the mine meant the end of the only way of life they have ever known. They were both brought up in this town and were married here when Hugh was twenty-one and his wife seventeen. Their fathers before them were coal miners, and Hugh went into the pit in 1943, when he was barely sixteen. In the 1956 explosion at the Springhill mine, when thirty-eight men were killed, he was trapped underground for nearly three days, and in the 1958 disaster, he survived a seven-day ordeal in the pit.

When the mine bumped last October, his wife, Margaret, a thin girl with a small face and pretty eyes, was in their small, pin-neat kitchen, giving her sister-in-law a home permanent. The impact of the bump was like an earthquake. Dishes in the Guthros' kitchen cupboard rattled and the telephone jumped off its table. Linda, their eight-year-old daughter, was looking out a window toward the mine, and when she saw a man blown up into the sky by the sheer force of the mine's inner convulsion, she began to scream hysterically. "I thought for sure Hughie was dead," says Margaret Guthro. "It just didn't seem possible that we'd be that lucky twice."

Now she is firmly determined that Hugh will never enter a mine again. "For a girl of twenty-eight, I look like forty, and any more of that kind of trouble would kill me altogether," Margaret says.

But after eight months without a paycheque, she and her husband were beginning to feel almost hopeless about the future.

Hugh Guthro had travelled all over the Maritimes, looking for work as a labourer, but without luck. "Living on the dole is just not living," says Hugh, "and besides, I'm a young man and I don't like being a charity case."

With their unemployment insurance exhausted, the Guthros are eligible for $25 a week from the Springhill Disaster Fund.

They are also faced with the realization that the disaster fund, which totalled almost $2 million in gifts from all over the continent, will probably not last any longer than May or June of next year, according to the committee that administers it.

If they're forced to, the Guthros will move to Toronto or farther west. But neither wants to leave their families or the home into which they've put all they've saved in eleven years of marriage. "I've never been away from Springhill in my whole life — we'd just go foolish in a city," Margaret Guthro explains.

The Guthros' reluctance to move is typical of the way most people who live in Springhill feel. Despite the bleakness of the town's future outlook, only seventy-five families had left by the end of June and not more than fifty others had any plans to move. In fact, some former Springhillers were already drifting back to their homes from other parts of the country.

The reasons for this strong loyalty to the town are hard to pin down.

The fact that 80 percent of the townspeople own their own houses — houses that cannot be sold now for even half their value — undoubtedly is an important factor. Many of the men who are in their sixties and fifties and even late forties feel they are now too old to find work elsewhere. Besides, few of them know any other trade besides coal mining. Most people want to stay here simply because it's home — they were born here, their relatives are here, they want to die here.

This strong loyalty to place that is immediately evident to a stranger in town has been widely described as a mystical something called "the Springhill spirit."

The Reverend Douglas Tupper, who has lived in Springhill for the last six years as minister of St. Andrew's United Church, tried to describe this spirit for me as it seems to a relative newcomer. He said, "There is a unique feeling here that is quite different from any town I've ever known. It's a mixture of memory and understanding and the security of knowing you can rely on your neighbours in bad times."

Seven days after the bump, workers rescued twelve men who had lived all that time in a 3-foot-high debris-strewn hole, a mile down in the shaft. Two days later — in what was later called the second miracle at Springhill — six more men were discovered alive. Maurice Ruddick was the leader of that second group.

Ruddick is a mulatto, a handsome, big man with an almost over-powering glow of good-natured vitality. When he was hauled out of the pit on a stretcher after the nine-day ordeal, he croaked to the crowd waiting outside, "Give me some whisky and I'll sing you a song." Ruddick was born forty-six years ago in a mining town called Joggins, thirty miles from Springhill, and has been mining most of his adult life. There are twelve Ruddick children, five boys and seven girls who range in age from thirteen to not quite one.

Maurice has appeared twice on the CBC-TV program *Front Page Challenge*, and has been interviewed on radio and television in several cities in Ontario and the Maritimes. He was named Citizen of the Year in a poll conducted by the *Toronto Telegram*, was feted on an all-expenses-paid holiday in Georgia with the rest of the eighteen rescued men, and has had one of his songs recorded by an American company.

Despite all this public recognition, Maurice has not been able to find a single day's work since the disaster. "I was offered a job up in Toronto to work in a car lot," he says. "But I don't know, I just have this feeling that if I leave, I'll let Springhill down — and I really believe in that old slogan, Springhill will never die."

Maurice looked uncharacteristically grave when he talked about his financial situation, then brightened immediately and said, "Oh well, we're making out all right now; when we get down to bread and molasses, that's the time to worry." He fills his days by going hunting or fishing, talking or playing cards at the miners' hall.

But he would far sooner talk about playing the guitar or singing in a quartet he formed ten years ago. ("My hobbies are singing and child raising," he's been known to say.) Or he may get to talking about the oddities of segregation laws in the South.

Shortly after the disaster, Marvin Griffin, then governor of the state of Georgia, offered the eighteen rescued Springhill miners and their families a week of southern hospitality in a Georgia resort on Jekyll Island. When he found out later that one of the families was Negro, he hastily said the Ruddicks could come to Georgia only on a segregated basis. The Ruddicks good-naturedly accepted his offer and were given a luxurious trailer in the coloured section of the same resort.

The other miners came over to see Maurice on two different evenings during the holiday, and both groups had an unforgettable time. But for Maurice the best moment of the whole week came one afternoon when Governor Griffin drove down to see him in a cavalcade of black limousines, escorted by state police on motorcycles. Ruddick and Griffin had a few drinks together, and Maurice persuaded the southern segregationist to pose for a colour picture holding the two youngest Ruddick children. The photo is one of Maurice's prized possessions.

I mentioned to Gorley Kempt, a miner who survived last October's disaster, a statement made to me that morning by Ralph Gilroy, the mayor, "Despite all the hardship they have suffered, I bet I could walk out this morning and find 400 men who'd go back to work in a mine tomorrow, if only one would open up," Gilroy had said.

Gorley agreed and explained, "There's nothing mysterious about it. People are always asking us how we could stand the life of a miner, but it's simple. There's good money in it. I used to make $20 on a good day at the mine. Now I get a dollar an hour, and I'm one of the lucky ones."

It's not the same either for Rose Leboch McLeod, the Kempts' good friend, who came to Springhill fifteen years ago as Robert McLeod's French war bride.

Rose was born in the small town of Grenay, France, 15 miles from Vimy Ridge. At sixteen she met Bob McLeod, a private in the Canadian Army. "It was a beautiful moonlit night in September," she remembers with wonderful Gallic gusto, "and that man was the best thing that ever happened to me." When Rose came out to her husband's hometown the next summer, she knew no English, and for the first months they communicated with each other by pointing at phrases in a dictionary issued by the army.

Now Rose and son Bobby, who is eleven, live there alone. Financially, they are reasonably secure. Immediately after the disaster each widow was paid $1,500 in compensation from DOSCO. From annuities set up for the widows by the Springhill Disaster Fund, Rose gets $40 a month (in accordance with the rule that allows $30 for the widow until she dies or remarries, $10 for the youngest child until he reaches eighteen, and $5 for each additional child). She also receives $82.50 a month from Workmen's Compensation and $8 a month in a baby-bonus cheque.

But as the months wear on, Rose finds that instead of recovering from her grief, she feels more and more lonely for her husband. "At first I was kind of numb and it was as though God had given me strength," she says simply. "But now I just go around the house looking at pictures of my Bob and I feel terrible."

"We didn't think she could ever manage without him," says Marguerite Kempt. "Bob did everything for her, probably because she was so young when they married, and a stranger to Canada. But she's shown a wonderful spirit in trying to pull herself out of her grief."

Rose can drive her car the 40 miles to Amherst to shop and she takes it on weekends to the McLeod cabin at Five Islands. "To some people that car might seem a big expense, but I told myself, 'Rose, for your son's sake, you've got to act alive,' and the car has helped me."

Her mother-in-law, Mrs. Robert McLeod Sr., has also been a big comfort to Rose. Six men with the surname McLeod were killed in the mine last fall, and two of them were Mrs. McLeod's sons. Two others were cousins. "She don't cry — she just says to me, 'Rose, it's God's will!'"

After I'd said goodbye to Rose and started down the gravel road from her house on Willow Avenue back to the pavement of Main

Street, I began to ponder the answer she'd given her family in France, when they wrote asking her to come home after her husband's funeral. The sentences Rose told me she had written seemed to sum up the reasons Springhill people won't leave their town: "Here I have friends, and because they know me and we've all lived through this terrible time, we have what I call an understanding together — now where else are you going to find that?" To almost everyone who lives in Springhill and wants to stay, the answer is simple: Nowhere else.

EIGHT

The New Power in the New West [6]

Saturday Night, September 1976

FOR NEARLY THREE YEARS now, before, during, and after the Great Canadian Oil Crisis, I've been travelling regularly to Alberta, making those hit-run-write forays that are the inevitable lot of the journalist who sets out to report this complicated federation we call a country. Every time I go there, as soon as the interviews begin — over lunch in the Owl's Nest at the Calgary Inn, say, with the interviewee sipping his first Bloody Caesar and people at nearby tables talking at the top of their enthusiasm range about wellheads, bull semen, rapeseed, drilling rigs, and riding rings — I get a feeling, both unsettling and exhilarating, that somehow I've strayed into a foreign land.

This sense of the "otherness" of the province has never been as strong as it was in July, when I spent ten days in Edmonton, Calgary, and points west and south, trying to get a handle on what Peter Lougheed has taken to calling "the spirit of the New West" and what I've come to think of as the very special style of the Independent Commonwealth of Alberta, Inc.

Nearly everybody I encountered, from the premier on his patio in Edmonton to the oil men on suede sofas in their office towers in Calgary, was as feisty as a colt let loose from a corral. In the rest of the country, people may have been worrying about prices, crises, scandals, scurrilities, and sundry other weaknesses of capitalism, bilingualism, and all we hold dear. But in Alberta, the natives were experiencing a self-congratulatory, barely controllable, super-duper high.

The federal government had been strong-armed at last into allowing domestic oil prices to move toward world market levels, with two increases this year making prices nearly triple the rates for 1973. The percentage of employable people with jobs was the highest in the country, the taxes levied on them the lowest, and the social services provided them the best. The estimated 1975 Alberta Gross Domestic Product showed an increase over 1974 of 18 percent, nearly double the rate of increase for Canada as a whole.

A newly established government-controlled fund of more than $2 billion in liquid capital, called the Heritage Trust, was causing the eyes of international money men to glow with greed. There was more drilling activity and more development and exploration money being spent in the oil business than ever before. The coal industry was gung-ho, despite a complicated new policy to regulate it just unveiled by the government. Foreign investors were flocking in to explore possible joint ventures in secondary industry or outright ownership of vast tracts of Alberta acreage as an inflation hedge, flagged on by favourable reports about Alberta's economic prospects and political stability in the international press, including papers as restrained as the *Financial Times* of London.

In brief, it was possible this summer for people in Alberta to believe they could get rich from a standing start, if not this year, well then next — an old dream that few Canadians outside that province have the heart or chutzpah to believe in any more.

Albertans love to talk about each other's triumphs. "He started with zip"— meaning nothing — they'll say, about some newly rich tycoon. "Zip, I tell you, and look at him now."

"What people don't talk about," says Kevin Peterson, city editor of the *Calgary Herald*, "is all the guys who started with zip and now have less, the ones who dreamed the dream, made the plays, failed, and have had to put their houses in their wives' names to escape bankruptcy takeovers." But then, that's Alberta — if you believe in tomorrow country, you don't count the candles or the failures. You hoist your belt and get moving.

To understand the mood of Alberta now, which sets it apart so markedly from the rest of Canada, you have to understand its peculiar political history; its economy, which is about to take off; its unique cultural style, which amounts to almost an ideology — and, of course, the importance of its premier, Peter Lougheed, who in his person sums up all three.

What the Albertans want is to control their own destiny and to be recognized for what they are — not seen as imitators of Texans or enviers of easterners, not as loudmouths, rednecks, soreheads, or cowboys, but as hard-working, urban-dwelling, richly deserving, sweetly reasonable SOBs.

In a way, Alberta is like a developing country involved in the first excitement of asserting its independence. In 1971, when the Lougheed Conservatives came to power after thirty-six years of Social Credit rule, the province was still a little like a colony whose political destiny was determined by a faraway paternalistic government that saw its leaders as manageable rubes.

Lougheed was known to have federal ambitions and was expected to look to Ottawa as a learning centre, a place where he would wind up eventually, as his grandfather, the senator, had before him; though what he had in mind was not the Red Chamber but the PM's office.

But to their chagrin, Lougheed and his colleagues found when they first went to federal-provincial meetings at various levels, they were plainly outclassed and rudely outmanoeuvred by the Ottawa politicians and their bureaucrats in a way that seems to have singed their pride and made them determined not just to get even but to outdo. They still tell tales of the times in the early 1970s when federal cabinet ministers kept their Alberta counterparts cooling their heels in anterooms, or patronizingly quieted Alberta's urgent requests with what amounted at times to outright lies fed to them by their mandarins.

Exchanges between Don Getty, who was then Alberta Minister of Intergovernmental Affairs, and Donald Macdonald, who was then federal Minister of Energy, were particularly tense during the autumn and winter of 1974–1975. A neutral observer recently described their encounters as "clashes between two very different kinds of guys who were the same age but came from very different backgrounds and totally misunderstood each other. Macdonald seemed to view Getty as some kind of dumb pro-football quarterback, and Getty saw him as a combination snotty private school prefect and big-time Bay Street lawyer." (Getty is still called a hawk in the Alberta cabinet vis-à-vis Ottawa. "I keep telling my colleagues," he said in conversation this summer, "that they're relaxing too soon. It's like being way ahead at half-time — that's when you can let down your guard and that's when you can lose the ball game.")

After the first shock at the treatment they received was over, the Albertans decided to fight back not blindly or noisily but with a calculated strategy they're still developing. The federalists plainly misjudged the man they were dealing with. Lougheed and his colleagues aren't intellectuals, and they aren't "civilized" in the way Ottawa reckons civility. (They never talk about Ken Galbraith, Château Lafite Medoc versus Château Haut-Brion, or the next candidate for GG.) But they do belong to the first generation of a different breed of western Canadian, rapidly forming into a class that is urban, educated, affluent, and bloody-minded.

In Lougheed's current cabinet of twenty-four, made up largely of the same people it comprised in 1971 (though they all now hold different portfolios), there are eight lawyers, nine businessmen, and only two farmers. Lougheed himself has a degree from Harvard. And Getty is an honour graduate of the business administration course at the University of Western Ontario. Merv Leitch, the provincial treasurer, was the gold medallist in his graduating year at the University of Alberta Law School, beating out for first place Ivan Head, Pierre Trudeau's principal foreign-policy adviser. Lou Hyndman, now the Minister of Intergovernmental Affairs and grandson of a judge, is a lawyer with lifelong political ambitions, and has experience as an executive assistant in Ottawa. The fifth powerhouse in the cabinet, Hugh Horner, though a member of the famous family of rootin'-tootin'-ranchin' Horners, was educated as a medical doctor and, despite his penchant for telling his enemies he'll tear their arms off, is said to be a sophisticated thinker in certain specialized areas. None of these men wears string ties or cowboy boots, except on their "spreads" or during Stampede week. In fact, a scientific foot count might show that there are more cowboy boots on Yonge Street these days than on Jasper Avenue.

In the last five years these men have strengthened resolutely their *indépendantiste* position, making moves that have caused complaint that they're covert separatists (notably from Senator Earl Hastings, who speaks for Alberta in Liberal Ottawa because there isn't a single elected Liberal MP from the province and hasn't been since Harry Hays and Hu Harries went down shaking their fists after failing to get anybody in Ottawa to listen to them).

When charged with separatism, Albertans answer unblinkingly that all they're trying to do is "redress the balance of confederation." To this end they've developed the intelligence network and negotiating skills of FIGA, their Federal and Intergovernmental Affairs Department, to the point where it operates like a miniature foreign office. FIGA has forty staff members in Edmonton in a non-line (i.e., one that doesn't deliver any services) department, plus resident officials in Ottawa to tell them what goes on there, and a routine engrained in their senior officers of phoning around the country every day to check out the action in the other provinces.

Every Alberta minister or bureaucrat has to clear through FIGA any statement or policy position he's going to take that affects federal-provincial relations so that when Alberta speaks, whether the matter is picayune or important, it's with one voice. In the last two years that voice has been heard loud and clear in Ottawa, with the Albertans winning big on the oil price rises and the Syncrude deal and coming out slightly better than even in the taxation on the provincial oil royalties situation.

Alberta isn't satisfied, though, with decolonizing itself politically. It's moving rapidly into a second phase that might be called economic liberation. Peter Lougheed gave public notice of this in a speech made in New York in June, when he said he planned to shift economic power west from the great centres of eastern Canada. What he was expressing was the Alberta business community's desire to be freed from the overriding financial control of Toronto and Montreal. To the outsider it sometimes seems that the hatred of eastern financial interests is bred into the bones of every true Albertan, in school if he was native-born and in the Petroleum Club if he was naturalized. Half the businessmen you meet — from Carl Nickle, whose father was a Calgary shoe salesman who became enormously rich during the first oil strikes of the 1940s, to Don Getty, who was born in the east but made his millions in oil in the 1960s before turning to politics — talk bitterly of how they were treated by officials in banks and investment houses on Bay or St. James Street when they went there seeking development money.

"They'd just look at us in those days and you could feel them think-ing, 'Alberta/oil/yeech!'" Getty remembers. "And then they'd smooth you over and turn you down. That's when I became a Westerner."

Sweet, sweet is the feeling of revenge these days. You can sense it in Calgary when old-style oil men, cigars stuffed between their chom-pers, the diamonds in the rings on their pinky fingers gleaming, let you know that T.O. is now the small time. Money waits for them in Zurich. Or you can detect it in the politicians, controlled and circum-spect in quiet suits in Edmonton, who describe benignly certain somewhat pleasing facts. Such as that representatives of most of the major banks have found their way out to the premier's office in recent months, suavely conceding that decision-making power on large loans won't have to be referred to head offices any more but will lie with local managers. Or that investment houses are beefing up their branches in Calgary with the hope of attracting the government's business. Young brokers fresh from the National or the St. James's Club say with awe that the money desk the provincial treasury depart-ment is running itself these days would put Wood Gundy's to shame.

Lougheed's ringing speech in New York, outlining his economic manifesto, was part of a ten-day trip he made through the United States, meeting businessmen, governors of western states, and several Washington senators from states bordering Alberta or doing business extensively with the province. That trip, in turn, fitted into what's obviously a master plan for Alberta to relate internationally to politi-cians and financiers without depending on Ottawa to represent it.

The European mission of last autumn, when sixty-five Albertans criss-crossed the continent, seeking venture capital and technological knowledge, was an even flashier display of the same kind of dogged planning. Before that, Lougheed had already journeyed to Japan and there is talk in Edmonton (acknowledged inscrutably by FIGA offi-cials) that next he's going to China. In the meantime Lougheed is making demands that tariff negotiations on petrochemicals (an important new industrial area opening up for Alberta) be made bilaterally with the U.S. rather than through GATT [General Agreement on Tariffs and Trade], a bold request but one he says is necessary "because if it isn't done that way, Ottawa will do the talking and Alberta's interests, as usual, will get lost in the buzz."

You can say to Lougheed or any of his three important ministers in the economic sphere — Getty, Hyndman, and Leitch — "Okay, you guys have leverage now because you lucked into the big time with the energy crisis, but what will happen when the oil runs out in ten or fifteen years — where will your economic power lie then?" But every one of them answers with optimism. Beyond the conventional oil reserves lie other wonders, they say — oil from the tar sands, natural gas by the trillions of cubic feet, coal by the billions of tons, forest resources, land resources. Beyond that is the Heritage Trust Fund, which is seen as energy changed into money and a continuing economic balancer.

All this makes it sound as though business and government work as one in Alberta. In effect, they do. There is some grumbling in Calgary, mostly among the executives in the multinational companies, that Lougheed is no friend of the oil business due to the price-fixing power he's vested in the Alberta Energy Commission. Businessmen in other endeavours croak occasionally about government interference in the private sector, meaning the takeover of Pacific Western Airlines by the government in 1974 and stringent regulations set for the coal industry this spring demanding hefty royalties and reclamation of land by mining companies, which previously got away with plunder.

But the complaints are perfunctory compared to the kind of hysteria businessmen in the province and elsewhere work up against Ottawa. (If you talk to corporate men these days anywhere in Canada you soon discover there is somebody called Him who looms so large in their consciousness he doesn't need a name. It isn't God they're talking about, or even the Devil, but Pierre Elliott Trudeau.)

In any case, Alberta is probably as close to a capitalist's paradise as it's possible to become in a democracy in the 1970s. The cabinet is like a board of directors of some vast corporation called Alberta, Inc. — secretive, self-contained, business-oriented, and run by a president-premier who practises an ideology that might be described as Aggressive Conservatism.

Listening to Lougheed — though they couldn't be more different physically or stylistically — one is reminded of de Gaulle. If the general could say, "I am France," then the premier can say, "I am Alberta." He gives the impression privately and publicly that he cares passionately about the province.

In return he's treated for the most part with the kind of deference usually accorded a symbolic icon, particularly by his personal staff, several of whom have been his friends since childhood. (Harold Millican, the deputy minister of FIGA, went to kindergarten with him in 1934 and to Washington with him in 1976, and they've scarcely been separated in the forty-two years between.)

One of the curious aspects of this regard is that Lougheed supporters won't admit to him having human flaws. If an outsider says he looks tired, they get huffy and tell you he feels great, he's been jogging regularly, he just needs some time in the sun, he weighs what he did when he was at the U of A, etc., etc. Once during the European mission last autumn, a young FIGA official, having been asked if an unexpected meeting with Lord Thomson could be managed, answered offhandedly, "Listen, we've plugged this little guy in everywhere he can be plugged." There was a ghastly thirty-second silence. Then a Lougheed staff man said, through thin lips, "He is *not* little."

Partly this adulation for The Leader is due to the way Albertans have always responded politically. Since the province's founding in

1905 they've tended to one-party dominance in their legislature. Their governing majorities, from the United Farmers to the Social Crediters to the Lougheed Conservatives, have functioned less like orthodox political parties than ideological movements, a situation that led to the famous thesis of C.B. Macpherson that Alberta doesn't have an alternate party system or even a plebiscitary democracy but a special governing style he called "the quasi-party system."

Dissent is distasteful to the true Albertan. Other than a small handful of political scientists at the Universities of Alberta and Calgary and an even smaller handful of nationalists (including Mel Hurtig, the Edmonton publisher, and Larry Pratt, a political scientist at the University of Alberta, who have publicly expressed outrage at the concessions the Alberta government has made in terms of energy resources to the voracity of the multinationals), few people seem even mildly disturbed by the size of the current Conservative majority.

Lougheed holds sixty-nine of the seventy-five seats in the legislature. Four dispirited Socreds make up the Opposition, along with one Independent and Grant Notley of the NDP, who's game but glassy-eyed at the enormity of the task he's trying to fulfill. Notley held onto his seat (Spirit River-Fairview) in 1975 by less than a hundred votes, and the Tories fought hard to bring him down, a fight made easier by the fact that the Socreds were persuaded not to put up a candidate, and the Conservatives' man was a prosperous Ukrainian farmer who cut into Notley's ethnic vote.

At his most hopeful Notley feels he can expect in the next election — the big breakthrough, he calls it — five seats. At that, he's more optimistic than the Liberals, who haven't held a single constituency for the last two elections and regularly lose their deposits when they run. So far there is no political leader in evidence who can challenge Lougheed's stature as a colossus.

Lougheed commands a response beyond the blind accord Albertans traditionally give their premier. He's not a great orator, and in person he's engaging though by no means flamboyant, original, or even egocentric. But in his compact person he sums up the qualities that Alberta admires, and they aren't the clichéd attributes of boosterism or pretension visualized in the East.

Primarily Lougheed is a doer and a winner. "He works hard," people say wonderingly, "twelve hours a day, doing his homework and feeding his internal computer and it *pays*." In his society — where important executives are in their offices ready to do business by eight o'clock, and everybody eats lunch sharp at twelve noon, clearing the expensive restaurants and club dining rooms by one-fifteen — hard work and hard-won success count for more than brains, looks, wit, and breeding combined. To most of the outstandingly successful business and professional men in the province, the premier is Peter, and Peter is perfect.

In answer to the puzzling question of why he decided not to run for the federal Tory leadership in February 1967, most of them reply vaguely that they don't really know — his family, maybe, perhaps the timing was wrong, though "he could have had it on the first ballot, I mean there was no doubt." But one man who's observed Lougheed closely for years looked at me when I inquired whether Lougheed didn't wish he were in Joe Clark's place, laughed, and said: "But we worked out the answer that night when we talked about it in Germany in October."

What he was remembering was a highlight of Lougheed's European mission, which had included a party at Lancaster House in London, a dinner at the Quai d'Orsay in France, and a dance at Edinburgh Castle, and would have involved a lunch with the Queen at Buckingham Palace if the premier hadn't been called home to eat that day at 24 Sussex Drive and hear the news of the Anti-Inflation Board.

This particular evening was a formal dinner given by Alberta itself at the Schloss Kronberg, a castle in the Black Forest to which more than a hundred West German businessmen — financiers, merchant bankers, and industrialists — had been invited. They had arrived from as far as 150 miles away in limousines that clogged the courtyards where their chauffeurs stood gossiping. They had dined on superb food in a huge room hung with medieval tapestries. Then they sat back with Turkish cigarettes and Cuban cigars, a sea of stout black backs, and turned toward the room's centre, where Lougheed stood to speak.

He made his standard we-welcome-foreign-investment speech, outlining Alberta's attractions in precise prose, saying that the dicta of the federal Foreign Investment Review Agency weren't really to be feared, and then deviated from the text for a moment and literally shouted, "I believe in the capitalist ethic."

There was a guttural roar of approval from the crowd; people jumped to their feet and applauded for what seemed like five minutes until Lougheed, flushed with excitement, held up his hand for them to stop.

Talking about it a few minutes later, as the Germans streamed out, clicking and bowing and galumphing into the night, I said to Lougheed's friend, "Wow, why would he want to give this up to hassle with Trudeau, to placate the Tory caucus, to try to win seats in Quebec?"

"The answer is he wouldn't, and he won't," said his friend, "because in Alberta he's got it all."

That turned out, of course, to be a truism that held — and will hold, the way things are going in the province, economically and politically, for as long into the future as any pundit can see.

NINE

The Long Ordeal of
William Wilder[7]

Saturday Night, June 1977

IF YOU SHOULD HAPPEN to find yourself some weekday morning this summer, at the unlikely hour of half-past seven, driving north in mid-town Toronto through the iron gates of Upper Canada College toward the landmark clock tower, you might catch a glimpse on the east side of the grounds of a man in a jogging suit resolutely circling a cinder track — his pace as steady, head as high, flanks as lean, as though he were a prefect just past eighteen and not a corporate titan pushing fifty-four.

The man's name is William Price Wilder — sometime president of Wood Gundy Limited, Canada's largest investment firm, and for the past five years chief executive officer of Canadian Arctic Gas Study Limited, the world's largest pipeline consortium — and he's running hard on home ground. UCC is his school and the school of all three of his sons. Bishop Strachan, where his daughter was educated, is a little to the west and the house where he lives is a little to the south, in that part of Lower Forest Hill where the old Anglo-Toronto money still owns the substantial houses with the Spanish tile roofs and the black maids in the kitchen brewing the coffee and the Yorkies out sniffing under the rhododendrons on the lawn.

You wouldn't know it to look at him as he runs, but William Wilder is nearing the end of a long ordeal. Since 1972, he's been attempting to get government approval to build the Mackenzie Valley pipeline, a project that's been described as the largest undertaking ever proposed by private enterprise in this country. That approval will be granted finally or denied by the Trudeau cabinet in the summer of 1977 in order to accommodate the deadline set by the U.S. government for its decision on the means of bringing desperately needed natural gas from Alaska to the American Middle West.

In 1972, when Wilder took on the job of heading Canadian Arctic Gas, the international consortium put together two years earlier to build a northern pipeline, he saw himself as a latter-day William Van Horne whose task was to open up the North as Van Horne's had been to open up the West with the building of the Canadian Pacific Railway. The corporations in the consortium, which included several giant oil companies, among them Exxon and Shell, saw Wilder as the perfect man to steer their project to quick completion. From all outward appearances, he had exactly the right political, financial, and social connections to bring these multinationals their hearts' desire.

But in five years the world in which Bill Wilder operated so surely for decades has been buffeted by radical reversals. Aroused Native peoples, irate environmentalists, hot nationalists, new and tougher government regulations, altered energy supplies and demands, and, most important of all, an unexpectedly broad official inquiry into his pipeline's social and environmental implications, conducted by a socialist judge, have all conspired against him. The outcome of his consortium's pipeline plans, which seemed so sure in the summer of 1972, is no longer sure at all.

This summer the look in Wilder's clear blue eyes is not exactly one of fatigue — he keeps himself in such good shape, what with the jogging and the skiing and the farming and fishing, that he rarely displays tiredness at all — but of puzzlement.

The story of Wilder's ordeal is interesting because it says a good deal about Canada in the' 1970s — about the centralized Establishment webs that used to control the country and now don't hold quite as firm; about our relationship with the Americans; about the burgeoning power of the regions; about our attitude toward our Native peoples, our natural resources, and our environment; and about the way the public interest is currently perceived. But more than anything else, Wilder's recent experiences symbolize the drastic change that's taken place in the Canadian business environment.

"The average businessman makes a rotten politician. If you're in business, you are used to getting on with things and to hell with compromise. The politician has to be flexible and pay attention to the public and the businessman doesn't understand that."
— Alastair Gillespie, Minister of Energy, Mines, and Resources, describing the differences he noticed when he left business for politics

Nobody, not even his good friend Gillespie, would say Bill Wilder is an *average* businessman. He is more like a prototype. His family background, his education, his experience, have all led him to believe ardently in the touchstones of capitalism's Darwinian creed: hard work, straight deals, maximized profits, minimized government interference, big is beautiful, the race is to the swift, and all's right with the corporate world. In a way, the story of Wilder's life is the story of Canadian capitalism in the past fifty years.

When he was born in the 1920s, his father was busy making money on a stock market that was bullish even for butcher boys and bliss for brokers like himself. The senior William Wilder was the son of a Methodist farmer from Prince Edward County in eastern Ontario who'd grown prosperous enough to send him to be educated at Victoria College in Toronto before the First World War.

At Vic he became fast friends with another young Methodist named Reginald Gundy, who helped him get a job in Wood Gundy, his family's firm, where he quickly climbed to the vice-presidency with the benevolent approval of the founder, J.H. Gundy.

A chauffeur used to drive young Bill when he was still a toddler from his parents' big house in Rosedale to pick up his father at the old Wood Gundy building on King Street near Bay, and he still remembers hearing the click of the tickers and savouring the bustle that infects the premises of the prosperous in palmy times.

On the day William Wilder Senior died, in the late spring of 1929, when he was just past forty and Bill was only six, his estate was valued at between $4 million and $5 million. But he had purchased not long before — at the urging of J.H. Gundy, who was doing the same thing himself — large blocks of Massey-Harris common stock, when it was selling at $96 a share, with the aid of a $1-million bank loan. After the crash the following October, when the lawyers got around to liquidating his estate, Massey-Harris was down to $6, and by the time everything was settled there weren't enough assets left to pay the succession duties. The case is still used as a dire warning to Ontario law students about how not to handle an estate, but all it meant for young Bill at the time was that "something terrible had happened," linking death and loss and money in one big wad of fear.

Mrs. Wilder had an inheritance from her father, a Scottish-Irish dry goods merchant put out of business by the similar, if superior, Toronto establishment of Timothy Eaton, and that turned out to be enough to send Bill to UCC and keep up the Rosedale house. All the same, the Depression affected Wilder in the way it affected so many men of his generation, making them anxious, acquisitive, and obsessively hard-working. "Some of my father's friends starved in the thirties and some of them jumped off the Glen Road Bridge," he says. "Panhandlers used to come out of the ravines and ask for food at our door. For as long as I can remember, I have been determined to have my share of worldly goods."

He set about acquiring that share, after spending four years in the navy and getting a B.Comm from McGill, by joining his father's old firm as a securities salesman in 1946. But he felt the advice he was giving clients was inadequate and he determined to get an M.B.A. at the Harvard School of Business, the fount of the new business gospel that was compelling the forward-looking among his contemporaries.

The school made a profound impression on him. "Everything I did before I went to Harvard was unfocused somehow. I learned to discipline myself there and live by a philosophy," he says.

The philosophy was provided by a sometime brigadier-general in the U.S. Army, a martinet professor named Georges Doriot. He told his students to look in the mirror every morning and say to themselves, "What are you going to accomplish today?" and to do the same thing every evening before going to bed, asking their reflections, "Am I better tonight than I was this morning?"

He also told them to read the *New York Times* regularly to see if it contained any news of interest to their companies (a revolution in a far-off state might alter the price of copper) or their careers (the death of an executive might mean an important opening up the ladder). Above all, he dinned into them his belief that to function well a good business has to be housed in a healthy body. Bill Wilder started to run a mile a day at Harvard and he's been running ever since.

During the next twenty-two years, back in Toronto, he gathered to himself all the other components of the Harvard dream. He married not just well but brilliantly. His wife, Judith Ryrie Bickle, was a

sunny-natured, athletic girl he met at a party, the only child of a powerful stockbroker named Edward Bickle, who functioned for years as
a bagman-cum-confidant for Ontario Progressive Conservative premiers and eventually left an estate of several millions.

When Wilder went to ask Bickle for his daughter's hand, the older
man saw fit to tell him that he had been "inquiring about you at Wood
Gundy, young fellow, and they say your prospects are good." And of
course they were. Wilder's connections and his hard-won Harvard savvy
and tireless ambition led him straight up the hierarchy until he became
president in his forties, fostering the growth of the firm from a family
business to a huge modern organization and at the same time outdoing
his father, pleasing his father-in-law, and making his personal fortune.
("If you marry a rich woman," he told a friend once, "you've got to have
money of your own. Otherwise, they lead you around by the nose.")

In the twenty-odd years he spent at Wood Gundy, Wilder got to know
almost everybody who mattered in the Canadian elite. He belonged to
important clubs (the York, the Toronto, the Badminton & Racquet, the
St. James's, the Tadenac Fishing). He had important friends (three of
the close ones from way back are John Aird, the Liberal lawyer and
fundraiser; Alastair Gillespie, who had also been at McGill and in the
navy and has a gentleman's farm close to the Wilders' place near Clare-
mont, Ontario; and Dr. John Evans, who married a Glassco and later
became president of the University of Toronto). He sat on important
boards (Noranda Mines, John Labatt, Simpsons) and espoused important causes (fundraising for the Hospital for Sick Children, the University
of Western Ontario, and Mitchell Sharp's leadership campaign). Best of
all, his company was at the centre of the Canadian boom.

Among its several functions, Wood Gundy raises capital for governments and large corporations. In the 1950s and 1960s, when Wilder
was making his climb, the firm put together the money for dozens of
huge deals in the hush of its Toronto offices, where the carpets are

thick and the china thin, where the walls are covered with the minor works of the Group of Seven, and where the senior partners wear beautiful shirts with collars that pinch, ever so gently, the pink flesh on their close-shaven necks.

Among those deals were several resource development schemes, such as TransCanada PipeLines, Interprovincial Pipe Line, Trans Mountain Pipe Line, and the giant Churchill Falls project. Wilder acquired a matchless reputation for being able to bring off intricate financial arrangements involving both the public and the private sectors, and this skill attracted Canadian Arctic Gas to him when its members were looking for a chief executive officer in 1972.

Canadian Arctic Gas was (and still is) a complex organization then made up of more than twenty Canadian and American corporations, several of them giant U.S.-based multinationals, which commanded billions of dollars in financial resources as well as intensive energy expertise and extensive industrial and consumer markets. They were combined in an uneasy alliance, bent on tapping promising sources of natural gas and oil owned by the U.S. in Alaska and by Canada in the Mackenzie Delta and bringing it to market via a pipeline along the Mackenzie Valley.

Under the pressure of the new nationalism in Canada in the early 1970s, the consortium's members came to recognize that they had to have a Canadian as CEO. Ian Sinclair of Canadian Pacific, one of the Canadian participants, in company with an agent of the multinationals, W.O. Twaits of Imperial Oil, is said to have sold the rest on Wilder as the safe choice to steer the proposal through the maze of the National Energy Board hearings into the pipeline's implications, which the Canadian government was committed to holding. (Long gone were the days when C.D. Howe could ram through the legislative process a trans-Canada pipeline on his own say-so — long gone, and, in this group, much lamented.) Still, before Wilder was approached, it was first ascertained that he was acceptable to the federal Liberals. In fact, the whole project, with Wilder at its head, turned out to be so acceptable in Ottawa at the time that the Canada Development Corporation, whose major shareholder is the federal government, became a member of the consortium.

On their part, the consortium's members were still living in the nostalgic era of supposedly endless energy resources. What they were doing by tapping the North was ensuring available supplies far into the future and at the same time guaranteeing themselves nearly endless profits. All they had to do was find out what the Canadian government expected of them in terms of environmental and economic safeguards, and they would build the pipeline through the tundra in jig time, bringing gas to U.S. markets by 1977.

On his part, Wilder saw his chance to escape from Wood Gundy before he was fifty, an age, as his Harvard mentors had told him, when a man needs to make a leap or go stale. He had accumulated his personal fortune; now, he saw his chance to make a public name. If a larger fortune went with it, well, that was the way of his world.

> "Wilder was naive. He really believed he was doing something great for his country, developing the North, creating jobs, serving the great god Progress. He thought he could control the consortium, including the American multinationals within it, the way he controlled Wood Gundy, and work the government system the way he had worked the business system. But even if he hadn't been naive, he couldn't have foreseen the disasters to come."
>
> — A Toronto businessman who knows
> Wilder and his milieu very well

Certainly it would have taken a sociologist-seer to predict the kind of problems Wilder would run into when he moved out of his secure place in the indigenous Anglo-Canadian elite into a highly visible role as *comprador* — to borrow the Portuguese word the nineteenth-century British imperialists used to describe their native agents in the outposts of the Far East.

Among the most obvious of his interrelated difficulties were these:

1. **The Kierans Kerfuffle.** Eric Kierans was the best known of the nationalists to challenge publicly the pipeline concept in its early stages, and all through his first years with Arctic Gas, Wilder had to appear on platforms to answer Kierans's charges, a proselytizing role he found alien and offensive. ("At Wood Gundy, I was sheltered," he says. "You never had to explain anything to the public.") It didn't take long for the Committee for an Independent Canada to sound its alarums, and later, a specially formed group, the Public Petroleum Association of Canada, added its hues to the citizen outcry.

2. **The Bob Blair Breakaway.** Robert Blair, a Calgary engineer with a healthy ego (fuelled by the new juice in the New West — he and Lougheed were thick as Grits), had committed his firm, Alberta Gas Trunk Line, to the Arctic Gas consortium with some reluctance in the first place. But after Wilder was in charge, Blair's dissatisfaction with the group grew. He disagreed with the route chosen, with the size of the pipe to be laid, on the American exigencies he felt were overwhelming Canadian interests. Most of all, Blair resented being treated like a small-time operator by the multinationals and quarrelled bitterly with Wilder, whom he saw as their creature and an Eastern Arrogant to boot. The upshot of the conflict was Blair's decision to quit the consortium in 1974 and to put forward his own proposal for the Maple Leaf Line, a move that exacerbated an already complicated situation. It meant that the National Energy Board

now had rival proposals to weigh and that Bill Wilder's long-time reputation as a diplomatic deal-maker was eroded by his failure to hold on to his temper and to Blair.

3. **The spiralling cost, dwindling resource, and mounting suspicion problems.** The Arctic Gas project was hard hit by the inflation and energy shortage fears that resulted from the OPEC crisis in the autumn of 1973. Instead of being the lone applicant come forward to pipe gas efficiently from a grateful Canada happy to sell its resources to a huge American market, Arctic Gas had to face a new situation. Newly aroused caution in resource circles resulted in the revelation that there was far less gas in the Mackenzie Delta than originally had been claimed, and that it would be far more expensive to bring out than even the most pessimistic had imagined. The official estimated costs of the Mackenzie Valley pipeline eventually amounted to close to $10 billion ($7.9 billion to be spent in Canada) — though in the atmosphere of distrust that has grown thicker around Arctic Gas with every passing year even this figure is questioned. Investors and nationalists alike have been saying that since building a pipeline in the far North is an undertaking entirely different from any other technological feat ever attempted, costs can only be guessed at.

To make their guesses more plausible, Arctic Gas had spent, by the end of 1976, $130 million on research alone, including environmental studies, social and economic projections, engineering analyses, and construction planning. But the more they spent, the less they were believed. Academic economists dismissed the study commissioned from the University of Toronto's Institute for Policy Analysis with the faculty club joke, "He who pays the computer calls the printout."

4. **The protracted-hearing, expanded-inquiry delays.** The original Arctic Gas timetable called for official approval of their application by early 1975. By late 1975, the National Energy Board hadn't even begun regular hearings. This was partly because the changing situation had caused the board to expand its frame of reference, and hence its demands on the applicants, and partly because of a lamentable incident involving the NEB chairman, Marshall Crowe.

   Crowe was challenged by several public interest groups as to his impartiality in the matter of the Mackenzie pipeline on the basis that he had served as chairman of the Canada Development Corporation when it belonged to the consortium. Hearings had to be suspended for months while the case was reviewed in the Supreme Court of Canada. Eventually, Crowe's role as chairman was disallowed for these hearings even though Bora Laskin, the Chief Justice, said there wasn't a shred of a suggestion Crowe was biased — only an apprehension of that bias. The suggestion that Crowe might be pro-Wilder was a joke in the oil and gas industry for months, since he was widely known as a tough-minded, resolutely unbiased High Mandarin who held no brief for Arctic Gas.

5. **The shrinking consortium situation.** As the cost and technological problems grew and the original deadline for approval, construction, and full operation passed, members of the consortium began to quarrel with one another and then to drop away. From a high of twenty-six participants in 1973, the group had dwindled in 1976 to fifteen members. Among those who lost their nerve were Exxon (which at one point had the gall to ask the Canadian government to provide economic guarantees), Atlantic Richfield, and Standard Oil of Ohio, as well as the CNR and Canadian Pacific Investments. Remaining are the three Canadian branch-plant oil

companies —Gulf, Shell, and Imperial — that have reserves in the Delta, as well as Consumers' Gas and TransCanada Pipelines. The CDC is now only an associate member, having withdrawn its ongoing financial support while remaining committed to invest $100 million in the project if it's approved.

6. **The Berger constrictor.** While rival consortiums kept making the headlines with their competing proposals to ship liquefied gas down the Pacific coast (the EI Paso proposal) or build a gas pipeline down the Alaska Highway (the Alcan line) or an oil pipeline from Kitimat to Edmonton (the Kitimat line), Arctic Gas's most redoubtable antagonist was a silent and enigmatic social democrat who went about the North preparing a report on the pipeline's impact on people and the land. Judge Thomas Berger, appointed as a sop to the NDP during one of the frailer moments of the Liberals' 1972–1974 minority, took his placebo mandate to investigate the social and environmental implications of the proposed pipeline more seriously than anyone, including the Native peoples, had expected. Through the forums provided by the peripatetic judge, the Native peoples found their voice and the Canadian public in the south learned new concepts, such as that a pipeline might mean progress but it could also mean human destruction.

Still, until the first volume of Berger's uncompromising report was published in early May 1977, Bill Wilder and his group were still feisty. The Arctic Gas proposal had won over the judge reporting to the Federal Power Commission in Washington, although the FPC itself had split two-to-two, putting the Alcan line down the Alaska Highway equal in its preference to the Mackenzie River route.

Once Berger's report was out, though, the Arctic Gas spokesmen, notably Vern Horte, the second-in-command (Wilder having long since abjured most public appearances — it was said he didn't have a charismatic manner), began to sound less certain.

Even though the NEB report was still to come, a full parliamentary debate had been promised, and the Arctic Gas proposal still had its champions in the cabinet and the business community, the odds against it were clearly growing.

It began to look as though Bill Wilder had been acting all along as the front for an idea whose time had passed — using skills that didn't work any more. His financial acumen, expensive research, and skilful backup staff, even his friendships with the men in the important offices in Ottawa, had turned out to be of limited help in a world of regulatory boards, public interest groups, and official inquiries.

As he circles the cinder track at UCC these mornings, he must ponder the fact that though the school's green grounds may not have changed much in the last fifty years, the world outside its gates has become a baffling, unpredictable place that can no longer be controlled by hard work and big money.

TEN

Canadian Cities: Let's Cherish Their Safety While We May[8]

Chatelaine, November 1970

A YOUNG SECRETARY on the way to visit a distant relative of my husband's in a hospital in Upper Manhattan is threatened with a knife as she gets out of her car in the parking lot, taken to the roof of a nearby apartment block, and raped; and when she propels herself, distraught, to the local police station, the officer on duty tells her there are a dozen such cases in the neighbourhood every day and only the fact that she's white causes him to write the incident down on his blotter. A Toronto couple studying in Chicago for a year have their sixth-floor apartment broken into, and their housekeeper robbed and assaulted in front of their two-year-old, and the only advice the police can offer is to mount a loaded shotgun in the window of the child's bedroom. A friend whose husband has been posted to the Canadian embassy in Washington sends her seven-year-old to the public school in her prosperous neighbourhood and matter-of-factly deals with a mimeographed sheet from his teacher giving instructions on how to get rid of head lice. A saleswoman in Saks Fifth Avenue catches a customer watching her dab at her streaming eyes, looks out from under her apricot bangs, and says, "Listen, honey, it's just I've been out to lunch and got the air in my face."

All these incidents, and a half a dozen others like them, have been recounted to me in the last year by various complaining inhabitants of American megalopolises, in tones that indicate they're almost common-places — atrocity stories from that none-too-distant war known as the Urban Crisis in the U.S. Each time I hear one of them I'm jolted out of complacency into fear. Could it happen here? Is the fact that our cities are still relatively safe, still relatively clean, still liveable, only another indication of how "backward" we are in comparison to the Americans? In five or ten years will Toronto be like a northern Chicago, and Van-couver a smaller L.A.?

A few weeks ago, I took these and other questions to Jane Jacobs, who's one of the foremost urban critics in the world. A native of Pennsyl-vania who lived for thirty years in New York, Mrs. Jacobs has diagnosed the ills of contemporary cities in two brilliant books, *The Death and Life of Great American Cities* and *The Economy of Cities*. She now lives in downtown Toronto with her husband, Robert Hyde Jacobs, an archi-tect, and three teenage children. In the nearly two years she's been here, she's involved herself in the life of the city, serving as a consultant to the urban-legal program of Osgoode Hall (the law school of York Uni-versity) and campaigning ardently for the Stop Spadina! movement — a local anti-expressway group — as well as continuing to work on a third book about cities, this time focusing on their governments.

She greeted me at her front door, wearing the Churchillian boiler suit she'd been writing in all day, gave me a glass of sherry, and led the way out to her pocket-size back garden, where we sat under a crabapple tree while she treated me to one of the most stimulating discussions I've had in years. We talked at first of her theories about cities — why they thrive, why they decay — as described in her two books, which one critic said were "beautifully imaginative, insistently intelligent, persuasively human." To try to summarize what they say here would be an absurdity. I enthusiastically recommend that you read them.

Unlike most urban experts, who appear to regard cities as great monsters in whose coils we are involuntarily caught, Jane Jacobs loves cities, sees their strength as lying in economic and social diversity, and their vitality in the very disorder that conventional city planners find so offensive.

She is emphatically opposed to "urban renewal," those programs so beloved of city officials with tidy minds that involve the hacking out of whole areas in the city core, and the imposition of an arid order on them with unrelieved acres of public-housing projects, apartment towers, huge office buildings, places where people feel compressed and dehumanized.

As we began to talk about what is right about Canadian city life and what could go wrong, she suddenly said, in a burst of feeling, "I find all the threshing around that goes on here about a Canadian identity absolutely bewildering. When you come here from outside, as I did, you know immediately what 'Canadian' means and that it is this very Canadian quality that has so far kept your cities liveable. Your saving grace is common sense, an enormously valuable attribute that has headed off so many errors made in American urban areas. Canadians have been very lucky; they are able to respond with this good sense to what Marshall McLuhan calls 'the early warning system.' You can see what goes wrong in the U.S. and not repeat their worst follies."

In response to a question about whether sheer size is not the decisive factor, she said size is not as important as most people believe, pointing out that you can compare American and Canadian cities, say Buffalo and Toronto, which are within a couple of hours of each other and with Toronto twice Buffalo's size, and find the Canadian city far safer. "What is important," she went on, "is that Canadians in cities haven't been kicked around as much. They haven't seen their homes levelled, as have millions of Americans, to make way for huge new developments. They haven't been subjected to the building of quite so many expressways that slice through cities, leaving whole areas barren. They aren't suspicious of their governments. They still have, in other words, a greater sense of trust, a greater stake in the neighbourhoods where they live, a realization that what goes on in their cities can be influenced by them. It's this trust — of politicians and of each other — that makes cities safe; where people are mistrustful because they've been kicked around, they become apathetic and they take on a 'what can you do?' attitude that hastens city decay, causes frustration and an attendant violence that no police force can contain."

This doesn't mean that Mrs. Jacobs feels we will never have an urban crisis; Canadian cities could copy all the American "progress symbols" that have caused such havoc. What threatens our cities, she says, is not a series of big abstractions like Violence or Racism or Galloping Growth but an accumulation of small inept decisions: the building of expressways that are meant to solve traffic problems but add to them instead; the proliferation of suburbs as against an increase in the supply of downtown living space; the levelling of old buildings that are still serving important functions.

On quite a different level, she believes that our notoriously cautious attitude toward investing money in our own country could be very destructive to the cities, which she sees as dependent for their diversity and continuing vitality on new businesses. Such businesses that start small and can grow big are begun by imaginative, restless people, and require risk capital. "I can see an explosive situation developing out of the denial of loans to immigrants, for instance," she says.

"Supposing an Italian wants to start a frozen pizza business and he finds all the money is Anglo money — available only to long-time, resolutely English Canadians with certifiably safe ideas. The kind of bitterness he feels in response, if multiplied, can have destructive ramifications — a deepening ghetto philosophy, a tendency to borrow money from illegal sources like the Mafia, which in turn leads to increased crime and violence. Canadians have to extend their trust in cities to a trust in their economic future."

We then talked about what ordinary people can do to prevent the decline of cities, and she expressed the opinion that there is no single easy formula. In general, she says, it's important that people look at the concerns of and threats to their own neighbourhoods and band together to ward off those threats. If a mindless road-widening scheme will spoil your street or a greedy developer is bent on cannibalizing your neighbourhood, then you can and should fight City Hall.

A good and hopeful sign, she believes, is simply the new widespread recognition that cities are important. Another is that more ratepayers associations are showing muscle and more bright people are becoming involved with municipal politics.

"After I've said all this, though," Mrs. Jacobs concluded, "I have to return to my faith in the Canadian character, in your whole lack of hysteria as a people, in your refusal to be caught up in what I call 'righteous manias.' This shows itself in many ways. For instance, this past summer several Canadian cities were supposedly going to be threatened by a 'hippie invasion' — hordes of young students hitchhiking across the country. Instead of putting on more locks and calling out more cops, municipalities responded by opening armouries, school gyms, to give the kids a place to sleep. By this simple move heaven knows how many problems were prevented. This is what I mean by common sense."

Jacobs is banking so much on this common sense that she and her husband have just bought a house in Toronto and are planning to become Canadian citizens. "Every time I have to go to New York on business," she says, "I come back feeling as though I've escaped once more from an insane asylum. I don't think enough Canadians know how bad it is down there — or how good up here."

ELEVEN

Politics and Pornography: The Yonge Street Cleanup[9]

Globe and Mail, July 5, 1975

DICK BECKETT — who used to be the mayor of Brantford and still looks the part (slicked-down hair, toothbrush moustache, and white summer shoes) even though he's been an MPP since 1971 and a minister without portfolio in the Davis government for more than a fortnight — succeeded in steering Bill 107 through second and third readings in the Ontario Legislature this week.

The bill, An Act to Amend the Municipal Act, as it's called on its title page, has fifteen parts. The real zinger among them is Section Eight, on licensing body-rub parlours. No doubt it will be touted from election platforms across Ontario in months to come as *the bill that cleaned up the Yonge Street Strip and saved Toronto from moral turpitude — praise the Lord and law and order and vote for the Tories if you hate sin* — or words to that effect.

The saga of Bill 107 — empowering municipalities to regulate through licensing these peculiar emporiums called body-rub parlours, where young women in various stages of undress (outside on the billboards they often have silver stars pasted over their nipples, but inside this apparently isn't so) perform various services for men of all ages, also in various stages of undress (outside, gazing longingly at the silver stars, they're decorously belted into their permapress pants, but inside this apparently isn't so, either) — is long and complicated, and says more than it's meant to about the mind-sweep of politicians in Ontario in 1975.

It's a story peopled by a cast of characters that might have been imagined by Evelyn Waugh and includes:

· A populist mayor named David Crombie, who's a short man seized by a tall ambition. He wants to be a populist Leader of the Opposition in the federal House of Commons and is fond of J.K. Galbraith's dictum that "any industrialized country's leader in the late twentieth century ought first to have been mayor of a great city." A Torontonian born and bred, Mr. Crombie has a shrewd sense of what makes the city tick and a fine eye for the ironies of political manipulation which success has not yet dimmed;

· A worried premier named William Davis, whose government must face the electorate soon, though its doing badly in the opinion polls, is beset by basic economic and social problems (inflation, pollution, and urban sprawl) that it can't control, and has turned to peripheral law-and-order problems (television violence, pornographic 8-mm movies, and body-rub parlours) that it can't control either, but is pretending it can;

· Two prosperous Yonge Street businessmen named Peter Clark, president of the Downtown Council, who deals in shoes and hates sex (at least when it's turned into an industry that threatens the respectability of his three downtown stores), and Arnold Linetsky, president of the Yonge Street Adult Entertainment Association, who deals in sex and hates shoes (at least when they're sold by "the kind of old-style businessman who couldn't make a buck to save themselves if their daddies hadn't been rich");

- Hundreds if not thousands of bit players who do their numbers on and off Yonge Street. They include aldermen of every persuasion, from Liberal to NDPer to Reformer-Rad; city planners who believe the bill is a political ploy and plays into the hands of developers; sandwich-board carriers bombed on amphetamines; street musicians high on bad Beethoven; reporters hyped on righteous indignation; professional and amateur whores indistinguishable from each other in halter tops and platform soles; ladies from Scarborough with home perms and polyester pantsuits who stroll The Strip arm in arm with relatives from Saskatoon, seeking out the sordid sights, clucking all the while; girls from Sudbury and Barcelona with tiny brain-pans and huge derrières making a buck in the nude-photography-needlepoint-shower-topless-massage, you-name-and-we-do-it trade for which "body-rub" is a euphemistic catch-all phrase; distraught hippies left over from the sixties selling beads, candles, and second-hand cassettes who'll be movin' on to Vancouver when they can; panhandlers who urinate in doorways, sleep in the streets, and are as prone as the prime minister to uttering fuddle-duddle when thwarted in their desires; and policemen who say they feel powerless to regulate it because of the inadequacies of the law and patrol The Strip in the heat of summer evenings, looking tolerant if tired.

All these people will be affected one way or another by the passage of Section Eight of Bill 107, although few of them are aware that the bill's history goes back not just to early June, when its contents were first hinted at in the legislature, but far beyond that to the winter of 1973.

That January, shortly after he was elected mayor for the first time, David Crombie made a speech warning downtown merchants that they'd better "clean up Yonge Street" or the city would do it for them. At the time, parts of lower Yonge had been turned into malls for several weeks during the previous two summers. And word was out all across Canada that it was a great place for those who abhor the work ethic to spend the hot weeks of July and August. Self-described "respectable" merchants were already alarmed at the year-round growth of the sex industry in their midst.

All the same, the mayor's speech met a spate of criticism from civil libertarians, who said the street expressed the colour and human variety of city life and should be left alone. Chastened by this response from the very people who were his campaign supporters, Crombie announced he was adopting a "wait-and-see" attitude.

The Downtown Council, made up of the respectable merchants and urged on by its president, Peter Clark the shoe man, made representations to the police that spring about cleaning up Yonge; but the police said they were shackled in their attempts to deal with the street's essential "sleaziness" by "lax laws" and "lack of citizen support."

This seemed true enough, since the mayor's office had discovered that the controls Crombie originally had in mind weren't within the city's jurisdiction — and most people seemed to like or tolerate Sin Strip, in any case. City Council decided to have malls again that summer and once more in 1974, although some people now say the malls exacerbated what was already a bad situation, bringing into the area a rush of tourists and suburbanites, who, in turn, attract even more parasites and criminals.

Still, nobody but the Downtown Council and three or four old-guard aldermen seemed to be really alarmed by Yonge Street's "degeneration" (a favourite word of The Strip's opponents). City Council even hired, in the spring of 1974, a group of young planners and architects named The City People to study the feasibility of a permanent mall.

Then, last summer, the situation changed. There had been too many fights on the mall, too many handbills advertising body-rub parlours handed out to shocked citizens, too many complaints about the noise of loudspeakers that made the main street sound like a midway, too many winos lying on blankets disturbing the equilibrium of diners coming out of side-street steak houses after paying $50 for a meal. Metro Council decided to act.

A year earlier, Metro had asked Queen's Park for legislation permitting bylaws to prohibit body-rub parlours. But Metro had been turned down by the Attorney-General's office on the grounds that such legislation would require making "moral judgements" and hence was a federal matter that should come under the Criminal Code. On July 30, 1974, mindful of this caveat, Metro merely requested authority to license the body rubbers. Nearly a month later, the request was acknowledged in a perfunctory way by the province. Nothing more was heard of it until June, when a very special set of circumstances apparently moved the Davis government, which had pooh-poohed the need to legislate against Sin Strip in January, to change its mind.

In the meantime, City Council took steps to stop the handing out of street literature advertising the body parlours and brought the worst noise pollution under control. Among the opponents of the Strip, it began to be said hopefully that the building of Eaton Centre and the Trizec Development at Dundas Street, and the Eaton College Street development farther north, would eventually clean up Yonge in any case.

All at once, with the advent of hot weather — and it blew in this year in late April as suddenly as a chinook — sin on The Strip once again became an issue. Peter Clark of the Downtown Council started lobbying City Hall harder than ever to drive out the sex industry before it drove out respectable business. He openly fought with Arnold Linetsky, who runs Mr. Arnold's, a body-rub shop right next door to Clark Shoes' main store. Linetsky, who recently formed his own Yonge Street Adult Entertainment Association to counter the "discrimination" practised by the Downtown Council, gave interviews describing how responsible his operation was ("lots of money spent on decor and no prostitution allowed — I'm not saying it hasn't happened, I'm saying it isn't allowed"). City Council decided to shelve the idea of a permanent mall indefinitely, despite the recommendations of the City People report, and not to have a mall of any kind this summer.

Around the same time, the *Toronto Star* went on a moralistic rampage of the kind that has only rarely been seen in these parts since Joe Atkinson was in his prime. Day after day, the *Star* ran Yonge Street stories describing the horrors of The Strip at night (calling it, among other things "a gaudy haven for raunchy movie houses"), implying there was Mafia money involved, interviewing aldermen, architects, and passers-by, and issuing daily invitations to its readers to write to *Voice of the People* and express their views.

When questioned about the effect of the *Star*'s campaign, David Crombie, who's a Tory and a winner, says, "The thing was, the *Star* discovered the obvious. I don't know what effect their campaign had on Queen's Park; you'll have to ask that question there. But I couldn't have been more pleased."

"Look, you've got to be realistic about this," says Alderman David Smith, who's a Liberal and a former co-coordinator of the Yonge Street Mall. "Whenever you get that much ink on an issue, you get politicians gathering. Public opinion was already turning against Yonge Street. All the *Star* did was jump on the bandwagon."

"Most people who live downtown — and there are 30,000 people in my ward who live within two blocks of Yonge in the stretch from Bloor to College — are cynical about what the *Star* was up to," says Alderman Allan Sparrow, a member of the Reform Caucus who's dubious about the whole affair. "Downtowners figure the real problems of Yonge Street are not sin but carbon monoxide from all the cars; not strippers but the lack of green space and community facilities. But that's the kind of issue that you can't make headlines out of — or for that matter, gains in provincial political terms. So it's probably true the *Star* campaign turned the trick."

The trick it may have turned was to get Bill Davis, at the beginning of June, to call Metro Chairman Paul Godfrey and Reid Scott, the aldermen who had been asked by David Crombie to take over the Yonge Street problem before he left on a visit to Amsterdam, to come to his office to discuss the burning issue of licensing body rubs that had been lying around unheeded by his government for ten full months. The three men came out of the meeting promising that Yonge Street would indeed be cleaned up and Bill 107 was drafted forthwith (or nearly forthwith, the first draft of the bill was so loosely worded that it would have outlawed Vic Tanny's and the YMCA) and introduced into the legislature on June 13.

Another bill aimed at cleaning up Yonge, this one amending the Theatres Act by broadening the province's censorship powers to include videotape and other film reproductions, was introduced a few days later. On Thursday, the same day Bill 107 went through second and third readings in the legislature, the Theatre Acts amendment was the subject of an extravagant speech by Conservative MPP Frank Drea, who said that such laws would help ensure that "the standards of the social degenerates and their camp followers" would not be forced upon "millions of decent Ontario men and women, and the families they're trying to raise." Drea traced the rise of the dirty-movie trade and linked it to organized crime.

At Queen's Park nobody's saying exactly why these bills were drafted so quickly after the abuses they seek to correct had been ignored for so long.

The premier, caught between dealing with oil and gas price problems and attending Conservative constituency nominations, says only that personally he has "been concerned with morality and permissiveness for more than a year" and that he "feels greater public concern about such things is not unrelated to greater public concern about violence. My government is reflecting both of these concerns. Now, we've had a lot of flak and a lot of cynicism expressed, but in my view a politician should lead if you feel strongly about something."

Darcy McKeough, who is no longer involved with Bill 107, although as Minister of the Treasury, Economics, and Intergovernmental Affairs he introduced it into the House, has his office turn inquiries over to Dick Beckett, who inherited the bill when he became a minister without portfolio in the middle of June. And Dick Beckett said he can't really be of much help in revealing why the government decided to act against body-rub parlours right now, because he's new at his job "and doesn't know the background."

Alderman Reid Scott says sagely there is no doubt in his mind "but the whole thing had to do with the general anti-permissiveness tack the Davis government has taken this spring. Still, it was a good move and I couldn't be more pleased."

Which seems to be just about the way nearly everyone involved feels. Crombie, Scott, and even Sparrow, who figures "the body-rub bill shows how bankrupt of ideas the Davis regime really is," are all pleased.

Certainly, Peter Clark is pleased. "At least," he says, "it represents some kind of action on the problem, even though it took the politicians such a long time to get off their behinds."

And Arnold Linetsky is pleased, sitting on a fake white leather chair floating in the purple shag in his apartment in the Manulife Centre. He figures the body-rub licenses "should be worth at least as much as beer parlours in terms of resale value. Right off, as soon as I'm licensed, Mr. Arnold's could be cashed in for a quarter-of-a-million. A good law like this will drive off the fly-by-nighters and give us guys with the real investment room to breathe."

Even the civil libertarians must be pleased, since none of them are questioning, at least very loudly, whether Bill 107 is defensible in their terms, although it could be read as an attempt to legislate morality.

And nobody, pleased or otherwise, is asking whether Bill 107 will work. Can anyone, that is, abolish prostitution, end panhandling, stop porn book sales, shut down dirty-movie houses, and keep vast hordes of people home at night by one innocuous licensing section in one catch-all amendments bill?

Come autumn, there will be politicians telling the populace that you can, and the populace may believe them if what happened to public opinion this spring and summer in Toronto is any indication of the climate of the times.

TWELVE

Requiem for the High Life[10]

Maclean's, September 1971

ONE DAY LAST SPRING I was standing in the reception area of a fashionable hairdresser's in midtown Toronto, waiting to pay my bill ($12 for a stark haircut that made me look exactly like one of the Presbyterian aunts I'd spent most of my life avoiding looking like). Ahead of me in the line was this very slick, chic lady of maybe thirty-eight or so dressed exactly as such a lady should be when she is going to spend the morning at the hairbender's (that's what chic ladies call all those rickety-cheeky Cockney boys who've taken over big-time women's barbering in the last half-decade) and then on to luncheon with an old friend from school and maybe a meeting of the women's committee of the symphony. She was wearing a beautifully cut midi coat and dark stockings and a Kenneth Jay Lane bracelet and the kind of tan you get in Acapulco when your husband feels he just has to get away in that dreary time between the skiing and the sailing, and her hair was pale and perfect.

While the cashier was ringing up her $25 bill (pale and perfect costs more than stark and Presbyterian), she stood looking idly out the window. At that moment, passing in the street, was a couple in their late teens or early twenties, the kind of kids the chic lady doubtless calls hippies, though the way things are going now with kids they may very well have been graduate students in aerodynamics, for all I know.

The boy had a lot of hair tied back with a leather thong and one of those Iranian embroidered skin vests and very narrow hips and jeans that did them proud, and the girl looked like some kind of curly pre-Raphaelite Madonna in a long wool challis dress with a lot going on underneath that obviously had nothing to do with lingerie. She was sucking an orange and licking the overflow juice from her fingers, and he was holding on to the wrist of her other arm and laughing at her, and they both looked happy or sensually aware, as the Gestalt thera-pists call it — in any case, as though it was pretty good to be nineteen or twenty-one and with no underwear in the sunshine in late April. The chic lady turned abruptly away from the window and I caught a glimpse of her in the mirror behind the cashier and she was touching her hair with a little rapid patting gesture and in her eyes was this unmistakable look of fear, the kind of o-my-god-why-hast-thou-forsaken-me? look, her god being Good Taste or something like that.

The whole incident didn't take any more than a minute, but it was a pretty important minute for me because it left me wanting to rush out and phone somebody and say, "Listen, I think I've just been wit-nessing the death of slick."

Now, you may be too young, or too intellectually rarefied or too resolutely plain-Canadian, to care that slick was once alive, let alone that it lies dying. But to a certain group of people who grew up in the 1950s ("tastemakers," the ad men who merchandised slick used to call them, though the word made the slick wince), who had a certain kind of education and a certain set of aspirations, slick was not just a phe-nomenon of dress, it was an enveloping sensibility, a way of looking at life.

The sensibility of any era is always difficult to define. It goes beyond fashion, beyond politics, beyond social history, though it takes all of these into account and synthesizes them into standards that those at the top of the society achieve and those who are moving up through the society envy and try to emulate. Throughout the 1950s and part of the 1960s what most people wanted to be was slick, though they probably called it sophisticated or elegant. (It was neither. Slick was a middle-class interpretation of elegance; it was attainable by anybody who had enough money and could learn the rules. It wasn't sophisticated because there *were* rules.)

Slick was strictly an American phenomenon. Europeans disdained it for the most part and held fast to their own real elegance, which had been a thousand years evolving. Canadians got it as a spillover so that the women who roamed Bloor Street in the 1950s and 1960s didn't have an indigenous slick style but wanted to look as though they could be walking on upper Fifth Avenue or crossing Park at 57th. (Of course, counter-slick, the sensibility of the New Age, is also an American spillover. It comes out of street theatre in the anti-war movement, and Abbie Hoffman and Black Power, and it hasn't very much to do with Canadian realities even though it parades on every main street in every city and town in the country.)

Slick as a sensibility had its beginnings in the 1920s, when it played a valid role in American life. It represented a coming of age in America after the First World War, a moving away from the turgid provincialisms and rigid concepts of society that had dominated the U.S. in the 1890s and the early 1900s. It was the evolution of the jazz age, it was the morganatic marriage of American insouciance with European aristocratic insolence, it was café society killing real society, the coming of a form of meritocracy (if you were talented and socially acceptable, like Richard Rodgers, say, you could be an important part of the world of slick, but if you were talented and a shade déclassé, like Frank Sinatra, you couldn't). But slick didn't really become the prevailing sensibility in North American life until the 1950s, when it had hardened into a lot of meaningless rules and affluence allowed it to blanket the urban and suburban reaches of the continent. It probably achieved its peak at the end of that decade when the Kennedys got to the White House. (The slickest thing anybody ever saw may very well have been Jackie Kennedy on the night before inauguration, dressed by Oleg Cassini, on her way to the Inaugural Gala in a lighted limousine, as recorded by Arthur Schlesinger Jr. Remember, "it all began in the cold..."?)

Which brings us to a curious anomaly — that you could be slick and liberal at the same time. (Though you couldn't, of course, be slick and poor. Slick, after all, was firmly rooted in money.) In truth, liberalism was a slick philosophy; it had a set of rules, and acceptable terminology that allowed its adherents to recognize each other. It was comforting to the fearful, and it had very little to do with what was actually going on.

But all this is too solemn. It turns slick into pseudo-sociology, a way it never was. Perhaps slick is best defined in terms of things that actually were slick:

Slick was wearing strapless red velvet and a diamond necklace or black silk and three strands of pearls and knowing you looked exactly right.

Slick was saying things were "in faultless taste."

Slick was driving obviously expensive cars like Lincolns and Cadillacs without feeling in the least embarrassed.

Slick was *Vogue* under the editorship of Diana Vreeland, which served as the slick bible and was widely and imperfectly copied.

Slick was engineered breasts, pearl earrings, Fire and Ice lipstick painted on with a brush, alligator bags, black-tie dinners, and believing Ralph Bunche was the ideal Negro.

Slick was spike heels, Porthault sheets, and lacquered mannequins like Dorian Leigh and Wilhelmina, who were photographed smiling and unattainable in furs in front of large houses with circular drives.

Slick was calling the movies "the flicks" and saying actually you preferred "going to the theatre" and quoting old aphorisms from Somerset Maugham as though they were Truth. ("You can't expect marriage to be amusing. If it were, the law wouldn't protect it and the church wouldn't sanctify it.")

Slick was listening to Cole Porter be played on a piano in a cocktail bar on a hotel rooftop in the early evening in October. Slick was never saying your grandfather came to Canada in steerage with an immigrant tag pinned on his coat. In Canada, the world of social slick and showbiz slick never, ever mixed — nobody could imagine Fiorenza Drew talking to Joyce Davidson, though Roloff Beny did a masterly job of introducing the homegrown socially slick to slick people of all stripes abroad.

Slick was being impressed by the description, "She always looks as though she just stepped out of a bandbox."

Slick for man was not wearing coloured shirts after five o'clock and never appearing in suede shoes in town in case you might be mistaken for an actor or for someone who worked for the CBC.

Slick was sex without sweat, as with Gregory Peck and Audrey Hepburn in *Roman Holiday.*

Slick was knowing and caring that champagne should be served in tulip glasses.

Slick was an ad for face powder that featured a woman in a tiara in a gold coach (jewels by Cartier, the cutline read) that said in effect, you, too, can be a princess or look like one. And Grace Kelly really did become the Princess of Slick, though Jackie Kennedy was later its Queen.

Slick was pretending you often ate *filet de bœuf à la jardinière* and that you liked *œufs en gelée* better than a toasted Western with ketchup.

Slick was owning a designer's signature scarf, always wearing white for tennis, paying $400 for a copy of a Paris original, and taking holidays in Greece before Diners Club and the Colonels got there.

Slick started out innocent with slumming in Harlem in the 1920s and ended up naive with Black Panthers in Leonard Bernstein's living room.

On that last point, it might even be argued that a study of the factors that have come together to kill slick would define it far better negatively than anyone ever could define it positively. During the last four or five years, slick has been savaged from within and without. For one thing, it became so accessible through magazine articles and how-to books that women from Scarsdale, and even Forest Hill and West Vancouver, could understand it perfectly and emulate it successfully. As a result, the avant-garde of slick was forced more and more into abandoning "good" taste for camp taste or pop taste and into trying to take over the self-consciously lumpen proletariat enthusiasms of the very young — enthusiasms that were really so alien to slick they couldn't be encompassed. (People who believe slick can survive are still trying to do this; they were selling blue denim in the old expensive slick New York stores this summer for $115 for a skirt and jacket.)

Far more important to slick's demise, though, was that the young stopped believing in it and started saying things like "Let it be" (slick never let anything be). They started realizing that it was wrong to go around sad-mouthing about the ghettos while wearing a Mainbocher, that it was right to want to look like yourself instead of some unbelievably perfect Beautiful Person, that bad taste could be good taste if it meant I-put-it-together-myself taste. In brief, the young robbed the slick of an essential response: envy.

This is not to say, of course, that there aren't a few ghosts of slick around. The Nixons are the prototypes of the kind of people who've taken over slick and reduced it to its knees. Truman Capote's masked ball at the Plaza was the latest *great* slick event, done with a certain sly and campy grace. But Tricia Nixon's wedding, which was obviously meant to be slick, by its naive public espousal of all those dear dead principles turned into a piece of pure camp slick. The moribund nature of slick showed up in the reportage of that wedding. Only the most banal of the established newspapers and magazines even attempted to treat it seriously. The non-established press indulged itself in joyful sniggering, as with *Rolling Stone*, which titled its report "The Making of the President's Daughter." It may just be that poor Tricia will be written into history as a terrible example of the generation that falls between the two sensibilities of slick and non-slick. To be truly slick, you almost had to have been born before the Second World War. To be truly, unselfconsciously non-slick, you have to have been born after 1950.

One last definition. Slick in its latter days was degraded by writers who took a subject of sophistic complexity and turned it into a magazine article of glib generality. Like this one.

THIRTEEN

Cathedral of Chic[11]

Saturday Night, July/August 1976

IT'S A DULL AFTERNOON — very cold for May, people have been saying all day long — and outside in the courtyard, where the fountain is forlornly shooting little spurts of water in the chill, rain begins to spatter against the hastily opened umbrellas of people passing by.

Inside the store, the rain and the cold don't matter. The beachwear section, with the bathing suits from Israel and California, the Panama straws, and the Indian cotton caftans embroidered as elaborately as a maharanee's robe, is lit up like a terrace on the Côte d'Azur at noon. Fifty feet away, in the narrow section dedicated to the genius of St. Laurent, the hip rock keeps on beating subtly from the ceiling, saying: buy, buy, buy.

The salesgirl with eyes as old as Egypt has just whisked away on little clog feet to have wrapped in black and silver The Customer's purchases (a blazer, a pair of creamy trousers, a grey print afternoon dress that looks like something from a half-remembered photograph of my mother-in-law at Marienbad in the summer of '34).

The Customer herself is waiting with a friend, pick, pick, picking her way through the racks of belts (every one of them bearing a tiny gold medallion imprinted with the initials YSL that make a yard of rope worth as much as The Customer pays her cleaning woman for a hard day's work) while they're talk, talk, talking about — well, nothing much, that is to say, their lives.

They look curiously alike, with high, narrow shoulders and gleamer on their eyebrows, although The Customer has an apricot-coloured bobbed head and layers of clothing à la Sonia Rykiel on her back and the friend is not so *outré* in her Ultrasuede pant outfit and with six rings on four fingers, all gold. In the shimmery light you can't tell how old they are, thirty-eight or maybe close to fifty if they've been to Dr. Harry Silver for a lift, but in any case dieted, coiffed, and dressed to an approximation of the twenty-year-old perfections found in *Vogue*.

Their voices are not so much loud as relentless, the accents indeterminate. They've had too much caw-fee, after the two with lunch at the Courtyard and the cup in the dressing room here; the belts are stunning; the blazer will go with the skirt bought from the San-Lore-ente winter collection and should prove so useful on the ya(c)h-te.

Names, prices, places are dropped not in a murmur but a cacophony until finally, mercifully, the salesgirl comes back with a big black box and a little silver credit card and says thank you, thank you, as she extends her fervent wishes for a happy sailing holiday in France. The Customer pats the carved hair at the nape of her immaculate neck and answers, "Well, I hope so, dear, but it's hard to tell. You know how it is on the Med — it either blows or it doesn't."

Then she and her friend ankle off, trailing clouds of Aliage and Joy, leaving me standing under a big blow-up of the master designer, asking myself in a momentary rush of alienation angst, "Where am I, anyway?"

In the city of your birth, dear heart. In what used to be Toronto the Plain. In a store bearing the same name and standing on the same Bloor Street site as the one you used to hurry by on countless mornings in the 1950s, bound for lectures on the campus three blocks away, where academics in black gowns told gullible girls from Ontario towns that riches didn't matter and the truth would make them free.

This is Creeds. Not the old Creeds, which was primarily a furriers where people's mothers used to buy other fripperies sometimes after they'd been to Holt Renfrew and found there weren't any navy glacé kid gloves left in stock. But the new Creeds. In the new Toronto. Home of the new money, the new luxe, the new certifiable, un-Canadian, designer-labelled international chic.

After Creeds opened the full glory of its expanded facilities in the Manulife Centre last year, its advertising department mailed out to the customers an ecstatic six-page promotion that suggested that this was not just a store but "…a whole new world." For people with a long memory of how Toronto used to be, the statement seemed hyperbolic but somehow apt.

On the surface, of course, Creeds is just a store, a glass box dedicated to the vanities of human wishes, turning over several million dollars' worth of soft goods every year, making money on the merchandising moxie of its owner, Eddie Creed. But it can also be seen — if you're in search of uncomputerized sociological data — as a symbol of the rise of a new class in Canada that is most visible in Toronto but exists with modifications in every big city in the country.

It's a class composed of the beneficiaries of the big boom of the 1950s and 1960s, people who amassed minor (and in some cases major) fortunes by being the right age in the right place at the right time, who had their work ethic formed by the urgencies of the 1930s and 1940s, and their sensibilities skewed by the fantasies of the 1960s, and who continue even in the down times of the 1970s to believe their importance is authenticated and their existence reconfirmed by the volume and expense of what they're able to consume.

Not long ago, a man who started to climb the slippery ladder of the country's old moneyed establishment in the 1920s, and is still hanging on to his rung near the top in the 1970s, was trying to describe what this new class really means. "The thing is," he said querulously after a slice of rare roast beef and a single glass of wine in one of those upstairs rooms at the York Club where ladies are allowed, "that it used to be hard to get rich in Canada — and harder still to penetrate the preserves of those who had money. In my day you had to conform to a code, but now the country's full of millionaires nobody even knows."

What he meant, for a start, was that in his day you had to have an anglophone name, and if you weren't lucky enough to come from a family able to ensure your education in an appropriate private school, you had to attach yourself to the right sort of mentor in the right sort of business, a stockbroker's or a publishing house or a chartered accountancy firm. By careful application of your talents on the job and making the right connections through wheedling your way into the minor league clubs and onto the joe-job committees of the major league arts boards, you might, if you were very, very lucky and very, very smart, get rich.

But in the decades of the boom, conformity to the code was no longer necessary. Huge sums of money were made in land development, in the construction business and its various suppliers, in the transportation industry, in oil and uranium and drug chains, in hotels and discount department stores. When the boom was at its crest in the late 1960s, the slumbering old Anglo establishment discovered that scores of people with names like Desmarais and Reichmann and Del Zotto (or, for that matter, Peterson and Matthews) and backgrounds that included growing up in places like Timmins and Wetaskiwin without ever having seen the inside of a private school or a private club, were very, very rich, and hundreds of others (the ones no one knows) were rich enough, if not to threaten the establishment's equanimity, at least to live like lords.

Despite C.P. Snow's dictum that if you have enough money your background doesn't matter, the Canadian establishment didn't immediately take these people to its angular bosom. Sociologists (notably Wallace Clement of McMaster University) who analyze penetration into the economic elite according to class origin and ethnic background continue to find that the old establishment, in terms of membership on important corporate boards and in important social institutions, is constituted mainly as it has been for decades. And among old establishment members who still adhere to the code, attitudes haven't changed very much at all.

Major-General Bruce Matthews of Toronto, an Argus Corporation executive who embodies in his elegant person just about every virtue the old money admires, was once asked why it was that he and his colleagues didn't want Paul Desmarais of Power Corporation — who grew up Franco-Ontarian in Sudbury, Ontario, and began his business life running a bus line in his old hometown — buying into Argus. Matthews leaned back in the period chair in his Adams office, stared hard at the toes of his beautifully polished shoes, and said, "Well, the thing about Mr. Desmarais is that he has raw-ther too much energy for us," a sentence that, if anyone ever ran a put-down contest, would certainly deserve some sort of prize.

The thing about the new class, though, is that it decided not to care what the major-generals of this world thought. It could buy what it wanted. In Desmarais's case, if he couldn't have control of Argus, he could have prime ministers for weekends and premiers to dine. Or, in the case of new class members with less money and power than Desmarais (who can be seen as at the pinnacle of the new class), if they couldn't belong to the Toronto Club, they could buy diamonds by the yard, safaris by the month, and Maseratis by the pair.

For a while, most of their big-time spending was done abroad, in New York, principally, since New York is the mecca of the new class as London was the mecca of the old. But then gradually, in the 1960s, it began to be recognized in Canada itself that there were people in the country who wanted to spend big money and have fun while they were at it (in direct contradiction of the Methodist/Presbyterian ethos that had formerly prevailed), and there was no important reason why they shouldn't spend it here.

The place where most of the new fortunes are located is Toronto, and it was in Toronto that entrepreneurs — from the owners of art galleries selling Oldenburgs or Dines to the buyers for stores stocking bags by Hermès and clothes from Chloé — recognized that what the new class lusted after were luxuries imported from abroad.

Having propelled themselves into the position of being not just dreamers of the golden dream but in possession of the money to make it true, the members of the new class set out to live in dwellings that looked like spreads in *House & Garden* and to wear clothes seen in *Harper's & Queen* or the French edition of *Vogue*. In brief, they wanted most of all to be "international" in their style.

In this respect (though they may not realize it) they are quintessentially Canadian and not really different from the old establishment at all. Both groups are provincial in the truest sense; that is, they believe where they are doesn't count. In their styles they exist as pale ghosts of other country's cultures, meeting the standards of other people's lives. The Canadian elites, old and new, have always seen this country as a place they must struggle to transcend.

Probably no entrepreneur was better fitted by instinct and experience to understand the desires of the new class than Edmond Martin

Creed. Eddie Creed is a handsome man, now fifty-four years old, a first-generation Canadian born to an egocentric émigré from the Ukraine named Jack Creed, who made a name for himself in the old pre-boom days as Canada's Merchant of Mink.

Jack Creed had been apprenticed to a tailor when he was six years old and when he was still an adolescent walked across Europe from Kiev to Paris, where he got a job in a dress design house. After immigrating to Canada, he finally opened his own shop in 1916 in the front of a house on Bloor Street, just across the road from the "whole new world." He put ads in the Toronto papers to the effect that he was a "Parisian Tailor–Designer Supreme" and then sat back, waiting for the carriage trade to drive up in their newly acquired cars. They trickled in, attracted by the gossip that Creed could make "fabulous ensembles" trimmed with fur. Later, with the custom tailor business on the wane, Creed gradually moved more and more into the business of designing furs.

He was a tyrannical man, a perfectionist in his work, and a snob who had no difficulty in assessing the relative importance and insecurity of his customers. Once a woman came into the shop with an old silver fox jacket to ask Creed how it could be altered, phrasing her request in terms of "What would you do with this?" "Do you have an attic, madame?" Creed asked, and when she said yes, he looked her in the eye and rasped, "Then climb up there, open the window wide, and fling that thing out."

This combination of fashion skill and imperious style made Jack Creed very successful in good old British-colonized T.O., and eventually he was making furs for the likes of Lady Tweedsmuir and Princess Elizabeth, who was presented with an ermine by the Imperial Order of the Daughters of the Empire when her marriage was announced in 1947.

That same year, Jack Creed's son, Eddie, reluctantly joined his parents in the firm. He had been an indifferent student, the frequent object of his father's scorn, and had served in the navy and gone to the Ontario Agricultural College with the notion that he might run a farm. When he came to the store he was twenty-five and had existed all his life in a kind of ethnic no man's land. His family's Jewishness had been largely ignored at home.

("Jack Creed," says an old Toronto Zionist bitterly, "was one of those European Jews who tried to pass themselves off as French or Russian or anything but what they were in order not to frighten off the WASPs." Jack Creed was also one of those European Jews with an acute sense of *realpolitik*. He gave an interview to the *Toronto Star* after a trip to Europe in 1938 that was brilliant in its forecast of the horrors that were to come. It may be a measure of how much Toronto's changed that his son, thirty-five years later, was proud to be the chairman of the United Jewish Appeal.)

In his teens, Eddie had been sent to Pickering College, one of the minor Anglo-Canadian private schools, and entertained at resolutely anti-Semitic WASP establishments like the Granite Club — situations that were, as he once told the writer June Callwood, "kind of confusing" — and he had learned to ski and play tennis very well. Beyond this knowledge of the habits of the customers his father wanted to attract, his qualifications for merchandising were very nearly nil.

For most of the next twenty years Creeds was run much as it always had been, with Jack Creed in charge, his wife supervising (until her death in the late 1950s) the buying for the dress and accessories departments, which were adjuncts to the fur salon, and Eddie "drifting along, doing what they wanted me to, happy not to have much responsibility. In those days I'd sooner play golf."

He married in the meantime a girl named Edie Sharp, whose father was a builder. In 1959, Eddie, his best friend, Murray Koffler (who was then a druggist embarking on his Shoppers Drug Mart venture), and his brother-in-law Isadore Sharp decided they wanted to diversify their interests, i.e., make some big money in the land boom. They had travelled fairly widely and were convinced a downtown motor hotel would be a good investment, so they pooled their cash, bought up some rundown old properties on Jarvis Street, demolished them, and built the Four Seasons Motor Hotel. It was a smash. The media slick flocked to the bar and the dining room from the CBC across the road, and the new-style businessmen who were sick of the old King Eddie and the Royal York but wanted to stay downtown flocked to the rooms and the swimming pool.

The Koffler-Creed-Sharp trio went on to build, with a success that was astonishing and has been attributed both to business acumen and to luck, other hotels, called either The Four Seasons or The Inn on the Park, in London overlooking Hyde Park and in other lesser centres from British Columbia to Israel. (Four Seasons Hotels Ltd. now owns eight hotels, having sold the Four Seasons–Sheraton in Toronto this year in order to build a new luxury hostelry to open later in the decade in the Yorkville district, not far from Creeds. Sharp is the firm's president, and Koffler and Creed are vice-president and secretary respectively.)

What Creed learned from the hotel business was that "the new kind of people want to have an experience when they go to a hotel — you know what I mean? The old crowd, they stay at Claridge's or maybe the Berkeley or the Dorchester in London. But the new crowd would find Claridge's — that is, if they could get in — kind of conservative, maybe shabby. In our hotels we give them an indoor garden maybe, beautiful rooms, a great location, something special, a new kind of luxe — and they love it. Four Seasons is a family business. Just like the store."

By the late 1960s, when the new Manulife Centre, with its apartment complex and luxurious shopping mall, was being planned for the Bloor Street block where Creeds had been located for years, Eddie Creed felt ready to amalgamate the knowledge of fashion merchandising he'd acquired in the shadow of his father (who died at the age of eighty-six in 1971) with the Four Seasons aesthetic of the new moneyed class.

"In the old store," he says, "we had been maintaining a prestigious but conservative approach to merchandising and I was looking for the kind of excitement we had in the hotels. Everything had changed. Younger people had money and they were free about spending it. I wanted to create the finest store in North America, which would retain the feeling of prestige we had but bring in new people. It had to be posh and done in the best taste, with lots of space and light. I wanted the store to be an experience."

And an experience it is, created mostly out of Eddie Creed's single-minded drive. Creed wooed the important European and American designers who won't put their clothes into just any store. Creed went to Europe on every single major buying trip, working seven days a week, twelve hours a day, to bring in the kind of clothes the new money might admire. He saw to the minute details of the new store's decor with the aid of Jack Winston, an interior designer, and his wife's favourite decorator, Robert Dirstein, who also did the Creeds' French château at Schomberg in the countryside north of Toronto where the old and new gentry have their acreage with their horses and their cows.

Among them they turned the store into a château away from the château. The fur salon has English oak on the walls, saved from a house that stood on the Park Lane site where the London Inn on the Park was built. The dress salon is fronted with marble pillars, sportswear has antique commodes, and scattered throughout the premises are stained glass windows, period chairs, and crystal chandeliers, all from France.

Everywhere there is the most rarefied merchandise you can buy from the most expensive merchandisers in the world, not just women's clothes from the major designers but other luxury goods so exotically wrought and extravagantly priced they might cause a lump to rise in

Thorstein Veblen's gorge. Glasses from Baccarat. Mustard from Fauchon. Sheets from Porthault. Chocolates from Godiva. Ties from Gucci. Watches from Cartier.

"Ninety percent of what's sold in the store," Creed says proudly, "is bought outside Canada." What makes up much of the other 10 percent is medium-priced (i.e., $50 for a pair of unlined cotton women's trousers), American-designed clothes made under contract by Canadian firms.

"Eddie Creed buys abroad because he has a gut understanding of Toronto," says a man who's in quite another kind of business, not far from Creeds. "He knows that this is a huge, vibrant city full of people with all kinds of money who are scared. So he gives them big-name labels that make everything kosher. The medallion on the St. Laurent belt says I've got taste the way the three-pointed star on the Mercedes 450 says I've got $24,000. The price is different but the principle and the patrons are the same."

Even in this year of barely controllable inflation, labour unrest, alarming unemployment, and consumer buying patterns that the financial papers describe euphemistically as "uncertain," the rush to acquire the authenticated accoutrements of the new luxe has gone largely unabated, according to Creed.

"People are screaming," he says, "but they're buying all the same. At least the people who want what we have in the store. My father used to tell me that some of his best years were during the Depression. And you can take what you like out of that." Creed isn't given to theorizing; in fact, he isn't given to talking much at all. Abstract questions cause him to squirm with boredom behind the French desk in his office with the velvety brown walls. All he knows is what sells and who buys.

Although he and his staff are reluctant to name names, they're not averse to describing types. (When asked who buys at Creeds, an employee looked from left to right to be sure she wasn't overheard, leaned forward, and said, *sotto voce*, "Have you read *The Canadian Establishment*? Well that's who — Mrs. Roman and Mrs. Bassett, like that.")

In any case, the customers — or the Creeds Woman, as the store's advertising has occasionally described her — seem to fall handily into three categories and, coincidentally, three castes:

1. *The Ladies* (or the Over Sixties, as one employee delicately described them), a small, hard-core group of older women who used to buy dresses from Jack Creed twenty years ago and are still patronizing the dress salon, buying the same sorts of clothes from the same dragon-lady saleswomen who used to terrorize unknowns intrepid or naive enough to wander off the street into the old Creeds. These women belong to a type more frequently found shopping on the couture floor at Holt Renfrew, or better still at Harrods when they're in London on the way to fish in Scotland in the spring. They're often women with what is usually called "old money" — though, as a man I know, who comes from a family with a fortune founded in Canada in the 1860s, says with the scorn born of an Oxford education, a regular income from investments, and a radical-liberal frame of mind, "In this country there's no old money; there's only the older money."

2. *The Arrivées.* This is the huge group of women between thirty and fifty whom Creed meant to attract when he opened the new store — the wives of the new millionaires and the new $100,000-a-year corporate executives — although some of them are the offspring of the old rich who wouldn't be caught dead looking like their mothers, and some of them are what's called in the wilder reaches of York-ville "Italian Princesses," i.e., the pampered wives of men with big money made in cement, who have supplanted in

Toronto the Jewish Princesses so well known in New York. These women shop in Miss Creed with forays into the Miss Creed Designer Boutique and the sections devoted to St. Laurent, Courrèges, and Rykiel. The prices in these shops are so inflated they're nearly meaningless in real-life terms. "You start thinking," a customer explains, "that because they've marked a Jean Muir down from $650 to $475 that it's really cheap."

(To buy in these shops you not only have to be rich, you have to be thin. Lisa Dalholt, the store's chief buyer, says, in a sentence borrowed unadorned from *Women's Wear Daily*, "Miss Creed is not an age but a frame of mind." When pressed on this point — what frame of mind do you have to be in to pay $70 for a pair of jeans? — she elaborates: "Well, actually, you have to have a body." The incongruity of the fact that she herself has a body that would have delighted Claude Renoir but couldn't possibly be squeezed into anything hanging on the racks in Miss Creed hasn't clouded her radiant eyes. Lisa Dalholt started out eighteen years ago as the store's house model, and she believes.)

Some of the arrivées are so fashion-obsessed that when new shipments arrive from Europe, salesgirls will glom through the clothes as they're being unpacked in the stockroom and rush upstairs to phone favourite customers to tell them what's come in. Sometimes they'll hang up after an ecstatic conversation and send out clothes to charge account customers, sight unseen. More often, customers will turn up with their husbands on a Saturday or with a friend after the hairdresser's on a Thursday afternoon to be shown what's been kept for them "on hold."

3. *The Aspirants.* This is a group made up of what Jeanne Grierson, the store's advertising director, calls "your better class of working girl" — i.e., women as young as twenty-five who are teachers or

highly paid secretaries or step-in fetch-its in glamour trades like television or advertising, earning maybe $12,000 to $14,000 a year, who've cottoned on to the Parisienne's idea that it's better to own one good thing than six cheapies. ("You never know," a secretary said to me, riffling through her Courrèges bag for a ciggie over lunch, "you might meet a guy who'll ask you to Antigua for the weekend, and you'll feel a whole lot better dressed by Creeds.")

There's a concerted effort to woo these girls into Miss Creed, and the salespersons there are frequently told not to frost customers, not to size them up peremptorily as no-buys, but to encourage them to invest in the $25 T-shirt or the $100 summer dress, since who knows, next year they may be arrivées and come in for the $355 jumpsuit by YSL.

In the meantime, there are lots of them who'll save up for a Tank watch from Cartier ($1,500 in gold, $225 in plate), happy in the knowledge that one of the young Eatons bought for his wife the first such timepiece the store sold on the morning it opened in February 1975, or better still — distant heroes having more cachet than homemade billionaires — that John Fitzgerald Kennedy used to give them to his girls.

Any Saturday afternoon in Toronto you can wander through the several blocks of chic stores within walking distance of Creeds, where the new luxe is purveyed with Creeds' purpose if not quite Creeds' style, and then come into the "whole new world" itself and watch the three categories of customers stream by, all palpitating in one beautifully dressed, obviously prosperous, upwardly mobile mob. It's as good, as a French-Canadian friend of mine once said about sitting for an evening on the Boulevard St. Germain, as going to the zoo.

Still, if you're cursed with a reflective turn of mind, this scene may cause a certain ambivalent response. Sometimes it seems like a cause for celebration, denoting the extension of wealth through a broader segment of the society, showing the end of the old dowdiness, the old timidities, the old snobbism, the greening of grey Toronto in its prime. At other times it seems like a cause for concern, representing consumerism run wild (who needs a dress for $1,200 or a crock of mustard that costs $6?), the loss of the work-scrimp-save syndrome that gave the city and the country its underlying principle long ago, and, what's probably most worrying of all, the rise of a new provincialism not really any better than the old.

Eddie Creed, and the entrepreneurs who admire and copy him, are seemingly untroubled by these polarities. For them, the whole thing's simple. Feel bad, buy something imported and expensive, feel good. No matter where you place it in the Canadian mosaic — beyond, below, or parallel to the old establishment — that ancient axiom seems to represent the basic ethic of the brand-new class.

PART III

Feminist in Arms

IF CHRISTINA WAS not born a feminist, she was certainly turned into one by the family in which she grew up and the education system that formed her. As a little girl, she was furious when she was told that she could never hope to have a handsome leather apron like that of her father, a Mason. As an undergraduate, she resented the university's widespread disdain for women's brains. This section demonstrates her evolution as a feminist from the late 1950s, relating her personal development to the evolving political scene around her. This was journalistic terrain that she had largely to herself, since Michele Landsberg did not do full-time journalism until the 1970s, Doris Anderson's work was mostly as editor, and June Callwood approached feminism through a different prism. In those days, no male reporter was alert to the concerns expressed in this section, all of which are now acknowledged as mainstream by the media, in the political establishment, and among the general public.

As a subtext of her feminism, Christina had made her personal into the political well before the movement championed the slogan. "Strong Women Who Could Endure" is a bittersweet missive to a long-time friend, Madeleine Gobeil, who had also been an intimate of Simone de Beauvoir. Both Christina and Madeleine agreed with Beauvoir's "One is not born a woman, one becomes one." While admiring the stoic qualities of hard work and communal modesty that governed the mores of her childhood, which she believed still prevailed in rural Canada, this melancholy self-portrait recalls the claustrophobic and chauvinistic Ontario of the 1940s, whose anal parochialism was simultaneously anti-sensual and anti-intellectual.

Initially a sceptic about the Royal Commission on the Status of Women, Christina became an ardent advocate of this political landmark. Witnessing the often heart-wrenching testimony of many women at its public hearings allowed her to sharpen her structural critique of Canadian society as well as her feminism at a time when very few in the media mainstream were taking the commission seriously. In "Some Awkward Truths the Royal Commission Missed," she critiqued the often ineffectual, low-key way the commission brought its recommendations to the public.

Later in the 1970s, Christina reported perceptively on the training of lawyers, the appointment of judges, and the development of a socially active law — work not included in this volume, although an early indication of her interest in the need for law reform can be seen in "Down with Alimony!"

"The Split Syndrome" presents in a lighter vein, though still through her own experience, the harsher realities that awaited divorced working women in later life.

Christina was intrigued by power, how decision-makers — almost always male — exercised it, and what effect it had on marginalized groups, particularly women. "In Ottawa, Women Are Either Babes or Blobs" is a dispatch from the trenches of Trudeau's Ottawa concerning what little progress had been made there. "Women and Political Power: What's Holding Us Back?" critiques the stalled progress made in getting women elected through the partisan arena of parliamentary politics.

— *SC*

FOURTEEN

Strong Women Who Could Endure[12]

Globe and Mail, October 13, 1975

MY DEAR MADELEINE:

We promised we would write to each other as a kind of bicultural Canadian bow to International Women's Year, about what it meant for each of us to grow up in our different milieus — you as a French-Canadian girl in Hull, me as an English-Canadian girl in Toronto — and what effect our upbringings had in the formation of the women we've become.

I sit here trying to sort through a thousand memories and realize that although we belong to the same country and are instantly en rapport when we meet, what I will describe may be foreign from your own experience as though we had grown up 2,000, not 250, miles apart.

The societies we knew as children were remote from each other, of course — otherwise, we would never think to write these letters and "two solitudes" would have remained a phrase from Rilke and never have become part of the language of our national angst.

Despite all the revelations and interchanges of the last fifteen years, despite the Royal Commission and the shelves of books on the problems of French–English relations, despite the brilliant films and the folk songs that have come out of the Quebec turmoil, French Canada is mysterious to me still.

All I have are glimpses of what it must have been like to live within it, gleaned from the novels of Claire Martin and Marie-Claire Blais and from things you said yourself in passing, and it could be that I romanticize its "otherness."

But English Canada — or at least the way it was in the 1940s and 1950s, when I was a small child, then an adolescent and a university student — is as unromantic and as familiar to me as a taste of the cod liver oil we used to swallow from a kitchen spoon on winter mornings, with the reluctant being admonished to hurry please, don't gag, this is *good* for you.

I'm talking about the English Canada of the middle-class WASPs whose mores set the tone of the society in those decades and in some ways set it still. It's a group that has been much reviled for its parochial absurdities and its Puritanism, and God knows I laughed at it a lot myself in my teens and twenties when I was trying to wring its ethos out of my soul.

But I don't laugh at it any longer and when I go into small Canadian towns as a journalist and encounter it in an older, purer form than is found in big cities now, I feel a surge of affection and admiration crowding the exasperation that's been part of my response to it since I was ten years old.

For one thing, it was the society that produced strong women who knew how to endure. And strength along with humour and openness are qualities women are in need of now as we keep on raking our psyches in search of answers to what it is we want from ourselves and from men and from work.

In my childhood, what women wanted as far as I could figure out, while standing around in my navy blue tunic and knee socks and hateful black oxfords (they're *good* for your feet, dear, patent leather is only for parties), was to be thought honest, hard-working, loyal, chaste, and therefore lovable.

That these characteristics were what was expected of men as well may have been a form of equality, but in combination they didn't do much to heighten our sense of identity as sexual beings or our sense of joy in our humanity.

My mother was (and is) a pretty woman with long dark hair she wore in a bun, marvellous skin, and a quick sense of humour that was the obverse side of an essentially dark vision of life. Still, we were taught to admire not her loveliness or her laughter but her fortitude.

When I was very young, maybe five or six, a distant relative said I was a beautiful child and my father shushed her promptly with a warning that she would "turn my head" with such praise. A report card full of A's was duly praised, but always with the admonition that you must continue to "do your best" or next term you might fall into the ignominy of standing second instead of first.

Time spent in front of a looking glass was thought to be wasted, and I used to sneak into the bathroom, lock the door, climb up on the plumbing, and gaze gravely at my legs in the mirror over the sink, hoping to confirm my hunch that they were rather fine.

(The idea that it was important to have good legs came from paging through *Life* or the *Saturday Evening Post* while waiting for the dentist and trying to forget about the drill, which was applied to the molars without any preliminary nonsense such as freezing the nerves. Once in the dentist's chair, I used to grip the arms hard while he ground away whistling, and at the end of the appointment, he would look at me approvingly and say, "Aren't you the little stoic!" High praise.)

Clothes played a serious and important part in our lives. We had English coats that were bought at Eaton's and came with leggings and roll-brim hats and were passed from child to child (they *never* wore out) and donned on Sundays so we could go, properly clad, to the Presbyterian Church, where you sat in your pew and listened to the minister praying interminably for England to achieve a glorious and quick victory over the hated Hun.

For parties and recitals there were silk dresses with smocking, long white stockings worn with garters that dangled from a cotton vest, and silver barrettes from Birks. These were necessities, part of being properly got up, and not really discussed much in frivolous terms as adornment.

No woman was ever described as sexy, but those who were might be sniffed at as "vulgar" or even "loose" if dark secrets were known about their lives. What one yearned to be was not sensuous like Betty Grable or Lana Turner but sophisticated and witty like Katharine Hepburn or Rosalind Russell, who once played, in a movie I saw, a wisecracking, brilliant journalist in a black pinstripe suit with a long silver fox fur flung around her neck, a part that fuelled the fantasy I never really got over.

But that was not real life and anyway it took place in America, where all sorts of glamorous things happened that couldn't possibly occur this side of the 49th parallel. In real life, in Canada, the ideal role for women was to be a wife and mother with an impeccably run household, its food cellar stocked with preserves, its laundry whiter than the neighbours', and its children better than good.

Any woman who didn't fit this circumscribed pattern was an "old maid." No grace of gesture, quality of mind, freedom of spirit, or worldly accomplishment could possibly make up for the horror of being identified by that phrase, which clearly damned a woman to be unloved, asexual, and lonely forever.

Old maids were librarians, nurses, or our teachers at school and at the conservatory, where piano lessons were given joylessly, their purpose not pleasure in music but accomplishment in the form of passing exams. (If you "got your grade eight" in music, it counted as a subject for university entrance. I got my grade eight one morning in May when I was sixteen, closed the piano, and never played it again.)

My music teacher was the old maid of our nightmares, one of a trio of sisters who looked after their tyrannical mother. This woman, the middle daughter of the trio, always wore cake rouge and blue dresses because, as she once confided, her mother disapproved of both. But this was about as far as her defiance went. For the most part she was, at forty-odd, a dutiful daughter still, childlike, dependent, and somehow pathetic even in the eyes of a docile eight-year-old playing five-finger exercises on the keys of her piano, which had yellowed like her teeth.

One year she travelled to Europe, and I thought she would come back transformed by a passionate encounter with a man or an idea. Instead, she talked about how dirty it was in Venice, how Catholic in Rome. "When we were sailing up the St. Lawrence on the way home," she summarized, "I stood at the ship's rail, turned to my sister, and said, 'Jenny, this really is God's country'" — God, as we both understood implicitly, being a grim old man with a long white beard and a firm hold on the Protestant work ethic.

I knew there were other kinds of women who worked and had lives separate from their families. But they were oddities in some way or another, possessed of unusual qualifications that made them "half a man," it was muttered obscurely, especially if they could drive a car.

The mother of one of my close friends was a classical scholar from Cambridge. M.A. (Cantab.) it said after her name. Oh marvellous! I thought. During the war she taught courses in Greek at McMaster University, travelling to Hamilton by train, reading her lecture notes as she went. After VE day, she gave the job up, though, so a man could rightfully hold it again. But she remained special in my mind because she was politically active and ran for a seat on the board of education and seemed close to the "women of spirit" who existed in the English novels I read but not in the world I inhabited.

In her household, girls as well as boys were encouraged to express themselves forcefully. She'd get us to discuss Laurence Olivier's film version of *Hamlet* and to compare it with the Donald Wolfit production we saw at the Royal Alexandra. And she understood perfectly when I told her, after I finished reading a book of essays by Bertrand Russell my brother had given me for my birthday, that I felt I could fly the several blocks from my house to hers in a state of intellectual excitement that was close to ecstasy.

But she was a rarity in my young life, and I didn't encounter her like again until I went to university at seventeen, although even there, most of the girls who sat in lecture halls with me were already programmed to think they were enrolled to get, as the dreary joke had it, a MRS. along with — or even instead of — a B.A. or B.Sc.

All this is too simplistic. There are a hundred other memories that might evoke my childhood more clearly were there space enough or time. But I hope this will give you some idea of what it was like to grow up being me, and of the dicta that I had to fight against, lean on or cast off in the long struggle to become my own person, which is far from ended yet.

By coincidence, the impact of my childhood on my consciousness was never clearer to me than on an occasion when I was talking about you to a mutual friend in Ottawa several years ago, before we met. He was a Québécois, a ministerial assistant, a warm-hearted man. I had seen you at a large, glittery party. You were dancing something like the boogaloo (it was the mid-1960s) with long blond hair falling over your shoulders, looking wonderfully alive, and when I was told you were a professor of French literature, I momentarily found it hard to believe.

"Not only is she brilliant," our friend went on, "she enjoys life," which he seemed to regard as the ultimate accolade. It was that phrase "she enjoys life" that really affected me. No English-Canadian girl of my generation that I knew of was expected to enjoy life. We were taught to tackle it head on, to accept with modesty its triumphs, and swallow with equanimity its disappointments because they were *good* for you.

It's taken me many years to learn to enjoy life. But the pleasure I take in it now is heightened by memories of my childhood — which you could almost say gave me the fortitude to appreciate the very real rigours of joy.

Affectionately,
Christina

FIFTEEN

Some Awkward Truths
the Royal Commission Missed[13]

Chatelaine, March 1971

WHEN THE REPORT of the Royal Commission on the Status of Women
was finally published in December, my response was one of sharp disappointment. It isn't that it seems superficial (in fact, a careful reading
shows it to be astonishingly thorough) or weak in its recommendations
(it makes some very tough demands on governments and institutions
despite the complaints of critics who say it asks for "too little, too late").

The fault I find with it — and I think it's a vital one — lies in its
tone and presentation. It's a formidably bleak and awkward document,
so lacking in passion that it might be a report on freight rates, so
devoid of personality that it could have been punched out by a computer.
When I read it first, I wanted to personally shake the commissioners
and say, "Look, ladies and gentlemen, you were charged with exam-
ining an aspect of the human condition that affects every man,
woman, and child in the country. You had a duty, though the Privy
Council Office may not have stated it in legalese, to engage Canadians
with your subject. After four years, 468 briefs, forty special research

projects, and $1.9 million, you ought to have been able to produce a report that nearly every literate person in the country —not just a few sociologists, ardent feminists, and snickering editorial writers — would want to read."

This may seem a picayune complaint, a question merely of style. But along with that supremely practical politician, Pierre Trudeau (remember his use during the Liberal leadership campaign of the French epigram *Le style est l'homme même?*), I think that style is often an important, and in this case possibly a crucial, factor in mass persuasion. What's too often forgotten is that publication of a Royal Commission report doesn't mean the problems it describes are solved; action has to come out of a change in public attitudes, which the commission supposedly fosters and the government hopefully heeds.

Almost from the beginning the Status of Women commission has been without a powerful advocate in government circles. Judy LaMarsh, whose cabinet influence got it established in the first place, was out of politics months before even its hearings were completed in 1968, and the general disinterest and/or ridicule the commission has been subjected to in the press made it unlikely that any other hard-headed pol would be imaginative enough to see it as an important vote-winning cause. That's why the onus was on the commission itself to engage the attention of the only possible — and potentially enormously powerful — lobby the report could have: women themselves.

It's my contention that this could have been done if the report had been written more forcefully, if it had been infused with the humanity that was so evident in its hearings. I sat in on those hearings for one week of the six months they lasted (though I listened later to many of the sessions held in other cities on tapes in the commission's office), and I found it one of the most engrossing, moving, and involving experiences I've ever had. The women who appeared before the commissioners weren't silly suffragettes in defensive hats or mannish harridans seeking unearned privileges. They were professors, farm women, nursery school teachers, Aboriginals, deserted wives, nuns, disaffected suburbanites — all real women with real problems of poverty, alienation, loneliness, and prejudice. Surely, something of their quality as human beings should have been imparted in the report, some part of their individual stories should have been told so that all those who couldn't attend and hear for themselves would have been affected, as were the audiences at those hearings. At one session in Ottawa, for instance, when an Aboriginal woman from the Caughnawaga reserve was eloquently describing the hardship of her life, another woman in the audience, the very model of a Rockcliffe matron in an expensive dress and careful hairdo, sat with tears rolling down her face. Something of the eloquence and the tears should have been in the report.

This could have been done by presenting the same material in a different, more human, form and by including a foreword that displayed some involvement with their subject on the commissioners' part. (The only commissioner who seemed roused was John Humphrey, who declined to sign the report and in the back explains why.) Instead of being merely a tiresome list of numbered items, maybe the findings reported in each chapter could have been synthesized into a lively essay. Instead of 596 (count 'em) disjointed paragraphs on "Women in the Canadian Economy," we might have had some real person's analysis of just what women have to put up with in the world of work in the way of prejudice, whether they're waitresses or barristers, an analysis that would have leavened the statistics with the kind of human anecdotes that were presented to the commission by the score. What do you find more moving personally — a story about a distinguished scholar (presented in a brief to one of the hearings but not included in the report) who was told by her department head, "Your students speak very highly of you, they say you have nice legs," or a statistic that shows men are thirty times more likely to be promoted to higher posts in academe than women? For me, the statistic is far more telling when presented in conjunction with the anecdote.

I also wish the commissioners had possessed the nerve to write some kind of eloquent foreword addressed largely to the women of the middle class (which means most of us), putting forth some home truths that would have pleased a few, offended some, roused many more into a recognition that no matter how many tough recommendations are made on behalf of women to governments, corporations, and public institutions, unless we ourselves get off our plump behinds, stop undermining each other's ambitions, cease whining about our burdens, and start working toward equality for women, that happy state is never going to be achieved in this or any other century.

A few such exhortatory ideas are tentatively expressed, tucked away throughout the report, but I think they needed to be massed together and emphasized. Women have to be persuaded that equality brings responsibilities, that we ourselves have to get over our inferior feelings as a "psychological minority," that we have to stop pointing our daughters, through education and emotional conditioning, toward a life confined to the home and then being surprised that, while at sixteen, a man and three babies seem all they want of life, at thirty many of them are already sick of playing Barbie and Ken.

Furthermore, I wish the commissioners had been able to point up some awkward realities that most of us know about but few of us mention — for instance, that women do each other great harm through jealousy, which often is nothing more than an outgrowth of insecurity. Women tend to be unfailingly kind toward the old, the weak, the dispossessed, and the male, but they have a god-awful tendency to sheer witchery when confronted by a woman of accomplishment.

Working women are the most obvious targets of jealousy. I'd hate to have to count how many times I've been told that the children of such and such a well-known woman have suffered horribly because of her career or that none of the operating-room nurses want to be on a surgical team that's headed by a woman doctor or that schools run by women principals are riddled with staff dissension. The envy flows the other way as well, though. I remember once standing with a woman writer while we waited to serve ourselves to a gourmet buffet that had been prepared by the total-homemaker wife of a colleague and having her say, in a whispered aside, "Of course, it's the kind of dinner only a woman like her can stage — she has nothing better to do with a day." The truth was that neither one of us could have prepared that meal in a week. But then, the put-down has been raised to a facile art by women through centuries of practice.

The commissioners might have pointed out as well that so much of what motivates women is the sheer fear of being thought undesirable by men; maybe they could have promoted an aphorism like "Smart *is* sexy!" that might help us overcome the effects of generations of training girls in the belief that the dim-witted draw the diamonds. (My own mother, who for her time was relatively enlightened — i.e., she believed in higher education for women — was fond of quoting to me Charles Kingsley's poem with its saccharine absurdity, "Be good, sweet maid, and let who can be clever!" while at the same time displaying delight when I brought home a report card full of A's.)

I could go on like this, complaining about the omissions in the Status of Women report (as what woman who's thought a little about the new feminism could not?). But perhaps the very fact that it has roused this much passion in me by its own absence of passion is a favourable augury for the long-term success of its proposals. Maybe women's clubs and women's editors by the dozens will be sufficiently goaded by its sober statistical approach into trying to reach other women by the thousands. Maybe a slow groundswell of support for its recommendations will build into an uproar legislators will heed. Maybe it will be worth the money spent and the effort expended. Holy Emmeline Pankhurst! I hope so.

SIXTEEN

Down with Alimony [14]

Chatelaine, December 1970

OF ALL THE ADVOCATES of women's liberation who've crowded my
television screen in the last six months — from the embattled whisky-
voiced matrons who've turned themselves into harridans for the cause,
to the young and grave-eyed bearers of placards (MALE CHAUVINISTS
BEWARE!) with their bobbling bosoms and straining jeans — the only
one I can actually bring myself to wholeheartedly like is the New York
writer Gloria Steinem. It's not only that Miss Steinem is intelligent,
articulate, and beautiful (so are a number of the sisters, despite what
businessmen, driven by nervousness into nasty innuendo, may be saying to each other over Bloody Marys at lunch). It's also that she appears
to be able to advocate liberation for women while at the same time
continuing to like men.

In fact, the feminist cause has never seemed more sympathetic to
me than it did last June, when, invited to give the graduation address
to the Vassar College class of 1970, Miss Steinem set out to explain
why liberation for women also means liberation for men — liberation
from the economic burden of being the sole supporters of women and

children until a punctured ulcer or a massive coronary do them part. She ended her speech by suggesting that a great rallying cry for the movement — symbolic of a new freedom for both sexes — might be NO MORE ALIMONY! and if I'd been in the Vassar daisy chain, I'd have stood up and hollered "Huzzah!"

For alimony has always seemed to me to be the ugliest of the spoils of the war between the sexes. It's precisely defined in dictionaries as being "an allowance for support made by a man to his wife pending or after her divorce or legal separation from him" and roughly in law as the obligation of a husband to provide for his wife in perpetuity in proportion to his ability to do so. Both are long-winded ways of describing matrimonial usury. It's my contention that alimony is usually unfair to men and always demeaning to women. It reinforces, by its very nature, the ancient premise that women are the helpless chattels of men and that marriage is essentially an economic alliance, as the feminist philosopher Kate Millett has pointed out: the woman as the weak partner contracts to give her services, sexual and otherwise, in return for financial support, which the man continues to provide whether he wants those services any more or not. He can put his wife out to pasture like an old horse, but he still has to provide the grass whereon she feeds.

In case these generalizations make you want to fling down your magazine, declaring, "I got married for love, not money, and I'd be too proud ever to ask for alimony anyway, and what about those poor women on welfare who can't get their husbands to help them with the kids and what about those rich men who run off with young bunnies and buy off their wives with alimony of $5,000 a month, how is that demeaning or unfair, eh?" — let me explain what I mean.

First of all, I'm talking about the alimony laws as they affect the middle class, the majority of us, you and me and the commercial artist down the street. (The matrimonial antics of the rich make great gossip but they don't have much to do with most people's lives, and the poor rarely get alimony anyway since they can't afford lawyers to haggle it out; instead, they get family-court support orders — which often prove unenforceable, but that's another injustice.)

Furthermore, the woman who's too proud to take alimony is still a rarity, as lawyers who practise in the field of what's euphemistically called "family law" will attest. Once a broken marriage reaches the final bitter stage when the financial details of separation are being worked out, too many women see money as a balm for their wounded spirits and too many men are prepared to pay it out of guilt. The alimony law is designed to feed these sadomasochistic impulses, since the rock-solid principle behind it is that the wife is entitled to alimony to allow her to live on the scale to which she has previously been maintained.

What happens in practice is that the money doesn't assuage the woman's hurt or the man's guilt; it usually makes her vindictive and him hopelessly angry. Take the case of a television producer I know. He left his wife, a girl with a private-school education and social expectations, after several years of mutual misery, agreeing to pay her $8,500 a year, or a little less than half his annual income. (One-third a man's income is a kind of rule of thumb in alimony, though it isn't entrenched in law, and agreements often go as high as a half.) What's happened is that the producer's *second* wife is working furiously at a demanding job in order to help make up the money paid to the *first* wife, who spends her life caring wanly for her only child, an eleven-year-old, and croaking to her friends in the Junior League (to which she still belongs) about how hateful it is to be abandoned and poor.

As the law stands, the only way out of this situation would be for the first wife to find herself a new husband or to get up the gumption to take a job and renounce the alimony, a highly unlikely event. Even so, a career doesn't mean that a woman will waive support rights. I've just heard of a professional woman who was married to a statistician and, when they split up, agreed to a very small alimony since she herself was making a good salary. She did get total possession of their house and support for their two teenagers: now she talks about the statistician (who had the luck to find himself a cosy blonde) as "that criminal" and has been heard to say darkly that her newly developed sciatica is going to cause her to give up her work and reopen the alimony arrangements, which the law entitles her to do.

There is widespread belief that the reforms of the Canadian divorce laws, which were brought in with such fanfare in 1968, put a stop to the worst abuses of alimony. The truth is that the laws governing the financial arrangements for broken marriages — alimony, maintenance of children, division of property — were affected very little by the revisions, which had to do mainly with widening the grounds for divorce itself. Alimony arrangements are so complicated, and so intertwined with the still torturously complex laws governing divorce, as to be almost unintelligible to the layman. I recently spent a couple of hours listening to a highly knowledgeable young lawyer named Malcolm Kronby, who practises in Toronto and has written a legal book called *Divorce Practice Manual*, trying to explain just their rudiments, leaving aside the wrinkles that an industrious lawyer can find in them. In the end, Mr. Kronby developed a hoarse throat and I developed an eye tic and found myself only able to nod vigorously when he stated in summation, "Look, there is a large body of opinion among lawyers practising in this field that either we need a further substantial revision of the divorce laws — which also means a revision of the alimony laws — or we need to go the whole way and completely rewrite the law.

"In the latter case," he went on, "we would have to freely admit as a society that people are entitled to a divorce if they don't want to live together any more, without trying to establish who's the guilty partner to be punished, and then make the actual procedure as simple as possible."

One country that is seeking to do just this, in a highly sensible manner, is West Germany, which is bringing a divorce reform bill before its parliament early in the new year. This bill is based on two vitally important premises: that marriage breakdown should be the only grounds for divorce and that both men and women have equal rights and responsibilities in marriage. In brief, it recognizes the equality of women by saying that they are and should be able to fend for themselves in today's industrial society. It provides that alimony will be given to the disadvantaged partner (usually the woman) only until she is able to be self-supporting. In practice, the way it will work is that when a marriage breaks down, if the wife can't support herself, the husband will give her money while she undergoes job retraining. There is a time limit on this support (two years, though it can be extended), and both partners are responsible financially for the care and education of their children.

Such a law, though eminently fair, would be tough on a lot of women who've grown up twittering about equality while taking all the advantages that inequality brings. But I suspect that if it were on our statute books, it would cause a lot of young girls to stop regarding a marriage licence as a lifetime meal ticket, to recognize that they should be trained for a productive role in society and should go out to fight for the right to fulfill that role. And I'm all for that. Aren't you?

SEVENTEEN

The Split Syndrome[15]

Saturday Night, April 1977

WHEN I WAS STARTING out as a journalist, I was required occasionally to ghostwrite articles for people whose experiences were more interesting than their prose. Once I was a Doukhobor, telling in shamefaced sentences what it had been like to ignite a neighbour's barn and then strip and stand there watching it flame, with a little bundle of clothes hugged to your bosom and goosebumps clearly visible on your backside in the light. Another time, I was a fisherman's wife, lauding old days and old ways, and for one blissful fortnight I got to be Roloff Beny, describing his adventures with the rich or famous in the capitals of the world.

Still, there was one article in which I just couldn't immerse myself no matter how hard I tried. Its working title was "Divorce: A Woman Describes the Trauma of a Broken Marriage," and its purpose was to recommend reform of the then vindictive laws.

The divorcee had two children and seemed old to me (she was close to thirty-five), with her sad eyes and her hair dyed an unbecoming red. Somehow I didn't have much empathy to bring to her experience. I was twenty-three that winter and as happy as I've ever been, making plans to be married later in the year. My life stretched out in front of me, full of places to see (I'd never been to Greece), books to devour (I'd never read the Russians thoroughly), and people to write about (I meant to seek an interview with Malraux as soon as there was time).

So I gave the divorcee's article only perfunctory attention, deciding that sheer trauma was not yet within my range, and soon put the whole collaboration right out of my still untroubled mind. But for reasons whose ironies are scarcely impenetrable I've thought about the woman with the dyed red hair several times in recent months.

It's eighteen years later. I've been to Russia but not to Greece (the colonels came to power, and I went to Paris or Barbados or someplace else instead). Dostoevsky still defeats me; Malraux's dead and I never met him; and now I find I am about to become a divorcee too.

These are very different times, though, and that designation now seems quaint. People call the once-married "liberated women," and divorce is no longer something that happens to the isolated few. Newspapers are forever printing statistical forecasts proving that half the· marriages entered into this year will be dissolved in court. Big law firms have four or five specialists in family law who go to war with one another to make advantageous property settlements for their clients. YMCAs offer courses in "Creative Divorce," as though the juxtaposition of those antithetical words could make the experience part of the human potential movement.

Some days I figure half the people I know are either contemplating, enduring, or recovering from a marital separation. Contemporaries regularly ring me up and say in sprightly voices, "You'll never guess who's split!" and I answer warily, "You're right, I never will," in the hope they'll move on to safer subjects, such as where we'll meet for lunch.

Sociologists keep saying this is a healthy development, that it's not that more people are unhappy in marriage but simply that they're unwilling to endure misery for convention's sake. For all I know, they're right. But the increasingly casual acceptance of mass marriage breakdown seems to me to trivialize what is still a terrible trauma, no matter how commonplace it has become. Having experienced it myself, I watch other people in the situation with very different eyes.

The radical activist, still engrossed in Marxist theory and anti-development politics, and the soft-voiced artist he's lived with for eight years who have decided to part by rational mutual consent. The middle-aged lawyer from a Fine Old Ontario Family, with his thirty-foot sloop and his corporate wheeler-dealering, whose wife left him for a better sailor though a lesser dealer. The one-time medical secretary who hadn't worked for a decade, until her husband took up with the chickie in the brown lip gloss he met at a sales conference, and is now juggling a job, the house, the kids, and an affair with her roomer, a graduate student who's into hash.

It doesn't seem to matter how long people have been married, whether they leave or are left, whether they are job-engrossed, child-free, extroverted, or shy, they all seem to suffer what I've come to think of as the separation syndrome. A sense of awful loss, a questioning of self, a remembrance of good times past, rage, manic gaiety, depressive withdrawal, and the eventual brave statement, "I think I'm getting over it now. I'm entering a whole new phase."

Any time now social scientists will codify, and thus authenticate, these symptoms. Right this minute, an interdisciplinary group at the University of Virginia is working on a study of separation that will no doubt be published as a tome with subheadings such as "The Influence of Ethnic Background on the Duration of Distress." Who knows, they may even come up with palliatives for this new pervasive grief.

In the meantime, what we're left with are some very old homilies ("Time cures all ills," my mother says) and some folk remedies amazingly similar to those that were current in the 1950s when I was ghostwriting articles and divorce was still a subject remote from most people's lives.

This was brought home to me one day this past winter when I went to get my hair cut by the man who's been doing it for three or four years, a Sicilian who likes to talk about Italian communism, Mafioso infiltration, Milanese supremacy in the world of design, and his sympathy for women.

He was standing behind me, towelling my head reflectively and looking at my face in the mirror. Suddenly, he called out to his colourist, "Hey, Luigi, what do you think? Shall we break out the henna and dye Mrs. Newman's hair red?"

The twenty-three-year-old inside me started to laugh, and I could hear her clear voice retorting, "Don't bother thinking about it, Luigi. Ms McCall likes her hair just the way it is."

They looked as though they figured I was acting a little nutsy. I knew I was entering a whole new phase.

EIGHTEEN

In Ottawa, Women Are
Either Babes or Blobs[16]

Chatelaine, September 1970

ON THE WAY HOME from his kissing and cavorting Pacific tour last spring, the prime minister is reported to have complained to a newspaperman that his advisers had tried desperately, if unsuccessfully, during the three weeks of his journey to keep him from being photographed "with the babes."

To most readers this must have seemed a characteristic turn of phrase, just one more manifestation of Pierre Trudeau's penchant for putting on his playboy-of-the-East-Block mask. But to me the remark was indicative of an attitude toward women that pervades not just the Prime Minister's Office, but the whole of official Ottawa as well. It shored up my long-held contention that to most of the men who run the country, women are "babes" if they're pretty, blobs if they're not, and in either case, people of no consequence belonging to a minority with only token power.

Lest that sound like the rhetorical rage of a new convert to Women's Liberation, let me say straight off that I'm too old to be militant (if still too young to be resigned) and that this conclusion was reached in a spirit of rueful realism after more than a decade of watching politicians turn a bland, blind eye on women both in public and in private.

It's a conclusion supported by some easily ascertainable facts: that since the only woman in the current House of Commons, Grace MacInnis of the NDP, doesn't belong to the government party, there is, of course, no woman in cabinet; that among the prime minister's senior advisers there are no women at all; that in the very top rank of the civil service — at the deputy minister level — no woman has ever served and that in point of fact, as a recent study commissioned by the government itself (called "Sex and the Public Service") reveals, 90 percent of its women employees have low-level jobs paying less than $6,000 a year, and of 343 government employees who are termed "senior officers" (count them and rail, O Feminists!), only *three* are women.

Not as overtly significant but just as telling to me are countless remembered disparaging remarks made about women's abilities and any number of distressing incidents when women have been put down by Ottawa men in my outwardly acquiescent, if inwardly rebellious, company. I'll content myself here with three that are fairly typical.

Item: While everybody knows how shabbily Judy LaMarsh was treated in Ottawa — she told it to the world in a dozen furious speeches and a bestselling book — few people realize that the same kind of attitudes prevailed in the treatment of her fellow Liberal MP, Pauline Jewett.

Professor Jewett was a parliamentarian with impeccable qualifications as a political theorist (a Harvard Ph.D.) and campaigner (she took a seat from a Tory in 1963 in the Conservative heartland of Ontario) and one would have thought an equally impeccable asset in the fact that she was an old friend of Trudeau's and an early supporter of his leadership candidacy. Yet when the riding of

Northumberland, which she'd contested three times, was redistributed out of existence before the '68 election, no real effort was made by the central Liberal Party organization to find her another seat, although all the important men in her party who had suffered similar losses were smoothly found suitable spots. "The thing is," a political organizer confided at the time, "if Pauline gets elected, she would have to be a minister and let's face it, women in cabinet have caused more disasters than the Red River."

Item: During the mid-1960s, one of the most intelligent, progressive, and ill-used men in the Liberal cabinet was Maurice Sauvé, the Minister of Forestry. The main charge made against Sauvé by his many detractors was that he was too openly ambitious (although ambition is the engine that drives any politician worth his seat); the second was that he was said to give unwarranted weight to the opinions of his wife, Jeanne, who had been a student with him at the University of Montreal, the London School of Economics, and the Sorbonne. She had also carved out a notably successful career on Quebec television, which was terminated when her husband became a cabinet minister and television producers were reluctant to use her talents because of a fear of Opposition charges of political influence in the CBC. No politician was ever willing to explain why Mme Sauvé shouldn't contribute her ideas to her husband's enterprises, but I'll never forget hearing an exchange on the subject between a new man in town and an old pol. Said the new man innocently, "Well, just what is the relationship between Sauvé and his wife?" Answered the old pol, with one of those short barks that in his world are used to signal a really wickedly witty sally: "Why, the same relationship Madame Chiang Kai-shek has to the Generalissimo." A dragon lady. Get it? I never did.

Item: Last June, when anniversary assessments were being made of the Trudeau regime's achievements, one of the young men on his staff was asked why, in this holy participatory democracy, so few women were close to the prime minister either as political advisers or as public servants with sufficient clout to have their opinions heard. "Well," he said thoughtfully, poking at his cold salmon garni in the Château Laurier Grill, "it's very simple really. There just aren't many possibilities around. Every time we unearth some woman who has suitable qualifications on paper for the Privy Council Office, say, she's liable to go before a [civil service appointments] board and blow the whole thing by getting *emotional*, for God's sake." Still, as irritating as this old slur of emotionalism may sound, the very need the young man had to articulate it indicates a slight change in the general Ottawa climate, a certain nervousness in the face of all the complaints that were aired during the hearings of the Royal Commission on the Status of Women and all the noise that's been made by Women's Lib protesters.

It's even possible to make a case that women, as a minority group, are in somewhat the same position as the French Canadians were a decade ago, just as the Quiet Revolution started to get noisy. It used to be said, for instance, that Quebecers had put too much emphasis on education in the classical colleges and hence were not trained to achieve success in a technological society; it's now said that women have tended to get their university degrees in the humanities and so are without the "career-relevant education" (in civil service jargon) necessary for the heady heights of power. It used to be the conventional wisdom that French Canadians wanted to bury themselves in their own insular society and had no desire to share in governing the country as a whole; it's now stated that women cling to the security of marriage and don't really want to come out of the kitchen and into External Affairs. In other words, men in power in Ottawa, as elsewhere, are beginning to spin out the same kind of defensive excuses for inequities perpetrated against women as they used to in the face of French-Canadian complaints of inequality. They're also, interestingly enough, making a few pallid gestures toward improving the situation.

In the Prime Minister's Office, for example, there is a young woman named Gwen Clark who's an assistant to an assistant and is engaged in making what she calls "a catalogue of competent business and professional women" who might serve as possible appointees to the many public offices that come under the federal government's jurisdiction; yet in the two years Trudeau has been in power, the only female order-in-council appointment (as distinct from a public-service-commission appointment) of any consequence so far is that of Judge Réjane Laberge-Colas to the Quebec Superior Court.

In the public service, the administrative arm of government, which is supposedly quick to reflect the political will, the situation for women is said to be getting better all the time. For one thing, after a long fight put up by militants within the service, women are now allowed to enrol in a management training scheme called the Career Assignment Program; last year — oh, wow! — one in every thirty-five such trainees was a woman.

An even more important talking point for the "look-we-really-do-treat-women-exceedingly-well" excuse-makers was the appointment last year of Dr. Sylvia Ostry as a director of the Economic Council, a job that carries assistant-deputy-minister status and means there is a woman only one rung down from the top. Dr. Ostry is an economist with high academic honours earned at McGill, Cambridge, and Oxford; six years' experience in the government service; and general intellectual qualifications so impressive that, as one of her male colleagues remarked, "If you covered up her sex on an application form, she was

better equipped for the job she got than anybody else in the country."
Yet in the press at the time she was named, and on the Ottawa party
circuit ever since, her appointment has been boasted of (or denigrated,
depending on the prejudices of the speaker) in the true tradition of
tokenism: as a tribute to her sex.

"What I'm looking forward to," another Ottawa woman said recently,
after hearing this cliché expounded for the twenty-second occasion,
"is the time when half a dozen Sylvia Ostrys are given important
appointments every year without sexist comment of any kind. Think
of it, a newspaper heading reading 'Brilliant Economist Appointed to
Economic Council' instead of 'Brown-Eyed and Glamorous Mother of
Two Makes It to the Top.'"

Sisters, it's an idea that blows the mind.

NINETEEN

Women and Political Power: What's Holding Us Back?[17]

Chatelaine, December 1982

ON THE SATURDAY of Thanksgiving weekend in 1974 — after I had been writing about Canadian politics for nearly eight years, first as the Ottawa editor of *Saturday Night*, the oldest and probably most respected periodical devoted to current affairs in the country, and then as a member of the editorial board of *Maclean's*, in those days a general monthly magazine with a circulation close to a million — I went to a dinner party that was to profoundly affect my life.

(I'd like to add that I set out for the party full of foreboding, but the truth is that I ran up the stone steps of the imposing Toronto house where it was being held thinking something like, "This is probably going to be entertaining, and even if it's a bloody bore we can certainly leave by eleven so I can still get up at seven and stuff the turkey for tomorrow.")

The host was a newspaper publisher, Richard Malone, a widower at the time. The guest of honour, Bruce Hutchison, was a famous old editor/reporter visiting from the West, a man renowned for the lyricism of his prose and the liberalism of his viewpoint. The other people around the table were a handsome couple in late middle age, the husband a pillar of the financial world and of the Liberal Party; a considerably younger editor/reporter, also of some renown, to whom I was married at the time; and myself.

The food was acceptable, the wine was splendid, and the conversation a civilized *tour d'horizon* centring on the events of a week the guest of honour had just spent in Washington, where he could still command entree to important senators and congressmen, as well as the respectful attention of the Canadian embassy's staff. Just before the coffee was poured and the brandy handed around, the handsome couple rose regretfully to take their leave; the wife had been ill, and their chauffeur was instructed to come for them at ten.

While the host was seeing them to the door, the old journalist turned to my husband and asked him, with the particularly avid interest of an old Ottawa hand, what was going on in the Canadian capital now.

My husband murmured that he hadn't been in Ottawa for months but that I had spent the previous week there doing research for a book we had contracted to co-author. "Ah, gathering 'the colour,' I suppose," said the older man, who had grown up in an era when women journalists were sob sisters or society columnists and "colour" writing was all they were thought to be fit for.

I shrugged off his patronizing tone and, warming quickly to my subject, began to talk, describing conflicts between Pierre Trudeau and his Minister of Finance, John Turner, that were already rattling the Ottawa establishment. Just as I got to a particularly affecting piece of news about what Turner's deputy minister thought of Lalonde's social welfare ideas, our host came back into the room.

Hutchison, eyes bright with interest, turned to him and called out, "Dick, come quick and sit down. *Peter* is telling me some fascinating stuff about what's going on in Ottawa." All three men began to immediately discuss sagaciously the implications of what had just been said — without ever acknowledging the fact that I was the one who had said it — while I sat there holding my demitasse so tightly I thought it would shatter in my hands. Nearly an hour later, when we made our own goodbyes — and the publisher and the editor had each pecked me on the cheek and remarked on how *lovely* I certainly looked — I was still in a state of shock. It was one of those famous "clicks" that feminists used to talk about in the early heady days of the women's movement, although the way I was living that autumn, on the edge of changing my life, I was experiencing a click a day. Suddenly, things that had been bothering me for months about my marriage and the conditions of my working life, which involved a close career partnership with my husband, came sharply into focus.

Within weeks, the ideas crystallized by that climactic click had been firmly acted on, and now, eight years later, the consequences have long since been absorbed. I was legally separated and then divorced, worked even harder at other, tougher journalistic jobs (the kind formerly the preserve of men) while bringing up my daughter alone, met and married an intelligent man who not only said he believed in the equality of women but acted on that belief, formed a new family, and dared to nourish at the same time larger ambitions for myself as a writer and to set out on the long road to their realization.

In brief, my life has been greatly altered since 1974, as have the lives of so many other self-directed women I know. But that episode remains with me and still has great pertinence to what I see as the situation of women in relationship to the world of power politics.

For most of the men at the centre of that world — the politicians, businessmen, and media managers who make up the great combine of elites that runs this country — women still exist at the periphery, inconsequential guests at the feast of the mighty, largely unheeded voices at the councils of the powerful.

"How can you say that?" I hear you asking. After all, there are a record number of women now sitting in the House of Commons, and two of them are in cabinet. Every provincial legislature has its quota of female members, as do most city councils. The major parties boast women presidents in their riding associations and women members on their national executives. Surely, the millennium's approaching. How can you say that women are only at the periphery of power still?

I say it because these portents so widely hailed as important continue to smack of tokenism. I say it because I don't think women have anything even approaching the real political power that's their due as people with the legal right to parity in a democratic state. I say it because I've spent more than fifteen years watching from a front-row seat the way power politics — what Pierre Trudeau once described to me as "the great game"— is really played in this country. What I learned from observation, conversation, and reportage in that time has been reinforced further by my experience in the last few years spent researching and writing a book that involved a detailed analysis of the power game based on hundreds of interviews with its chief players, attendance at dozens of political meetings, and journeys of thousands of miles — a book about the denizens of the federal Liberal Party, the people who have held power in Canada for all but twelve of the last sixty years. What I've learned has led me to the inescapable if sobering conclusion that, even with all the advances women have made — and I'll grant straight off that it's a lot better to be heading up a riding association or sitting on the backbenches of a provincial legislature than to be typing the letters in an MP's office or cutting the sandwiches in a candidate's headquarters — we are still amateur players in politics, still serving on the second-string teams or, more often, sitting on the sidelines as spectators, cheering hoarsely (or booing fiercely, in the case of the confrontationist feminists) while we wait to get into the game.

In fact, there wasn't a woman in cabinet at all during the early Trudeau years, when we were first governed by a prime minister who was on the record as an appreciator of women's beauty and off the record as a depreciator of their brains. (He liked to call women "the babes" in those days before he married his own.) It wasn't until 1972 that Jeanne Sauvé became the first woman in a Trudeau cabinet.

To be short, sharp, and blunt about it, at the rate we're going it will take several hundred years for women to achieve political parity in Canada; to move out from being the support staff who organize men's campaigns, run men's offices, prepare men's briefing papers, or, as the rare MPs scattered on the back benches, applaud the important male ministers during televised Question Periods; to become the candidates who get the plum "winnable" ridings, the key jobs in cabinet and in the Prime Minister's Office, the ones that bring real power with them and real impact on the government's direction.

It's as though, some sixty years since women were enfranchised, politics is still a sport whose rules we don't precisely understand. Or to use an analogy more pertinent to our situation as a politically under-represented group, we are in a position similar to that of the French Canadians before the ferment of the Quiet Revolution led to dramatic social and political change there.

We back the ruling federal party loyally (the women's vote has been disproportionately higher for the Liberals than for either the Tories or the NDP) as French Canadians did (and do). In return, we get two or three acceptable portfolios to keep us happy, appointments to a few key boards, some token high positions in the public service, though not quite up there at the top, and several seats on the party's executive, where the power definitely isn't. But for the really important jobs, as the anglophone male power group used to say soothingly of French Canadians (and the francophone/anglophone male power group now says soothingly of women), they "aren't educated for the big portfolios or the crucial decision-making roles; they're not interested in exercising power since they're too caught up in their own rich culture/church teachings/provincial hierarchy (read families/love life/career) to go for broke to the top."

I don't believe those statements about women any more than Pierre Trudeau and his friends in the 1950s believed them about Quebecers. I think women are educated for and capable of political power now. But if we are to alter our political lot radically in the next thirty years, as French Canadians have altered theirs, then we're going to have to change the way we behave.

Before I try to expand on this discomfiting contention, I had better briefly describe that great male "game" whose intricacies govern our lives. If I could reduce its complexities to one central premise, it would be a line from *Men in Groups*, a book published by the Canadian-born anthropologist Lionel Tiger in 1969. Tiger's thesis said simply, "Males bond." What he meant was that modern men bond together in groups, as they did as hunters in primitive times, forming close attachments and going after their goals as a collective. In those days, it was a deer or a bear; in the political world now, it's a constituency nomination, or a policy deal, or a big portfolio to match their big ambitions, or a carefully plotted electoral victory to meet their party's needs. They support each other's ambitions and share each other's moxie, cover each other's errors and applaud each other's strengths until the day when they do battle with rival groups in order to elevate to the leadership the most promising member from their ranks.

Whether you believe, as Tiger did, that this behaviour is biologically imprinted, or, as I do, that it's only culturally induced, the fact is that men in groups do behave differently from women. They know how to stick together to get what they want for the benefit of them all.

Lest you think I've simply bought a piece of debatable academic theory that's probably out of date, let me illustrate its veracity from life in the here and now. In the summer of 1979, when the Liberals were briefly out of office and Trudeau's retirement was imminent, John Roberts, the former cabinet minister, went to see Keith Davey, the senator, and asked him how he could improve his leadership prospects. How could Roberts burnish his image and get himself a favourable press, and hence a following among the potential delegates to a future leadership convention?

The senator explained patiently, as he had often done before, that this wasn't the way to go about it. What you have to do first, he told Roberts, is get together a dozen guys whose interests meld with yours and figure out a long-term strategy for winning the leadership race. You may be the one to get the nomination or it could be someone else, but the important thing is to make common cause.

Davey knew what he was talking about from intimate experience. As the longest-lasting, permanent floating backroom power in his party, he had been part of two great Liberal coalitions for power in the previous twenty years and had closely observed a third. When he was a young man in the late 1950s, working for a Toronto radio station, he had joined a group of reform Liberals called Cell Thirteen (eleven other men and Judy LaMarsh), who made common cause with Lester Pearson and his old friend Walter Gordon, and helped them all win power in 1963. Five years later, Davey had been forced to sit back in the Senate and watch, after power was taken away from his group by the men around Trudeau, a new Liberal male collective of a very different complexion. Its chief players, besides Trudeau himself, were Marc Lalonde and Michael Pitfield as the important figures behind the scenes, along with Jean Marchand and Gérard Pelletier, who were out front, and half a dozen lesser figures, French and English, all male.

(Not the least absurd of the myths about Trudeau so widely perpetuated in English Canada is that he's always been a loner. On the contrary, from the time he came home to Montreal from his studies and travels abroad, he has always belonged to a group whose ties were based originally on an intensely felt shared ideology and who are commonly called the *Cité libristes* in Quebec, after the magazine in whose pages they originally expressed their ideas. This group expanded to encompass others just before and just after Trudeau went into Liberal politics in 1965, but if you examine its members' lives, some thirty years after it was first formed, you soon realize that they still hang in together. Its leader has power and he continues to deliver what his followers need, in this case jobs of the highest importance, such as Minister of Finance, clerk of the Privy Council.

When the Trudeauites faltered in 1972 and nearly lost the election, a remnant of Davey's old band of Pearsonian Liberals came to their rescue, and the two groups melded into a new and bigger band, the one that's kept the Liberals in office ever since, except for those few months in late 1979 and early 1980 when poor Joe Clark wrested it briefly from their grasp.

When Keith Davey responded to John Roberts, he was repeating a piece of ingrained male wisdom that he had seen proven again and again and will doubtless see proven once more when Trudeau finally does step down and another male power group with John Turner, or Donald Macdonald, or Jean Chrétien, or James Coutts, or some other dark horse at its head takes over the Liberal reins. Every one of those groups that's serious will include a couple of women, just as every combine used to include a couple of Québécois. None of them — that's serious — will have a woman as contender.

I get it, I hear you saying, she's talking about networks. Well, women have networks too now. Yes, I know they do. But from my observation, and from the observations of several women who view the three major federal parties from within, they're not the same as male networks. The bulk of them are comprised of "supportive" or "survival" groups that grew out of the women's movement and that still operate outside the mainstream of political life, gathering their forces periodically for the occasional guerrilla raid, like the two mounted in 1981 with so much publicity and so little effect over the question of the Constitution and then falling back without consolidating their gains.

Younger working women of the kind who have been pouring out of the universities in the last six or seven years with degrees in law, economics, and business administration are gathering regularly in big cities to exchange information and make contacts, to talk about bond issues or new wrinkles in the real estate laws. What they're not talking about is how to get and wield political power for women. Most of them are too busy learning the intricacies of the business world to have time left over for the intricacies of politics. Even women who do have the time to join the ranks of the major parties find discussions there are rarely concerned with the large questions of women's advancement or even the specific questions of concern to themselves, such as the horrific widespread poverty among the elderly that our pension policies exacerbate. Women rarely make common cause in the parties even now. Political women are too engrossed in how to keep their individual footholds on the shifting beachheads that have already been established, how to decide who is the male figure with whom they should throw in their political lot, how to circumvent the worst of the male chauvinism that still surfaces occasionally like an oil slick from a submarine.

A prize story in this category, still being told in political circles three years after it occurred, involved a very well-known Liberal who was representing the government at an important international function. She was standing talking in a circle when a prominent member of the interest group she was meant to lobby lurched up, grabbed the bodice of her dress, and, peering down the front, said accusingly, "Hey, I heard you had big tits, and they're really not big at all."

The woman who recounted this anecdote to me shivered a little as she talked; she was one of several people representing all three major parties whom I talked to at length this fall trying to unravel once more the whole question of the general alienation of women from the masculine world of power.

Interestingly, the reasons given for our backwardness concentrated far less on the antagonisms of men, as it would have in the 1970s, and more on the limitations of the way women view themselves within the political process.

"Women are held back by their own fears," said an NDPer. "They wind up in the sacrificial lamb seats because they're afraid to go after the winnable ones. They expect a party to be a 'fathering' institution, to provide them with workers, money, policies, everything, whereas men are aware of the need to look after themselves and to press on from dawn till dark."

"Women don't seem to realize they need an independent base, if they're to move away from the support roles," said a Tory who was lamenting the fact that, despite her leader's interest in fostering women, there is no solid woman candidate emerging for the party's presidency at its January convention. "What we have is many more women in the middle but no more women at the top. Men move on from being aco- lytes, they learn from their mentors and eventually become mentors themselves. But women either cling or quit. Ever since I read Colette Dowling, I see so many political women's careers in terms of the Cin- derella Complex — the need to be rescued by a strong male."

"I sometimes have the feeling that it will be another generation before women really catch on to team playing," said a Liberal who's adept at the art herself. "Something goes wrong at a level below the rational. We haven't been taught accommodation or turf-sharing. Women can be supportive of each other emotionally on an egalitarian level, but once a woman moves out ahead of the pack, other women get nervous about supporting her. *Why isn't that me?* they start thinking, instead of *How can that help me?*— which is the equivalent response of the male. Women even have trouble using male networks if they're lucky enough to work their way into one. They either fall back on occasional confrontations, which get them precisely nowhere, or they are so anxious not to offend, they do a self-effacing fade."

In trying to weigh where women are politically now, one woman shrewdly summed up: "What we're doing in the 1980s isn't always exhilarating. These are times for retrenchment, for carefulness and cunning, for making minor gains. No woman in any party has the positive power of the men. But there are two women who have something women never had before. Flora [MacDonald] and Monique [Bégin] haven't a hope in hell of winning a leadership race. But all the years of battling and hanging in have brought them enough respect among women and the more liberal-minded men that they have a kind of negative power, the power to stop someone else. Come the conventions, the candidates will have to court their support."

Then she leaned forward to deliver the clincher: *"That means the men will have to listen when the women get up to talk."* Looking back eight years, I had to agree that represents progress of a sort.

PART IV

The Drama of Politics

BEYOND ALL ELSE — beyond her perceptions of the wider Canada, beyond her insight into the unfolding urban scene, beyond her steely-eyed but compassionate feminism — Christina wrote about politics. Her dream had been to be a theatre critic, since she loved drama and knew writing was her destiny. But life took her to Ottawa when her first husband, also a writer at *Maclean's*, was moved there to cover the federal government. While first feeling in exile in this remote city, she was bemused by the theatricality of federal politics, which, at that time, was enlivened by the pyrotechnics of John Diefenbaker's doomed incumbency and then morphed into the dreams, debates, and soap-opera scandals of the Pearson years. Soon, she accepted that her fate was to write about the human exchanges taking place at what she often referred to as "the bloody crossroads where literature and politics meet."

I have organized the selections around four topics: the Pearson years, Canadian nationalism, Quebec, and the Trudeau era.

Initially dismissive of Prime Minister Lester Pearson's incumbency for its political bungling and administrative ineptitude, Christina later gave "Mike" credit for his progressive achievements — Canada's distinctive flag and medicare, bilingualism, and the modernization of laws on homosexuality and divorce. For a conference of historians considering the era, she composed a bemused assessment of the unlikely Diefenbaker-Pearson combo: "The Unlikely Gladiators."

Christina wrote about the present, but her perceptions were informed by a deep historical sense of conditions changing and eras ending. One such transition was the slow but sure decline of the Ottawa mandarin caste, which encompassed such figures as O.D. Skelton, Jack Pickersgill, and Mitchell Sharp, great civil servants who shaped the postwar liberal welfare state. Although the mandarinate's decline was inevitable given the changing zeitgeist, she nevertheless recalled with wry fondness the ethos of this dedicated elite. The subtitle of her review of the memoirs of Michael Ignatieff's father, George Ignatieff, "The End of an Era," conveys her argument: "the story of a singular man, a remarkable generation, and Canada's golden age of innocence in international affairs."

As much a nationalist as a feminist, in "What Was Important About the Gordon Commission" Christina responded viscerally to the much-loved maverick Walter Gordon's civil, intelligent, and devoted commitment to rescuing Canadian capitalism — and so Canada — from U.S. domination. Christina's nationalism came naturally to her in the 1950s and 1960s, free from either paranoia or superiority. She loved New York for its cultural riches, enjoyed Washington for its political excitement, and took great delight in seeing an aging John Kenneth Galbraith shuffle into the Harvard Faculty Club to lunch with his cronies. She knew she was good enough to have written for *The New Yorker*, but was proud to have written for Canadians. "How Mel Watkins Brought Socialism to the NDP" plunges us into the fevered politics of the Canadian left at the end of the 1960s, and "Growing Up Reluctantly" gives her obituary for "the birth and brutal death of the new nationalism." Canadians' enduring inferiority complex vis-à-vis the United States is explored wryly in "The 10 Percent Solution: Canada's Colonial Neurosis." The tension in the delicate Canadian-American relationship at the end of the Trudeau era is addressed in "The Unquiet American," the profile of Ronald Reagan's always blunt, often clownish, larger-than-life ambassador in Ottawa, Paul Heron Robinson Jr., who wanted to visit the Arctic because that's where he believed World War III would break out.

Although Christina suffered from a tin ear and regretted that she had never got beyond a reading knowledge of French, she was fascinated with the great divide between Quebec's francophones and the rest of the country. In "De Gaulle's Gaffe Was a Pivotal Point for Canada," she and I revisited this crisis that had burst onto the world stage following the French president's provocative "*Vive le Québec libre!*" in 1967. "Learning French Is No Longer a Courtesy in Ottawa" assesses how Trudeau's official bilingualism was transforming bureaucratic careers. "Ten Years: From the Quiet Revolution to the Apprehended Insurrection" reports on the crisis that provoked the War Measures Act and put Canadian soldiers on the streets of Montreal. "Bridging the Great Canadian Divide" sums up the disappointing persistence of the enduring two solitudes.

When we worked together in the 1980s on Pierre Trudeau's biography *Trudeau and Our Times*, I was constantly amazed by two facets of Christina's prodigious talent. In one moment she was the social anthropologist, extrapolating from the responses of the politician or bureaucrat we had just interviewed where he or she stood in terms of class or ethnic background. In the next, she was the novelist, seeing deep into the psyche of those we interviewed. The Alice Munro of Canadian nonfiction (she preferred the more positive "reality writing"), she explained not just the workings of Canada's elite-dominated democracy but the motivations and psychology of its movers and shakers.

With bookstores currently selling four new treatments of Pierre Trudeau by Max and Monique Nemni, John English, Robert Wright, and Bruce Powe, I need to justify reprinting Christina's writings from three decades before, when she had no access to the family archives' dark secrets and no knowledge that he would make a comeback from the steady decline that was taking him to defeat in 1979. Right from the start, her take on Trudeau was as remarkably dispassionate as it was sharply analytical. At the time, Trudeau drew media coverage that tilted to three extremes — uncritical praise (George Radwanski), betrayed adoration (Peter Newman), or irrational distrust, whether from the left (Walter Stewart) or the right (Peter Worthington). Christina's work was distinguished by her rejection of these testosterone-dominated, two-dimensional slants.

The pieces here exhibit her ability to detect early on what a conventional, unradical politician he was — despite the crusade atmosphere of his leadership campaign, the over-the-top Trudeaumania of his first federal election, and his scorn for the media. Time and again, her reports transcended the period, making it worthwhile to look at the early Trudeau as if he were preserved in aspic. Embedded as she was in Liberal Ottawa's politics, these articles provided eyewitness reporting from the front lines.

"Our Heroes on the Russian Front" was the first piece of reporting to puncture the romantic balloon that had inflated Trudeau's image following his surprise marriage to Margaret Sinclair. In the light of Stephen Harper's somewhat pathetic efforts to cast Canada as an "energy superpower" at international summit meetings, Christina's straight-up reporting on Pierre Trudeau's pretentious but aimless prime ministerial tour with his bride in the Soviet Union gives us some perspective on Canada's endless search for a role in the world.

"The Exotic Mindscape of Pierre Trudeau" discusses the character traits that account for his disturbingly authoritarian beliefs as a young man: his loner quality, his self-engrossment, his pride, his need for self-dramatization. Later, his persona of a hero wandering in the wilderness while performing feats of endurance exposed behavioural patterns that revealed the narcissist in search of a mission. Christina was critical of the flawed leader but sensed that his formidable intellectual skills and his underestimated yet superior strategic sense would give him the upper hand when dealing with Quebec's separatists after René Lévesque's victory in 1976.

Our "Bowing Out: John Turner's Resignation" revisits the failure of Pierre Trudeau's successor as Liberal leader to develop a consistent policy stance and hold on to power. It also views his campaign in the 1988 federal election against Brian Mulroney's deeply flawed trade deal with Reagan as his finest hour.

Christina had an innate sense of what was fair game in her portraits of living politicians. Nevertheless, some of her subjects were deeply hurt. James Coutts was wounded less by the chapter she wrote about him for her great book *Grits* than when it was excerpted in *Saturday Night* as "Jim Coutts and the Politics of Manipulation." The damage was done not by the text but by the accompanying grotesquely distorted photos, taken with a fish-eye lens.

— *SC*

TWENTY

The Unlikely Gladiators: Pearson and Diefenbaker Remembered [18]

From *Pearson: The Unlikely Gladiator*, Norman Hillmer, ed. (McGill-Queen's University Press, 1999)

WHEN I FIRST HEARD the title of Jack Granatstein's paper, "Pearson and Diefenbaker: Similar Men?" it seemed to me a mind-boggler. How was it possible that those warring titans whose palpable differences defined the public discourse in my green years as a political writer could be seen by such a renowned historian as being even vaguely alike? But after I had turned the notion around in my head for a few minutes, looking at it upside down and sideways, I realized that there was a time in the 1950s when I would have accepted Professor Granatstein's hypothesis with ease.

After all, both men belonged to the generation of Anglo-Canadians who were born before the turn of the century, were called to the defence of the British Empire in the "war to end all wars," and energetically engaged in public life thereafter as members of the young dominion's small educated class. Men whose responses to the exigencies of the Depression and the Second World War led them to prominence in the old Canada — that long-lost homogeneous society whose citizens were connected to each other not by six degrees of separation, as the American playwright John Guare would have it, but by only one or two.

For many people in the Anglo-Canadian middle class of the early postwar period, Diefenbaker and Pearson were as familiar as distant relatives and talked of in much the same terms. Certainly, they were in my parents' house in Toronto and in the houses of my friends.

My father was an Ulsterman who had immigrated to Canada as a boy and had involved himself in the Presbyterian Church and the Conservative Party. John Diefenbaker's maternal uncle, Duncan Bannerman, was a member of the same Tory riding association, an adopted Celtic cousin who shared my father's prejudices and his hopes. They both loathed the condescensions of the English, the boosterism of the Americans, and the perfidies of the arch-Liberal William Lyon Mackenzie King.

To the barely pubescent me, Bannerman seemed a scary old character, with fierce pale eyes and the noxious habit of smoking cigars while expressing his immutable opinions after a roast-beef Sunday lunch. He convalesced at our house once from a mysterious operation. ("What was wrong with him exactly?" I asked my mother. "It's nothing for you to worry about," she replied. "It can only happen to men.")

When Diefenbaker, then an Opposition MP from Saskatchewan renowned as an advocate for the underdog, came to Toronto to make a political speech — probably part of his doomed attempt to beat out the Ontario premier George Drew for the leadership of the federal Conservatives in 1948 — he fitted into his schedule a duty call on his uncle Dunc. In a fit of shyness, I hid in my room while Diefenbaker was in the house, but I could hear his voice reverberating up the stairwell as he addressed his tiny Tory audience of three while consuming tea and cakes. (Diefenbaker was a Baptist teetotaller and, out of respect for his convictions, my father and Mr. Bannerman must have decided to forgo the dram of whisky they occasionally enjoyed.)

After Diefenbaker left, waving grandly from a taxi, I listened while the adults talked about John's anti–Bay Street ideas and eloquent concern for the unjustly accused and unfairly disadvantaged— the very first time I ever heard an expression of western rage against the central Canadian hegemony.

Five or six years later, when I was studying at Victoria College in the University of Toronto, Lester Pearson, then leading a charmed life as the peripatetic secretary of state for external affairs in Louis St. Laurent's Liberal government, was much talked of in the college as its illustrious graduate, the honorific college chancellor and a power in cold-war diplomacy.

One Hallowe'en, students from Burwash Hall—the men's residence where Pearson himself had lived as an undergraduate — burned in effigy the red-baiting American senator Joe McCarthy. After their prank was reported in *The Varsity* and picked up by the Toronto dailies, the college buzzed with the news that Pearson had written censoriously to the college principal about this profoundly illiberal act, even though— or perhaps because— he himself was suffering from the scrutiny of McCarthy's senatorial committee on American security. That episode —and the fact that Pearson's radiant face could be seen occasionally in American news magazines as he went his conciliatory way in the world— seemed to connect us directly to great events beyond parochial Canada. Undergraduate women seeking political sophistication as members of the university's international relations club could bask in Pearson's reputation when we toured the United Nations headquarters in New York; and undergraduate men — gangly boys from the same Ontario towns where Pearson had grown up as the son of a Methodist preacher — talked of the possibilities of "going into External" after they graduated and "making a difference in the world, just like Mike."

My parents looked on Pearson as a man who transcended party politics; he might have been a protegé of the hated King and a favourite of the suspect St. Laurent, but they knew a good man when they saw one. A close friend's parents, Cambridge classicists turned Canadian academics who were founding members of the social democratic Co-operative Commonwealth Federation, sympathized as Pearson tangled with the forces of American reaction. At the same time, they approved of Diefenbaker's advocacy of a citizens' bill of rights.

The cosy postwar Canadian consensus that this "approval across party lines" represented began to crumble as the 1950s wore away, with the bitterly fought pipeline debate of 1956, which proved to the electorate that the Grits were as arrogant as the Tories claimed, and with the Suez crisis later that year, which brought both Lester Pearson's Nobel Peace Prize and the disaffection from him of die-hard British Imperial Canadians who saw his role in that tangled affair as a heinous betrayal of "Mother England."

These events, thought to be cataclysmic at the time, led to the Liberal Party's fall from grace and to Diefenbaker's electoral triumphs of 1957, when he defeated the sadly aged St. Laurent, and 1958, when he overwhelmed the still boyish-looking Pearson, by then the Liberal leader.

When Pearson displayed embarrassing ineptitudes in his first two years as Opposition leader, a job he approached with well-founded misgivings, and Diefenbaker enjoyed surprising successes in his early years as prime minister, a job he had been longing for most of his adult life, it looked as though the heyday of the old consociational Canada, elitist in its democracy and centred on the alliance of Ontario and

Quebec, had passed forever, and that it would be Pearson's unenviable lot to oversee the steady decline of the Liberal Party that had been so instrumental in its creation.

By the time I began to work in Ottawa in early 1960, as a young magazine writer recently married to a political journalist reporting from the Parliamentary Press Gallery, anybody expressing the bizarre notion that Diefenbaker and Pearson were "similar men" would have been laughed off Parliament Hill. Pearson was viewed as an overly genteel has-been, Diefenbaker as the harbinger of a more egalitarian Canada, fuelled by the rambunctious energy of the emerging West.

Animosity between the two men burgeoned as Pearson tried to adjust to being out of power and confined to dealing with mostly local (i.e., Canadian) affairs, and Diefenbaker struggled to wield power while turning away from traditional Tory ideas and traditional Tory supporters in the business community and seeking to appeal to both the emerging multicultural middle class and his natural agrarian constituency.

Among old Ottawa hands left over from the King–St. Laurent era, it was thought to be only a matter of time before some suitably important job abroad would be found for Mike by his international friends, since his foray into domestic politics was so clearly a disaster.

But before 1960 was over, *Fortuna* began to turn again in Pearson's favour. That was the year when Diefenbaker's errors of judgement in foreign and economic affairs, his ineptitude in managing his cabinet and caucus, and increasing alienation from the intertwined business and bureaucratic elites began to tell. The year when monetary policy conflicts between the prime minister and James Coyne, the bloody-minded governor of the Bank of Canada, began to surface. The year when the Opposition Liberals were heartened by their provincial counterparts' victories in Quebec (under Jean Lesage) and New Brunswick (under Louis Robichaud); by the election of the liberal Democratic candidate, John Kennedy, as president of the United States; and by the demoralizing

effect their determined attacks in Parliament were having on Diefenbaker and his inexperienced front bench.

Senior mandarins in the bureaucracy and senior commentators in
the press gallery began to express in private their grave concerns about
what would happen to Canada if the renegade Diefenbaker wasn't
stopped before he did Canada irreversible harm. As they toyed with
their oysters at the communal table in the Rideau Club at noon and
sipped their dry martinis in the bar of the Roxborough at nightfall, the
Ottawa men began to tell each other, and their attentive junior colleagues, that only Mike could save the country.

For reasons particular to my circumstances, I watched this drama
unfolding from one of the best seats in the house. The man I was married to then and I both wrote for magazines — still a powerful national
medium — he for the old biweekly *Maclean's* and I for *Maclean's* and
Chatelaine, with some side excursions into CBC radio and television. I
also functioned as his researcher and editor, an extra pair of eyes and
ears. In that guise, I went in his company to Question Periods, private
bureaucratic briefings, and off-the-record interviews with politicians
of a kind that women rarely attended and at which I listened mutely
to constant talk about the urgent need for change.

Because of the restrictions on the subjects that women were thought
capable of writing about then — commenting on cabinet decisions of
consequence, particularly when they had to do with the economy or
international affairs, was thought to be beyond our scope — I also saw
the Diefenbaker/Pearson era from the perspective of voters who were
not privy to confidential briefings but were experiencing this need for
change in their everyday lives as the postwar consensus faltered along
with the postwar boom.

Some of the suitably "soft" issues that had not yet become central
to the public policy agenda and could safely be assigned to a woman
writer like me included proposed reforms of the archaic divorce laws;

the failure of the social welfare system to meet the needs of the growing numbers of the unemployed; the problems experienced by the
Inuit trying to leap for their lives into the twentieth century as white
men brought their technology, their addictions, and their diseases to
the North; the ideas of the sociologist John Porter on how the class
system worked against the interests of Canadians of non-British backgrounds; the causes and consequences of the brain drain to the United
States; or — and this one came closer to home, or at least to Ottawa
insider briefings — the hard lot of politicians' wives.

Researching major articles on Olive Diefenbaker and Maryon
Pearson was at least as revelatory of the marked differences in their
husbands' experiences and attitudes as listening to the two men rail at
each other across the Commons floor or observing them closely at
press conferences, political meetings, and social gatherings. Blair Fraser, the great liberal gentleman journalist of the postwar Liberal era,
told me once that official Ottawa was a village where everybody knew
everybody else, and it was important for political writers to be aware
of its dangers as well as its charms, a perception that took on a heightened acuity when I interviewed the leaders' wives.

Encountering Mrs. Diefenbaker at 24 Sussex was like visiting a prairie parsonage presided over by a sweet-natured minister's wife who
had an unexpectedly shrewd eye for the vagaries of his parishioners
and the ways in which they might do him harm. After discussing with
disarming frankness the details of her everyday life, she showed me
the separate bedrooms where she and her husband slept; took me into
the prime-ministerial kitchens and introduced me to the domestic
staff; displayed for my admiration the best set of dishes used for queens
and presidents, and the second-best set, used for practising politicians
and assorted lesser lights; retrieved from the safe the modest jewellery that had been given to her as the Conservative leader's wife; told
me confidentially —"I know you'll understand"— how hard it was for

her to watch her painfully unilingual husband try to politic in Quebec despite his party's huge majority there, won in 1958 with the aid of the still-powerful Union Nationale machine of Maurice Duplessis.

"*They* are so different from *us*," she said, smiling into my apparently credulous twenty-five-year-old face. Oh God! thought I — and it wasn't the implacable Taskmaster-in-the-Sky of my Presbyterian childhood I was invoking — she thinks we're *alike.* How can I tell this nice woman I find such notions noxiously racist?— a response that was as reflective of my generation's naive one-world idealism as hers was of her generation's sectarian tribalism.

Paradoxically, interviewing Maryon Pearson was a far more difficult task, though superficially we *were* alike, at least in several of our private interests. She had a reputation as "*une dame formidable,*" as the wife of a Quebec Liberal MP warned in advance, advising me to watch out for an ambush.

In the cold light of a November morning, Mrs. Pearson seemed less formidable than I'd feared. She was far more sophisticated in her conversation than Olive Diefenbaker and far less circumspect in bemoaning the problems of political wives, which she described with a wit she had been honing for decades and that by now had achieved a razor-sharp edge. She talked of the ennui she experienced at political events where she had to play the wife of the leader; of the pleasure she took in the work of the Canadian painters David Milne, Lawren Harris, and Joe Plaskett; and of her taste in literature (the novels of Muriel Spark, the short stories of Katherine Mansfield, and the poetry of Edna St. Vincent Millay, though she disparaged Millay's verse by saying it reflected the attitudes of "sentimental girls of my generation.")

While Mrs. Diefenbaker had introduced me to her seamstress and her cook, Mrs. Pearson treated her domestic staff as though they were automatons and basked instead in the flattering attentions of the *Maclean's* photographer, a glamorous figure who drove a Jaguar, played the piano with brio, and described his experiences publishing pictures in *Paris Match* and *Life* while clicking away like mad.

In the wake of the articles' publication, Mrs. Diefenbaker sent me a graceful note, written in a rounded hand on a flowered card; Mrs. Pearson had a secretary ring me up and then came on the line to deliver four or five sarcastic comments in rapid succession, attacking my perfidy in having repeated in print some of her milder dissatisfactions with her lot. In summing up, she said witheringly, "You're just so young. Only someone as young as you are could be so indiscreet."

Thirty-five years later — in an era of adversarial journalism and confessional celebrity, when revealing the dark secrets of public figures' lives is commonplace — both my article and Mrs. Pearson's reaction to it seem to me to be touchingly restrained, redolent of a period when punches were pulled, privacies were respected, and to be called "too young" was considered an insult. At the time, I was first unnerved, then furious, and, finally, amused. The "youthquake" was coming, and I figured my cohort was on its leading edge.

John Porter–inspired visions of class-based differences between the Pearsons and the Diefenbakers began to bounce around in my busy head. Superficially, the two couples would seem to belong to the same social echelon. Olive Freeman was the adolescent daughter of a Baptist minister in Saskatoon when she met her second husband-to-be, the young lawyer John George Diefenbaker. Maryon Moody was the offspring of a Winnipeg doctor, studying at Victoria College when she encountered her future husband, the young history tutor Lester Bowles Pearson. But fate had treated the two women and their husbands very differently.

Widowed in her thirties, Olive had supported herself and her daughter by working as a high school teacher before marrying in late middle age the doughty Dief, who had suffered many reverses both personal and political, which he privately blamed on the fact that his paternal ancestors were German and that his education had been hard-won at raw institutions on the western frontier. Maryon Pearson had danced and dined in embassies around the world, affecting a cigarette holder and engaging in repartee with the great men of her time while her husband had climbed with seeming ease the slippery ladder of international success as a diplomat, leaning only a little on his status as an old Oxonian and a familiar of the internationally well-connected among the central Canadian elite.

Diefenbaker had grown increasingly suspicious as he aged, convinced that this elite was out to sabotage his every effort, and given to refuting criticisms of his government in a desperate, bombastic style. Pearson had become ever more urbane, maintaining, even in his darkest travail, his endearing self-deprecatory manner and his habit of showing consideration to all comers.

He phoned me up once after watching a CBC interview I conducted with a specialist on foreign aid and discussed the subject as though he and I were equals, a capacity he had developed as a diplomat when he conversed confidentially with worldly journalists from important British and American newspapers who were eager to hear what had gone on behind closed doors at international meetings.

Remembering that phone call and one or two other conversations of the same ilk with Pearson, I found his wife's rudeness inexplicable until a Jungian psychoanalyst, with whom I had collaborated on an article on modern marriage, told me she thought that the women were the men's alter egos in both the Diefenbaker and the Pearson partnerships. The saintly, optimistic Olive balanced the dour, pessimistic Diefenbaker, urging him to function according to the tenets of their Baptist youths; the acerbic Maryon acted out the concealed animosities and vented the darker feelings that the always-charming Mike could not let himself express.

In my early years in Ottawa I had viewed the marked differences between Diefenbaker and Pearson as having to do mostly with matters of style. But now I began to see their continuing confrontations as did so many of my elders and my peers — as embodying an historic struggle between the old inward-turning, backward-facing, repressive Canada, refusing to fade away, and a new cosmopolitan, outward-looking, more confident modern country struggling to thrive. Diefenbaker's original freshness of approach to Canada's problems had vanished, despite valiant efforts made on his behalf in the early years of his regime by his professional civil service, while Pearson in opposition had become increasingly open to new ideas being expressed by both old and new adherents to Liberalism.

Pearson had gathered around him a remarkable group of policy advisers, political aides, and would-be candidates, people who wanted to rebuild the shattered Liberal Party as a preliminary step toward putting into effect the legislation necessary to bolster their plans for a transformed Canada more socially generous and more economically independent.

The problems that befell them and their leader as they went about this gargantuan task — the three hard-fought, mind-numbing, body-breaking elections of 1962, 1963, and 1965 that failed to produce a Liberal majority; the series of farcical scandals that exacerbated French-English problems as the Quiet Revolution in Quebec turned noisy; the quarrels over foreign investment and medicare within the Prime Minister's Office among Pearson's advisers, and around the cabinet table among his ministers, quarrels that were leaked to the press almost as soon as they occurred — diminished Pearson's reputation for composure in the face of crisis and his party's reputation for competence in the management of public affairs.

As his tumultuous prime ministership lurched along, Pearson began to be viewed in much the same way his nemesis Diefenbaker had been in the same job — as a man out of step with his times. When his government's many positive accomplishments were subsumed in the

Trudeau phenomenon, Pearson left office in 1968 without being given his due. Louis Robichaud, then the premier of New Brunswick and later a Liberal senator, remembered telephoning the prime minister to protest his resignation as detrimental to Canadian unity, and being told by Pearson that he could not go on in the face of his government's difficulties. He explained that every day he got up and cried a little before he could force himself to go into the office.

It's only in recent years that the achievements of the Pearson era have begun to be recognized— how innovative it was and what far-reaching changes it set in train. Changes in the way the Canadian-American relationship was perceived as a consequence of the impact that the economic nationalist ideas of Pearson's first Minister of Finance, Walter Gordon, had on the public discourse against the background of the Vietnam War; changes in the way social policy developed as a consequence of the influence on Pearson's thinking of his left-liberal advisers, Tom Kent and Allan MacEachen; changes in the way the French-English relationship was seen as a result of Pearson's willingness to try to understand the Quebec viewpoint and to accommodate his French lieutenants, from Maurice Lamontage to Guy Favreau, and Jean Marchand to Pierre Trudeau and Marc Lalonde.

These accomplishments — and many others — are being described now in memoirs and detailed scholarly studies of the period. What no analyst has yet taken much note of, as far as I am aware, is the impact of the Pearson era on what's been called the longest revolution: the struggle for greater equality for women.

It's not that Pearson was a secret feminist, a latter-day John Stuart Mill. In their private discourse, a mild misogyny was as endemic among men of his class and generation as their carefully concealed ambitions. But that this civilized, decent human being liked and respected women was apparent in his relationship with his mother and his wife, both of whose opinions he heeded; in his friendships with the intelligent wives of his peers, women like Elizabeth Gordon and Alison Ignatieff, whose views he routinely sought; in his respect for the political savvy of his assistant, Mary Macdonald, who managed his riding of Algoma East; in his often-expressed admiration for the writers Barbara Ward and Barbara Tuchman; and in his treatment of Judy LaMarsh, whom he appointed to the important portfolio of health and welfare, treated with understanding when the male-dominated political system caused her grief, made secretary of state in charge of the centennial celebrations, and whose demands for a Royal Commission on the Status of Women he acceded to, albeit somewhat reluctantly.

At a seminar comparing the development of feminism in various Western democracies that I attended in Italy last year, an English historian asked me whether the roots of the Canadian women's movement were the same as those of American feminism. My spontaneous response was an unequivocal "No, they weren't. American women took to the streets. Canadian women took to the government." And the government we took to, of course, was the government of Lester Pearson.

In this area of women's rights, as in so many other aspects of national life, it was not so much that Pearson turned Canada leftward, as right-wing analysts would have it to this day. It's that he helped consolidate a political culture north of the American border that centred on the value of government, rather than on its venality, entrenching in the Canadian consciousness a view that even in the 1990s accepts deficit-cutting measures only if their main intent is to restore fiscal balance, rather than to attack the state itself.

Decades after I first encountered them in person in the 1960s, Pearson and Diefenbaker still seem to me to have been distinctly dissimilar men. But their individual qualities and ideas were nevertheless historically complementary. In retrospect, their curiously symbiotic regimes can be seen as having generated innovation while assuring continuity. John Diefenbaker's prairie populism was a creative force that challenged the old consociational consensus by confronting the business and bureaucratic elites' hammerlock on government and by calling for better treatment of the disadvantaged. Mike Pearson in office became as catalytic a force domestically in the mid-1960s as he had been internationally in previous decades, filling the policy void left behind by his predecessor with far-reaching initiatives.

Both Diefenbaker and Pearson maintained the federal finance department's prudent postwar Keynesianism, which incurred social spending only when it was affordable. (In the 1960s, deficit spending was a temporary budgetary device, not the permanent practice it became in the 1970s and 1980s.) Both men grumbled about American domination while keeping Canada within the North Atlantic alliance, as the Western world faced the pervasive fear of a nuclear holocaust that the Soviet threat represented.

The chaotic conditions that these two prime ministers' governing styles produced — and that gleeful journalists made such sport of — have proven in hindsight to be highly productive. Diefenbaker was a populist prophet, Pearson a liberal agent of progress. Both were very Canadian men of their times.

Together, they ushered the country into its second century, ready to embrace, for better and for worse, Pierre Trudeau's siren call to create a just society within a bilingual, multicultural state.

TWENTY-ONE

The End of an Era[19]

Saturday Night, June 1985

IN THE LATE AUTUMN of 1978 rumours ran around the upper reaches of the federal Liberal Party — and the remnants of the old White Anglo-Saxon Anglican Toronto elite that was still connected to it — that George Ignatieff would be appointed Governor General of Canada before the year was out. To almost everyone who had any knowledge of the country's history in the previous forty years, Ignatieff seemed a perfect choice for the job. A distinguished former diplomat who had become the provost of Trinity College at the University of Toronto, he was superbly educated, deeply versed in international affairs, unusually attractive in his demeanour, and well connected at home and abroad. Furthermore, as one of Ignatieff's Liberal admirers told me at the time, crinkling his eyes with amusement and fingering his Sulka silk, polka-dotted, Lester B. Pearson bow tie, "We see George as the 'bohunk' candidate for GG, don'cha know." Lest I miss the joke, he added some information that every WASA and many Grits already had absorbed: that Provost Ignatieff was the son of a Russian count who had fled St. Petersburg with his family at the onset of the revolution in 1917 and, after many adventures, fetched up on Canadian shores.

This background qualified him as the first "ethnic" candidate for the viceregal office, which had alternated between the anglophone and francophone native-born ever since Vincent Massey became Governor General in 1952. With this extra fillip to recommend him, Ignatieff was seen as such a sure thing that his wife, Alison Grant Ignatieff, had been asked to do a stint as a lady-in-waiting to the queen and the provost himself was included in ministerial deliberations on the constitution that fall.

It was with some surprise, then, a couple of months later, that I read news of the appointment as Governor General of Edward Schreyer, the former NDP premier of Manitoba. The politics behind Pierre Trudeau's change of mind (the viceregal appointment being a prime ministerial prerogative) immediately became the cause of wide speculation. But to me — as a sometime critic and frequent chronicler of the accomplishments of the old Ottawa public-service establishment, the remarkable group of men who held sway in the capital from the days of Mackenzie King to the time of Pierre Trudeau and in whose ranks George Ignatieff belonged — one thing was immediately clear: the appointment of Schreyer instead of Ignatieff marked the end of an era. The influence of the Ottawa men on Canadian life had been declining for more than a decade. Now it was over and done.

This recognition was accompanied by an acute sense of loss that I filed away in the back of my mind as part of the detritus of advancing middle age. It wasn't until this spring, when I read George Ignatieff's newly published memoir, *The Making of a Peacemonger* (University of Toronto Press), that I began to sort through just what this loss entailed. Ignatieff has enlisted the aid of Sonja Sinclair in writing his autobiography, and they've produced a book that's the story not just of a remarkable man but of a remarkable generation and period for Canada in international affairs, a period that Ignatieff calls the golden age of diplomacy but that in hindsight looks more like a golden age of innocence.

It's a period that's been documented in a flood of reminiscences and analyses, some by public men who participated in the great events of their time (Mike Pearson, Jack Pickersgill, Arnold Heeney, Charles Ritchie), some by scholars who have analyzed those men and events (Jack Granatstein and James Eayrs), and others by participant-scholars who've done both (John Holmes and Escott Reid). But never before has it been written about in a manner so accessible to the nonspecialist or with such clarity and self-effacing charm.

For roughly a quarter of a century, from just after the beginning of the Second World War until the mid-1960s, when Pearson ran afoul of Lyndon Johnson over the American involvement in Vietnam, the Ottawa men as policy-makers were able to envisage for this small country a large world role. In that brief period, just as Canadians were getting out from under the British and had not yet recognized that we'd be forced to become American dependents, it was possible for our governing elite to believe that we could be "peacemongers," as Ignatieff was once described.

This idealistic view of Canada's international role was rooted in the attitudes of the highly cohesive group of men who staffed the Department of External Affairs in its early days and dominated the top levels of the civil service and Liberal cabinets in that crucial quarter-century. Ignatieff, of course, didn't share with his colleagues their surprisingly homogeneous background as the children of hard-working, God-fearing families in the provincial towns of English Canada. He was the child of aristocrats who had important careers in the service of the tsars, and he writes about his family's adventures both in Russia and in flight with wonderful good humour. (There is a brilliantly detailed scene in which his mother faces down a marauding Bolshevik who is searching for the Ignatieffs' hidden valuables while sporting a purloined ring, and several others describe his father's efforts to run a dairy farm in Sussex with the aid of a band of dispossessed White Russians, princesses, counts, and generals all, every one of them ignorant of agriculture.) But once the Ignatieffs immigrated to Canada in the 1920s, the influences on the adolescent Count Georgi Pavlovich (as Ignatieff was christened) were strikingly similar to those that affected his generation of Ottawa men.

When the Depression wiped out his family's small remaining store of capital, he was enrolled first at Central Technical School and then at Jarvis Collegiate in Toronto and found a summer job working as an axe man in the Kootenays. He then attended the University of Toronto and studied political economy and history under Harold Innis and Donald Creighton with such success that he went on to win a Rhodes scholarship in 1936 against the stiff competition of his contemporaries Claude Bissell and Saul Rae. At New College, Oxford, he endured the chill inflicted on colonials by the snobbery of the English dons as well as the rigours of the English climate and survived to pass with distinction the entrance examinations to the Department of External Affairs.

The early years of the war found him serving in the Canadian High Commission in London under the aegis of Vincent Massey and Mike Pearson. It turned out to be an enviable apprenticeship during which Ignatieff learned how to handle gracefully both the routine tasks of a foreign-service officer's life and the unexpected events that make such a life exciting.

Once, after he had been sent to 10 Downing Street to tender a belated invitation to Winston Churchill to attend a celebration at Westminster Abbey commemorating the seventy-fifth anniversary of the Canadian Confederation, he wound up walking up the main aisle of the abbey with Mrs. Churchill on his arm. He looked on in fascination while Vincent Massey's wife, Alice, charmed Charles de Gaulle out of a foul mood and into a frame of mind that made him receptive to the Canadian government's request for a Free French force to occupy Saint Pierre and

Miquelon. His happiest evenings were spent at "just-for-ourselves" dinners given by the Masseys, gatherings at which he often encountered a lively young Canadian named Alison Grant, who was working for the British War Office. She was also Mrs. Massey's favourite niece and was later to become George Ignatieff's witty and much-admired wife.

All in all, it was an apt beginning for a career that over the next thirty years saw Ignatieff intimately involved in one crucial international event after another. He was there at the founding of the United Nations, serving as an aide to General A.G.L. McNaughton, the Canadian delegate who tried desperately in the months after Hiroshima to find a means of containing nuclear technology within an international body. He engaged actively in discussions about the partition of India, the founding of the state of Israel, and the beginnings of the Korean War. During the Suez crisis, he served as an aide to Pearson while Pearson worked out the idea for a Middle Eastern peacekeeping force that solved the immediate crisis and won him a Nobel Prize.

Ignatieff knew Jan Masaryk, the last foreign minister of a free Czechoslovakia, as well as George Drew, the last premier of a backward Ontario, and Burgess, Maclean, and Philby, the British spies, too. Nikita Khrushchev took pleasure in getting him sick-drunk on vodka, and when he conferred with Marshal Tito he made sure he was wearing striped pants. He served as Canada's ambassador to the United Nations and as the country's permanent representative to NATO and to the disarmament committee in Geneva.

All these events and encounters are described in a lively prose that disguises how much meticulously researched detail about international affairs is being revealed. At the same time, the book is permeated with the kind of Methodist idealism that the Ottawa men evolved as their group ethic during the 1930s and 1940s. Ignatieff himself was first infected with it during the London Blitz when he and Pearson stood together one Sunday morning watching fires burning out of control all around them in Whitehall and resolved then and there to work for world peace. And work he has toward that chimera ever since, in ways that have won him many honours, including a brief period as Canada's ambassador and adviser for disarmament during the Turner regime last year.

It's probably this idealistic attitude more than anything else that stirs in me feelings of loss when I read about those men and their times from the bleak vantage point of the 1980s. It was possible for the Ottawa men (or the "Pearsonalities," as John Diefenbaker bitterly described them) to think of Canada's being able to evolve an independent foreign policy, to play a middle power's brokerage role, to make a difference in world councils. Their relief at escaping from the British, who were both their mentors and their scourge, and the general ignorance of the full meaning of the nuclear threat, allowed them the dreams that were embroidered on by those of us in the generation immediately behind them. (When I was an undergraduate at the University of Toronto in the mid-1950s, I used to go down to New York in the autumn with a campus international-relations club to attend the UN General Assembly proceedings in much the same spirit as the students of the 1960s went to rock concerts. Half the bright young men I knew wanted to go into External so they could help Mike Pearson save the world.)

The subtext of Ignatieff's descriptions of what happened in Canada's glory days of internationalism shows how inexorably this country was drawn into the American nuclear web. When he analyzes our first involvement in NORAD, when he tells about Diefenbaker's spluttering ignorance of the implications of accepting the Bomarc missile, when he remembers how Pearson, the arch pacifier, came to terms with NATO's realities, he's setting the scene for our situation now. Those are the decisions and events that led us to a prime minister (in Brian Mulroney) who's giving the U.S. the benefit of the doubt on Grenada, Nicaragua, and El Salvador, and on the testing of the cruise missile, and a secretary of state (in Joe Clark) who's being forced to pick his way gingerly through Washington's Star Wars scenario like a Mackenzie King with the gout. What Ignatieff is really describing is the period when we went, in Kenneth McNaught's phrase, from colony to nation to colony.

For me, part of the value of *The Making of a Peacemonger* — and it is a valuable book — is that I finished it thinking not just, "What glorious times they had," but, "What amazing naïfs we were." We thought the road to the nirvana of independence as a nation could be paved by civilized men.

TWENTY-TWO

What Was Important About the Gordon Commission[20]

Saturday Night, June 1977

I'VE ALWAYS THOUGHT of 1957 as a time when Canada was both euphoric and a little defiant, which may be simple projection since the description fits my own mood that year. I was just out of university, working in Toronto at a job I loved as a magazine researcher, squandering my small salary on clothes I hoped were slinky or at least far removed from the cashmere-sweater-pleated-skirt-college-girl uniform I had been wearing for so long.

I remember going with a stuffy young lawyer one Saturday night that winter to a dinner dance at the Badminton & Racquet, wearing a black Chinese dress slit thigh-high on both sides and pretending not to care at all that the other girls at the party, dressed in pearls and taffeta, were frosty because their stuffy young lawyer/broker/doctor beaus were giving me a rush on the dance floor and holding me a little too close.

One of the half-dozen men in the group (they had been friends at Upper Canada) was a new recruit at Clarkson, Gordon, the establishment accountancy firm. When the talk at the table inevitably got around to Walter Gordon, the company's star partner, who was winding up his Royal Commission into Canada's Economic Prospects at the time, I immediately turned glassy-eyed and deaf-eared. Politics and business were drear-ee (a favourite word that season, though I've seldom felt less drear), and Walter Gordon must be drear-ee, too, if he was anything like these men who were so in thrall to his reputation.

The kind of people I wanted to know more about were the writers and artists I saw in the magazine's downtown offices, men who were *outré* and imaginative, marvellous "big dirty men" as one of the other researchers wistfully described them.

What I didn't have the sense to realize, of course, was that what Walter Gordon was doing in Ottawa was as imaginative and maybe even as daring as anything the big dirty men were contemplating in their midnight dreams. He was questioning some of the most important economic shibboleths of the era, and setting out on a public career that soon would see him pilloried in places like the Badminton & Racquet as a traitor to his class.

Gordon was then fifty-one years old, in the prime of his time, and as much an establishmentarian as any Canadian can be. His mother belonged to the third generation in Canada of the illustrious Toronto family the Cassels, and Gordon had followed his father, the Colonel, to UCC and RMC and into the family firm.

Furthermore, he had grown very rich on his own account, having made a great success at Clarkson, Gordon, and later as a management consultant working with some of the most important corporations in the country and on some of the federal government's thorniest problems. He was married to Elizabeth Counsell, an elegant, witty woman, and they had three children, some of the liveliest Canadians of their generation among their many friends, an impressive art collection, a house in Rosedale, two devoted Irish maids, and a farm called Seldom Seen.

Still, behind his armour of English suiting, impeccably trimmed mustache, and unassailable self-confidence, Gordon had a concern. It seemed to him that despite the booming economy, there was too much foreign capital (and with it too much foreign ownership) coming into the country under the encouragement of C.D. Howe, the Liberals' powerful "minister of everything." Gordon had determined, two years before, that something concrete should be done.

The way he went about "doing something" was indicative both of the era — when Canada's affairs were conducted almost entirely through agreements made among friends — and of Gordon's particular style, which is to seek unconventional ends by reassuring means.

He was chairman of the executive committee of the Canadian Institute of International Affairs that year, and he prepared an article for its publication, the *International Journal*, expressing his concerns about the economy and calling for a royal commission. Lest the article upset his confidants in Liberal Ottawa, he sent a draft to Ken Taylor, the Deputy Minister of Finance, a department where Gordon himself had served during the Second World War. Taylor showed the article to his minister, Walter Harris, who showed it to the prime minister, Louis St. Laurent, and it was decided between them that a commission could be just the ticket to provide the Liberals, a few of whom were vaguely aware that maybe they'd grown a little torpid after twenty years in power, with some new ideas to throw to the voters in the next election.

The only problem was to get the thing past "C.D.," who was not enamoured of Gordon and in any case would regard any investigation of the Canadian economy as an investigation of C.D. Howe. This feat was accomplished by finessing the order-in-council appointing the commission through the cabinet when Howe was out of the country and then letting it be known that Gordon's appointment as chairman was Mr. St. Laurent's express desire.

From the start, the commission was Gordon's show, despite the fact that there were four other commissioners, some thirty staff economists, including Douglas Fullerton, Simon Reisman, William Hood, and Irving Brecher, and contributions from important outsiders ranging from John Kenneth Galbraith to J. Grant Glasso, who produced among them dozens of studies that can be found even now fading in their bindings in the stacks of university libraries. As far as anybody knows, these studies don't contain a nationalist word.

Still, Gordon had his way by means both subtle and shrewd. First, he hired as research director and writer Douglas LePan, a distinguished poet and career diplomat who had versed himself privately in Keynesianism but as a man who had never studied economics formally was not a captive of that discipline's guild. (The way Gordon got LePan is pure Gordonometry. He went to his great friend, Mike Pearson, then the secretary of state for external affairs, and tricked him amiably into releasing his great friend, LePan, from an important post as minister-counsellor in Washington to take an arduous job that neither of them wanted him to have.)

Second, Gordon used the considerable powers of persuasion he had learned behind closed corporate doors to trade off his acceptance of points that were of individual interest to his fellow commissioners (a railway branch line in Quebec, say, or a new wrinkle in resource policy) for their support of his nationalist ideas.

As a result, even though the special study on Canada–United States economic relations written by Irving Brecher and Simon Reisman would suggest, with the naivety of the 1950s (before "multinational" became a dirty word), that "In the normal course of events...an international company behaves in essentially the same way as a domestic firm" and go on to praise effusively the contribution of American investment for its "uniquely heavy inflows of technology, entrepreneurial, and management skills," Gordon through LePan's superb prose and with the acquiescence of his confreres could conclude something different. In the commission's final report, it is clearly stated that the real concern about foreign investment was that it conferred on non-residents a frightening measure of control over some of our most important industries, so that there was a real danger eventually of "legitimate Canadian interests [being] overlooked or disregarded." Mild though that statement sounds in 1977, it was heresy in the 1950s — when America the Beautiful was the object of our complete trust — as the shrieks of orthodox economists immediately confirmed.

Other than sounding these alarms about foreign investment, the Gordon report was a solid expression of conventional economic research. It confirmed the wisdom of the time that, barring an atomic war or a major depression, Canada was destined to wax ever richer, like some solid, stolid widow who had unlimited resources and the benefit of impeccable advisers managing her estate.

Despite this — and despite all of Gordon's great connections and even greater diplomatic skills — the report met a stony reception from the politicians. The Liberals who commissioned it disavowed its preliminary report, released in 1956, because of their fear that taken holus-bolus it might provide more ammunition for the Opposition than reassuring planks for the Liberal election platform. The Conservatives who slid into office in June of 1957, five months before the final report was ready, buried it because of its Liberal taint and at the same time abandoned, apparently forever, their traditional economic nationalist stance because it had been co-opted by Gordon, whom Diefenbaker described as "the flossy Toronto taxidermist who stuffs the Grits with zany ideas."

In the end, what was important about the Gordon commission was less its studies (most of which were sound) or its predictions (many of which were accurate) or its recommendations (some of which were implemented later when Pearson was in power and Gordon was his

Minister of Finance) or even its beautiful prose (there has probably never been a government report so lucidly written as the chapters phrased by LePan), than that it represented subversion from within.

Commissioned by a resolutely continentalist government from a man they thought of as one of their own, it launched the nationalist movement by raising a question that has been nagging the country's elites ever since.

After 1957, Canadian politicians and academics and businessmen could no longer protest their innocence as to the meaning of the influx of capital from the south. They still haven't done much to stop this continuing rape, but since 1957 they haven't been able to lie back and enjoy it with quite the same élan.

TWENTY-THREE

How Mel Watkins Brought
Socialism to the NDP[21]

Saturday Night, September 1970

JUST TWELVE MONTHS ago now, in that week after Labour Day when
Canadians traditionally throw off the sensuous sloth of summer and
get back to the business of feeling cold and acting sensible, a radical
economist named Melville Henry Watkins issued in Ottawa his now
famous call for an Independent Socialist Canada. Thereby began the
Year of the Waffle.

On that same September afternoon, Watkins may have launched —
if the nationalistic movement he's come to personify continues to
evolve from its fervid beginnings — a whole new era in Canadian politics. It's somehow satisfying to imagine that future patriots may mark
September 4, 1969, as the day when we crossed our Rubicon, put out
more red and white maple leaf flags, spat in the eye of the American
eagle, and maybe even declared our positive existence after one hundred and two uncertain years.

For it was an exquisitely Canadian occasion. The Americans can
look back on Paul Revere riding though the New England night, shout-

ing, "The British are coming!"; the French cherish the image of a mob on the way to the Bastille, singing of *liberté, fraternité*, etc.; the Cubans have a vision of Fidel growing hair and drilling guerrillas in the hills. And what have we got? The memory of a wryly earnest, dangerously thin, bespectacled intellectual getting up on a platform in the National Press Building in Ottawa, clearing his throat, and issuing a mimeographed call to arms.

Historical fantasies aside, both the way in which Mel Watkins has become a minor folk hero among the young and what has happened to nationalism in Canada since he declared the existence of his own radical brand say a great deal about this country, how it works, and how it feels about itself.

The Watkins Manifesto and the debate that followed have turned nationalism from a marginal concern with a few reviled adherents into the seminal issue that may well set the tone of the politics of the 1970s. It detonated a whole series of reactions, both inside and outside the NDP, the party it was chiefly meant to influence.

For a start, we have had Joe Greene's sudden conversion on the road to Denver; Ian Wahn's proposal for an alien control agency, which would force the Americans to sell 51 percent of their holdings here; Robert Stanfield's halting call to combat continentalism (which he conservatively chose to issue in London, from the safety of the fallen bosom of the Mother Empire); the establishment of several citizens' groups to study the issue; and widespread enthusiasm among students, who've taken to asking embarrassing questions of their parents and their teachers. ("What did you do in the war, Dad?" is fast becoming "Where were you when the Waffle went up?")

The fever is gradually sifting down to the elementary school level. A University of Toronto economist who has spent a professional lifetime in the sympathetic study of foreign ownership of Canadian industry had a shattering experience last spring; his son came home from school, sobbing, "Daddy, the kids all say you're a continentalist." And even the most outspoken anti-nationalist of them all, Pierre Elliott Trudeau, has taken a firm stand on Arctic sovereignty and commissioned minister without portfolio Herb Gray to recommend legislation on foreign ownership for cabinet consideration.

Mel Watkins, the man who's been the catalyst for much of this passionate activity, himself remains resolutely unimpassioned. He seems to regard everything that's happened to him in the last year with a bemused if exhausted eye; he still behaves for the most part in the spare, laconic manner of the University of Toronto lecturer he became in 1958.

He does occasionally talk now in a low-key imitation of radical rhetoric and is fond of saying he had "working-class origins." His father worked all his life at hard manual labour in the Georgian Bay area of Ontario, scraping a living for five children from the bush in the summer and the sawmills in the winter. He managed, partly through working in a cordite plant during the war, to put together enough money to send Watkins (along with his twin brother) to the University of Toronto in 1948, when they were barely sixteen.

"I came from the kind of background where there was no talk about a liberal education," says Watkins. "If you went to university, you were meant to be something — a lawyer, a doctor, or, as it was decided in my case, a chartered accountant. And I accepted this. After I graduated from Commerce and Finance, I actually spent a year as an accountant at Price Waterhouse, much to our mutual dismay." He then decided to go back to university and won a fellowship to the Massachusetts Institute of Technology. He stayed there for four post-graduate years, becoming in the process a superbly well-trained professional economist — what he now calls "a competent technocrat."

During this formative decade of his life, when most young intellectuals sow the seeds of their radicalism, Watkins was, as he describes it, "an apolitical bookworm, working my tail off for seven days a week just to make it in an academic community that was very uptight about politics, determined after the ravages of McCarthyism to be uninvolved at any cost."

He came back to Canada to lecture at the University of Toronto with an American wife, vaguely liberal leanings of the madly-for-Adlai variety, and the strong continentalist, anti-nationalist bias that was the only acceptable viewpoint among academics at the time.

Within a couple of years he had become a close friend of a brilliant young fellow economist from Montreal named Abraham Rotstein. The process of his conversion then began. Rotstein is by all odds the most important nationalist theorist Canada has ever produced, and he turned out to be, by Watkins's own admission, "the most important single influence on my thinking of any man I've met."

Because Rotstein was disgusted with the apathy of the Canadian academic community in the early 1960s, he set about, with Watkins as an interested disciple, to involve young intellectuals in Canadian social issues. Together they reactivated the University League for Social Reform and published a collection of position papers under the title *The Prospect of Change*. It included a firmly continentalist Watkins essay, "Canadian Economic Policy: A Proposal," which concluded with the straight-forward suggestion that we should "stop harassing foreign investors."

The two men then moved on to a couple of other intellectual adventures: the teach-in movement, which was the first sign of radical stirrings in English-Canadian universities, and another ginger group that took over the old Canadian intellectual monthly, the *Canadian Forum*. All this time, Rotstein was tilting at the windmills of American imperialism and Watkins was following behind, like an emaciated Sancho Panza, gradually and subtly shifting his attitudes on economic nationalism.

By the time Walter Gordon got around to asking Abe Rotstein for the name of a man who could head his Task Force on Foreign Investment in early 1967, Watkins was acceptable to them both, even though he was only thirty-five years old and a still obscure associate professor in a faculty (political economy) that was disdainfully anti-nationalist and painfully pro-American. (At first Gordon, who was a nationalist in the 1930s when Watkins was still studying in a one-room rural school, had wanted Rotstein as his chairman. But they quickly agreed that Rotstein's known nationalistic position would damage his effectiveness.)

Before the task force — chaired by Watkins and made up of eight economists, including Rotstein — published its report the following year, Gordon told Watkins it would make him famous. And it did — chiefly because Gordon was phasing himself out of politics and Watkins was left to proselytize for the benefit of businessmen's lunch club audiences on the main tenets of what's now called the Gordon position, or the "old" nationalism.

It was during those eighteen months or so, while he gained a national reputation as the author of the task force report, that Watkins became radicalized. The process took place on two fronts. He was disturbed by the hysterical hostility toward the task force (which he personally felt had made a mild statement) shown by businessmen, who thought Gordon was a kook and Watkins little better. At the same time he was increasingly disgusted by Vietnam — which was, of course, the key radicalizing experience of the 1960s for so many liberals both younger and older than he. "I came to realize in that year and a half," he says now, "that radicalism in Canada has to mean nationalism, in the sense that we must survive outside the American orbit."

Even though by the spring of 1969 he regarded himself as a radical socialist, Watkins still had no more than a passing interest in organized politics. His whole involvement in the Watkins Manifesto came about as an accident. Late in April he was considering a book on socialism and was invited to a meeting of young radical New Democrats that included Gerry Caplan, a professor of education who'd been expelled from Rhodesia (which is even better in the

Movement, one gathers, than having been zonked in Chicago or gassed at Berkeley); Giles Endicott, a union worker and the son of an old radical Toronto family; and Jim Laxer, a graduate student in history at Queen's. They decided that night to draft a radical nationalist manifesto for presentation to the NDP's annual meeting in Winnipeg later that year.

Watkins promptly joined the NDP and set about redrafting Laxer's original manifesto. It ended up as something close to a Marxist document couched in strongly anti-American language, and it called for the nationalization of Canada's productive facilities.

This meant that in ten years Watkins had done a complete about-face on continentalism and that in two years he had turned away from Walter Gordon's program — as expressed in the Watkins Report — to save the country from American capitalism for Canadian capitalism. What Watkins wanted now was to save the country from American capitalism for the state.

By the time the manifesto was released to the press in September, it had become — through a process of elimination and scared-rabbit retreats by NDP big names — the Watkins Manifesto: he was now the only nationally recognized figure connected with it. (Nobody is quite certain how this name was modified to the Waffle Manifesto, except that the change took place during the NDP's October meeting, where the manifesto's proposals were scorned privately, screeched at publicly, and defeated resoundingly. Some say that Ed Broadbent, the NDP member of parliament for Oshawa, called it a waffling document in an excess of sarcasm because he figured it was so extreme. In any case, the Waffle it became and all those who adhere to its tenets are known, ridiculously, as Wafflers.)

As Waffler-in-Chief, Watkins has endured a year that makes his previous role as task-force chairman and Empire Club speechmaker seem almost languorous. As well as carrying a full teaching load and organizing Waffle affairs, he's been constantly hassled by the press, invited to meetings by student groups hungry for the sight and sound of any homegrown radical, asked to speak at institutions as diverse as the University of Chicago and the Just Society, and served as the hero of a handbook on nationalism called *Gordon to Watkins to You*, which was put together partly, as its young editor, Dave Godfrey, said in a press conference launching it in June, "to mythologize Watkins a little."

As a mythic revolutionary hero, Watkins is a distinctly odd sight. He still dresses in the kind of clothes that would have been appropriate to an impecunious graduate student at MIT in the mid-1950s — faded pink shirt, beige drill pants, loafers, sports jacket, topped by a shoulder-length head of hair that he keeps shoving out of his eyes and seems to have grown less out of protest than out of lack of time to visit a barber.

On a single afternoon in July when I was in the hot, cramped cubicle on St. George Street that serves as his university office, he coolly answered five demanding phone calls within a couple of hours. Among other things, Pierre Berton called to ask him to come on his television show for a debate with Dalton Camp, and a researcher for the Joint Economic Committee of the U.S. Congress telephoned from Washington to ask him to appear at one of its sessions and discuss multinational corporations in the Gallic company of J.J. Servan-Schreiber.

Just after he hung up on this call, a colleague knocked on his door to discuss a joint university project. When Watkins sat down again we began to talk about the effects of his notoriety and socialism on his academic career. Thirty years ago, when another radical socialist professor named Frank Underhill mildly hinted at the Couchiching Conference that British influence in Canada was on the wane, he was very nearly dismissed from his teaching post by an apoplectic university board of governors, who figured he was expounding a subversive doctrine; his job was saved only when he was able to present "incontrovertible evidence" that "he wanted Britain to win the war."

"Well, when you think back to the Underhill affair, the university has come a long way," Watkins said. "Certainly there has been no overt objection to my views. I was made a full professor as of July 1. I didn't, of course, get this for politicking but for publishing. But I suppose it's significant that it wasn't denied to me. I think there is a certain amount of scepticism among my colleagues, but nobody is harassing me."

One of these colleagues told me later that the chief response to Watkins within the teaching community at Toronto is "an incredulity that he would want to do such a thing, tempered by the overriding standard liberal intellectual agreement that he must be allowed to take any political position he wants. But as far as concrete support goes, I can only think of four people who actually signed the Waffle Manifesto, none of them in any kind of senior position and none in his own department."

Watkins feels that there might be more open hostility to his views within the university if he were taking part in radical activities on campus, especially the struggle to democratize university government. But he regards university affairs as having a very low priority; he's concentrating his politicking on the Waffle's assault-from-within tactics in the NDP.

Exactly what the status of Watkins (and the Waffle) is within the NDP is difficult for an outsider to fathom. The group has a mailing list of 1,500 names (with almost no representation from the Maritimes or Quebec), made up of radicals mostly in their mid-twenties and card-carrying members of the NDP, plus a few old pre-bossism union members and some disillusioned Trotskyites.

There is no doubt that the Waffle has turned the NDP upside down. After thirty-five years of assuring itself that "victory is within our grasp" and living down the stigma of nationalization, which has scared off two generations of Canadian voters, the NDP has now awakened to find that Watkins and his manifesto have made nationalization once more the party's central issue. Almost overnight, Watkins has returned the NDP to socialism.

This has so infuriated the party's determinedly pragmatic establishment that they have barely been able to contain their rage. David Lewis has publicly referred to the Watkins Manifesto as "horrible, indigestible rubbish," and his son, Stephen, says it gives him a feeling of "sheer, unabashed weariness."

But for all that, Watkins is a vice-president of the party and a member of its policy committee and he is determined to keep the Waffle group within the NDP. Like Walter Gordon in the Liberal Party, he may not be able to swing his party to his point of view, but he can't be ignored.

More important than its immediate influence on the NDP is the astonishing effect the Waffle has had, considering its size and disorganization, on the Canadian body politic.

Abe Rotstein, who emphatically disagrees with Watkins's view that you must have socialism to achieve meaningful nationalism, nevertheless recently pointed out: "Mel Watkins has already, in his own way, entered the imagination of the country. The great paradox is that the very brief existence of the Waffle Group in the NDP has already done more to break the logjam in the Liberal Party on the independence issue than any other single factor.

"In consensus politics," Rotstein elaborates, "which is the kind of politics this country has always practised, the fringe is important because it shifts the middle. In this way, the Waffle is altruistic politics at its very best."

Watkins was under pressure from the Waffle all summer long to declare himself a candidate for the NDP national leadership, but one sensed that in the bleakness of his back-country realism he knew he couldn't win and was, in any case, more interested in influence than in power. The Waffle was talking, after a policy conference held in

Toronto in early August, about a scheme to field a ten-candidate leadership committee; it sounded like altruistic politics at its worst.

Still, whatever happens to the Waffle in the second year of its existence, the very fact that its manifesto was issued not to overthrow a government but to stimulate debate within a long-established political party, and the further fact that it is being worked through accepted channels in order to broaden the political middle, make it a quintessentially Canadian document.

It ought to be reassuring even to the "unabashedly weary" among us that Mel Watkins is our answer to the world's Jerry Rubins, Che Gueveras, and Ho Chi Minhs. In a way, the Watkins phenomenon symbolizes what Canada is all about — not just the True North strong and free, but the true compromise good and sane.

TWENTY-FOUR

Growing Up Reluctantly²²

Maclean's, August 1972

ON THE FIRST TUESDAY in May this year, just before five o'clock in the afternoon, the prime minister of Canada left his office on Parliament Hill, wearing in his lapel a flower plucked from the Governor General's greenhouse, and at his elbow his Minister of National Revenue, a lawyer from Windsor, Ontario, named Herb Gray, who is in his early forties now but has something of the high school swot about him still, a certain air of dutiful, damp-palmed stolidity.

Gray is a long way from being among the prime minister's circle of intimates, and the special privilege accorded him on this occasion — that of walking a few hundred yards in the glowing presence of the Leader — was due to the fact that he was about to stand up in the House of Commons and read aloud from the text of the government's long-awaited bill on foreign ownership of the Canadian economy.

Inside the chamber, the MPs went quiet in their seats in heady anticipation, and the galleries above them were filled with the curious because the bill had been promised for many months and was meant to give some clue not just to the Liberals' policy on this torturously complicated subject but to the country's future.

Indistinguishable among the doubters and debaters in the crowd were little knots of hopeful Canadian nationalists, and one of them said afterward, "I'd been telling myself all day not to expect too much, but even so, as Gray droned on, I began to feel as though somebody was hitting me in the face with a wad of old White Papers. It took me several hours — until after I'd seen Gray and Jean-Luc Pépin [the Minister of Industry] run through their smug defence of the bill on television — before I could really define my outrage. It wasn't just that, after all these years of protest and all those learned studies showing just how much we're under the American thumb, the government was refusing to do any more than make a token acknowledgement of the whole problem. They actually seemed proud of themselves for putting forward a policy designed to *efficiently* sell us out."

But there were those of us who thought that what the country should feel for the government in general for putting forward this bill, and for Mr. Gray in particular for reading it, was gratitude. Because in those few minutes and with that dreary speech, the minister was able to freeze the Liberal ethos for a moment and peel off a Polaroid snapshot of it, showing us all how this country's government works and where it stands.

The trouble was that to really appreciate the picture you had to have a long memory and an understanding of the subtle absurdities of contemporary Canadian politics.

You had to know that in this election year, when the need for a show of independence has taken hold of the collective Canadian psyche in a way that four or five years ago nobody would have believed possible, the issue is still regarded in Ottawa as at best a bore and at worst an irritant.

You had to recognize that for the preceding six months, the Canadian government had been playing footsie with the American Treasury

Department in a desperate desire to placate both the Nixon administration, which was making tough trade demands on us, and the
American business interests in Canada, who own most of this country's industrial and natural resources and control the bulk of the
election campaign funds available to the old-line parties.

Most important of all, you had to remember that the Liberal Party
has operated with consummate success for more than forty years on
the theory that the price of power is accommodation, and there is no
way that taking a strong stand on behalf of Canadian independence
can be construed as an accommodating idea.

Liberal politicians, and the liberal mandarins who are their alter
egos and the source of their policy statements, still regard any display of
patriotic fervour as illogical, immoderate, and maybe even ill-mannered.
In this attitude they're the willing victims of a canard about Canada
that still has a grip on most members of the generation now in charge
here: that this is somehow a mildly embarrassing country to belong to,
a backward nation whose chief motivation should be to "catch up"
with what is going on elsewhere, and to be careful, oh so careful, not
to offend anybody in the meantime.

The roots of this attitude lie in our history as an adjunct to two
empires, in our educational system, and in our own heads. One sometimes suspects that the secret dream of every ambitious Canadian who
grew up in the 1930s and 1940s and 1950s was not to be a Canadian.
This was true of Canadian painters and writers who whiled away their
hopes talking about international standards, Venice Biennales, and New
York successes, and Canadian intellectuals who needed degrees from
Harvard and Oxford and the London School of Economics the way
plumbers need union cards. And it was truer still of Canadian businessmen, who've always spoken with awe about American know-how,
American capital, and the American dream. But it was truest of all of
Canadian bureaucrats and politicians of the elitist mould — members

of the Ottawa establishment or whatever you want to call that good grey group of people who've run this country for decades and who run it still, though the country has long since moved away from them and exists beyond the walled city of their lives and the limited calculations of their vision. To ask such people to defend Canada is to ask them to defend a country they've struggled for years to transcend. Most of them are prone, as Morley Callaghan expresses it, to spend their days "playing the role of colonel," existing as pale ghosts of other countries' cultures, meeting the standards of other peoples' lives. The essence of what is Canadian in them has been educated out, so that official Ottawa still views benignly the odd spectacle of a highly placed civil servant, born a Saskatchewan station agent's son, talking and living now as though he'd spent his childhood basking in the civil literacy of leftover high-table talk in the household of an Oxford don instead of delivering papers on dusty prairie streets, sped on by the determination to get the hell out of there as fast as a Rhodes scholarship and the CPR could carry him. Think of it: Lester Pearson wanting to be Dag Hammarskjöld, Gérard Pelletier visualizing himself as André Malraux.

This diffused image that our leaders have of themselves and their country was distinctly evident in the statement Herb Gray made that day in May—a statement that amounted to nothing more than a promise that the cabinet would make secret, undefined assessments of proposed takeovers of Canadian companies to see whether they were in the national interest, a move calculated not to offend anybody in Akron, Ohio, let alone Washington, D.C.

But the fact that the Liberals were forced into making any kind of statement, however pallid, about our foreign ownership problem, reflected the demands made by the new nationalists, a determined and growing group of Canadians who have come to represent a countervailing force against the neo-colonial pragmatism that's been the old liberalism's hallmark. What this group has set out to do is to cast some kind of strong light on the Canadian identity before it disappears into Baffin Bay, to try to convince the country's leaders that we have a right, as the movement's leading intellectual, Abraham Rotstein, expresses it, "to interfere in our own internal affairs," to show that after a century of living as bastard Englishmen and bastard Americans it's all right to be plain Canadians at last.

It's not that the new nationalists are all progressive visionaries or even that they're all like-minded. But in the last two or three years, nationalism has developed from a fringe cause espoused by a few dedicated eccentrics into a popular movement that's drawn to its banner Canadians of diverse backgrounds and disparate sensibilities: quiet professors turned radical tigers, upper-caste poets writing exhortatory rhymes, middle-class Marxists coining barricade cries, big-time lawyers, small-time publishers, ad men tired of reworking Madison Avenue slogans.

The chief focus of the new nationalism has been on economics, because it's in this sphere that our loss of identity and control has been most obvious. (The litany of how little we own of our industry and resources has become as familiar to every schoolboy as the tune of Ca—nada.) But there's also evidence of a growing awareness that economic domination means cultural domination, political domination, intellectual domination — in sum, external control of a country that's in danger of losing its independence entirely through a failure of the will to be.

The trouble is that the nationalist cause, like the country it's meant to defend, is still raw, ill-defined, uncontrived — and leaderless.

The closest thing the movement has to a founding father/patron saint is Walter Gordon, a beautiful loser of a peculiarly Canadian kind. Gordon is rich, witty, self-deprecating, opposed to melodramatics, and committed to working within the existing political system — qualities that might prove in any other country to be dire handicaps for a believer in an ideological revolution, but that in this one have constituted strengths, simply because they've allowed him to survive.

Gordon was stubbornly unconvinced that continentalism (which is what the Canadian brand of internationalism was turning into, as American money cascaded over the border at the net rate of $3 million a day) was as glorious a phenomenon as C.D. Howe and his cohorts thought. When he was appointed chairman of the Royal Commission on Canada's Economic Prospects in 1955, he set out to question the long-term impact on the country of our loss of economic control. Just as his mammoth report was published, the Liberals were thrown out of office in the election of 1957 and John Diefenbaker, who ought to have been at least rhetorically responsive to its anti-continentalist theories, tossed it aside as a Grit document with no place in his prairie prophetic vision of Canada.

Undaunted, Gordon decided the thing to do was to get into power a government amenable to his ideas, so he enlisted, or so he thought, his old friend Lester Pearson in the cause, raised money for the party, organized the leadership and election campaigns of the late 1950s and early 1960s, stood for election himself and finally, in 1963, after being named Minister of Finance in Pearson's cabinet, brought down his first budget. This budget, which was meant to put into effect some of his ideas about saving the economy for Canadians, was conceived in haste, attacked in hatred, and judged a total failure. Some of his provisions were impractical and others eminently sensible, but all of them were savaged by his enemies as the ramblings of a non-pragmatic man. The reputation that Gordon was tarred with because of its failure dogs the movement still.

Gordon eventually resigned from the cabinet after the election of 1965 and his nationalistic proposals were ridiculed publicly at the Liberal policy conference the next year by continentalists who were once again in the ascendancy in the party, and have remained so to this day. Gordon was enticed back into the government by Lester Pearson in 1967 with the promise that he could set up a task force to study the whole problem.

At this point, nationalism was at its lowest ebb and Gordon had nobody to turn to except a few loyal friends, some of them powerful (such as Beland Honderich, the publisher of the liberal *Toronto Star*, the only paper in the country that has consistently supported nationalism) and some obscure (such as Abraham Rotstein, who was then an assistant professor of political economy at the University of Toronto).

Rotstein suggested that he get another young University of Toronto economist named Mel Watkins to head the study, since his own known nationalist bias might prove a deterrent to the objective image the task force chairman ought to have. Watkins, who'd grown up in the bush country near Parry Sound, Ontario, but learned economics at MIT in Cambridge, had been a Harry Johnson continentalist for most of his professional life, though he was now reappraising his ideas. By the time the task force, which included Rotstein and seven other economists on its staff, had finished its job thirteen months later, he'd changed from what he called a "competent technocrat" into a committed nationalist and a radical to boot. "I came to realize in that year and a half," he said later, "that radicalism in Canada has to mean nationalism in the sense that we must survive outside the American orbit economically if we're to escape the political horrors of American imperialism of the kind we were witnessing in Vietnam. And in that context nationalism was not a piece of retrogressive xenophobic fancy, as the Johnsonian economists would have us believe, but a contemporary imperative."

Watkins's official task force report, a relatively mild document on how to limit the American takeover of the economy through certain carefully supervised government measures, was ignored in Ottawa and laughed at by businessmen elsewhere, an attitude that made Watkins feel so "p—ed off with the system I'd always worked so dutifully for that I figured something radical had to be done."

Gordon and Rotstein met for lunch one day the following February at the King Edward Hotel in Toronto with Peter Newman, who was then editor-in-chief of the *Toronto Star*. A longtime visceral nationalist, Newman had been brooding on the issue for months and during that lunch, which is now mythologized in some branches of the movement as The Beginning, Rotstein and Gordon agreed with Newman's conclusion that the formation of some kind of strong cross-country extra-parliamentary pressure group held the only hope of forcing the federal government to deal with the problem. The three of them decided then and there to establish an organization they named, in an excess of rhetorical fancy, the Committee for an Independent Canada. It was meant to provide a focus for nationalists with ideas less radical — though no less passionately held — than those of the Wafflers.

The importance of the CIC goes beyond its proselytizing and its press coverage. It was and is a middle-class movement made up for the most part of men and women who'd never before in their lives joined a cause and had always operated within the system to the degree that many of them were helping to run it.

For all that, the organization was not so much the wellspring of nationalist sentiment as an agency for its expression. "We were simply giving voice to an idea whose time had come, an idea you could see working in every segment of the society," says Rotstein.

The segment where the change could be seen most clearly was in the intellectual community, where there occurred, in the late 1960s, a series of conversions to nationalism among heavy thinkers in their young middle age. The most prominent of them were James Eayrs of the University of Toronto, who'd been a Harry Johnson continentalist, though his ingrained mistrust of cant had made him an odd cat in that crowd, and Robert Fulford, who wrote a confessional piece in *Saturday Night* pointing out how wrong he and all the other cultural internationalists of the 1950s had been in their conviction that the only thing for the talented to do was to "graduate from Canada."

Nationalism also took hold as a form of radicalism on university campuses in the late 1960s, but it had its most vocal expression in Ontario, as a result of the influence of Mel Watkins and his fellow Waffler James Laxer, and two professors from Carleton University in Ottawa named Robin Mathews and James Steele. Mathews and Steele made a speaking tour of campuses across the country in 1970 to raise an outcry against the takeover of Canadian university faculties by expatriate Americans and, in their wake, there were a series of student protests over the widespread use of American textbooks.

Still, there are a few businessmen who regard the nationalism phenomenon as something more serious than a chic trend to be exploited and among those who've displayed concern about the country's future if foreign capital investment continues unchecked are Jake Moore, the president of Brascan, Malim Harding of Harding Carpets, and David Kinnear, the president of the T. Eaton Co. The feelings they can express in public as Canadians in charge of Canadian firms are echoed occasionally in private by middle-level executives in multinational corporations who've taken to writing Walter Gordon and other known nationalists the kind of letters that begin "This is off the record but..." and continue with variations of "I've had it to the eyeballs with being told what to do by some guy in Chicago who skims up to my plant once a year, knows next to nothing about my employees' needs, and cares for nothing except taking out higher profits."

Why the hell is it then — it may sensibly be asked — if there is this much strong feeling in the country about maintaining Canadian independence and any number of methodically documented prescriptions for how to go about it, that Ottawa refuses to act?

The quick answer is that the opposition to nationalism is quiet but powerful and it rests on habit, inertia, and fear.

The people who control the Canadian economy at the civil service level have lived in Ottawa for a career lifetime and their thinking is dominated by intellectual views they formed in the 1940s and early 1950s when C.D. Howe was in his prime. They believe that, to prosper, Canada has to negotiate and renegotiate a continuing compromise with the Americans. This idea of amiable accommodation is as basic to their thinking as the notion, say, that French wines are the only wines, that women don't belong in the upstairs dining room in the Rideau Club, or that the *Times Literary Supplement* really tells where everything's at. For most of the period that they've known power, their commitment to continentalism was smoothed by the fact that the men they negotiated with in the State Department in Washington were in a very real sense their opposite numbers. They were liberals serving Liberals, talking to liberals serving Democrats, and sometimes they'd even played tennis together at Oxford or met on the squash courts of Harvard.

The fact that their sweet world vanished when Richard Nixon gained power and the U.S. Treasury Department put an end to the so-called special relationship between the U.S. and Canada with the invention of Nixonomics hasn't penetrated their emotions. For them, continentalism is still in Canada's best interest, and they bolster their beliefs with amiably expressed scare warnings to the effect that our standard of living will drop if we try to maintain our economic independence.

All this probably places too much emphasis, if not on the role, at least on the responsibility of the bureaucrats. They do proffer the advice on which the economy is run but, as they're fond of saying, they are "simply the servants of our political masters." The kind of enormous conceptual shift that a change from traditional continentalism to enlightened nationalism would involve must come from the political sector.

The trouble is that the ascendant politicians in the three major federal political parties are, for their individual reasons, reluctant to come to terms with nationalism.

The Liberal position is the easiest to comprehend. It's traditionally been the continentalist party. It has in Pierre Trudeau a leader intellectually and emotionally compatible with the mandarin view of economics. Its senior ministers from English Canada (Sharp, Drury, Jamieson) see themselves as the natural heirs of C.D. Howe, and its senior ministers from French Canada (Pelletier, Pépin, Marchand) have exhausted themselves for a decade fighting a form of nationalism in Quebec. In addition, among the prime minister's senior non-elected political advisers, there is no one with any personal commitment to nationalism or with anything to gain by risking the PM's displeasure through standing up to him on the issue.

The response of the Official Opposition was just about as wishy-washy, a situation that reflects the conundrum in which the Tory leader finds himself. Bob Stanfield is what one of his fellow Conservatives describes as "dubitante" on the issue. Intellectually, he would be willing to take moderate steps to control foreign investment and he knows he leads a party that's historically nationalistic, but emotionally he's still tied to the Maritime myth that you need unlimited foreign capital to keep the poorer regions of the country viable.

The NDP's position is odder still. Although the party officially espouses nationalism, the old-line elements within it are engaged in a desperate fight to render impotent its radical nationalist Waffle wing.

Where this vacillating leaves the nationalist movement this summer is in a fermentative pause. One phase of it, the very Canadian, polite, good-natured, work-within-the-system phase, is obviously ending as moderate nationalists begin to display the kind of disillusioned anger that, with other causes in other places, has led to revamped political alignments, to the formation of new parties and the making of new leaders.

What will trigger the next phase or what form it will take is as yet unknown. But nationalism has taken too firm a hold on the Canadian consciousness to quietly wither away. And whatever the gentlemen continentalists may think, the time of their time is over. If tomorrow's nationalists don't get them, Nixonomics will.

TWENTY-FIVE

The 10 Percent Solution:
Canada's Colonial Neurosis[23]

Saturday Night, **July 1977**

EARLY THIS SPRING a group of English-Canadian writers and academics published a manifesto calling for a new constitution. For me, its importance, and the reason why I signed it, was not just its sane acceptance of Quebec nationalism — a reality that most English Canadians have been incapable of coping with emotionally in their oh-my-god-the-sky-is-falling terror since November 15 — but the quiet affirmation it contained in its second paragraph: "We believe English-speaking Canada exists as a viable national community... [with a] will to survive as an independent nation regardless of the choice that the people of Quebec may make about their future."

This belief is something I've hugged to myself stubbornly since I was a child in the 1940s and heard my brother argue with my father that the Americans were a better model for us than the British ever had been ("Why do we have to be like anybody?" I kept saying inside my head. "Why can't we just be us?").

Still, it's a conviction that's been buffeted ever since by encounters with the inferiorities that dominate our lives. Never mind the nationalism of the last ten years, never mind the new fervour and the new excellence in the arts, never mind the timid legislation to protect the economy and the publishing and broadcasting industries, this is still a country where, in Abraham Rotstein's brilliant phrase, "meddling in our own internal affairs" is thought to be subversive.

Just in the three months since the Quebec/Canada manifesto was released I have:

- Sat boggle-eyed through a dinner party dominated by the noisily expressed anti-Canadian sentiments of one of the country's leading left-wing activists. A funny, juicy, lively man — leader of protests against every inequity known to the oppressed — he spent half an hour extolling the "infinitely superior" qualities of American political, social, and cultural life and then, spearing his fork with zest into a fat slice of lemon pie, delivered himself of that tired but apparently still potent adage, "There's nothing we do here that the Americans can't do better. When you compare us with them, you have to agree, this is essentially a crummy place."

- Sympathized with my twelve-year-old, who is a student at a progressive public school in midtown Toronto, supposedly the red-hot centre of Canadian nationalism, when she came home with the complaint that her history and geography teacher had asked the class to debate the resolution, "Canada should become the fifty-first state." What disturbed my child was that she was the only person in a class of thirty-two who would speak against the motion and that the teacher herself was an ardent believer that annexation "would be good for us all."

- Felt infuriated while I watched a performance of *One Night Stand*, a new play by Carol Bolt, an avant-garde Toronto writer who has been deservedly praised for her contribution to indigenous theatre. What she produced here was a slick, derivative comedy about urban alienation full of American phraseology, American pathology, and American movie mythology. By sticking in two or three Canadian place names (Kapuskasing, Winnipeg, Yonge and St. Clair) and a Canadian cliché or two (heroine as bank clerk, the prototypical job if you think of us a nation of small account savers), she and her director — and the critics and CBC, which has made a deal to co-produce the play for television — apparently assumed she had created a Canadian drama.

- Been amused by a phone call from a young writer asking me to talk about an article she was preparing called "New Girl Network." As we explored the idea I began to feel uneasy, but it wasn't until a couple of hours later that I realized why. Two weeks before, *New York* magazine had run a piece with exactly that title, describing the way women careerists are relating to one another in the U.S.

What all these examples have in common is that they come under what I call the 10 percent solution approach to Canada. The rationale behind it goes roughly like this: we share a continent with the U.S., we have 10 percent of its population, therefore we can claim 10 percent of whatever it is the Americans are experiencing, suffering, celebrating.

The way this works in its most simplistic form is that the Associated Press, say, will announce that there have been 100,000 cases of beri-beri reported this month in the United States. Canadian newspapers will run the report with the bracketed aside saying that sources here surmise there must be 10,000 such cases in Canada, paying no heed to the reality that the disease flourishes in the swampland below the Mason-Dixon line and can't possibly take hold in the bush garden.

I first found out about the 10 percent solution when I was writing big survey articles on social problems in the early 1960s. The American magazines would announce a rhetorical crusade to solve the problems of the "Other America," say, pointing out how unacceptable it was to have 20 million Americans living below the poverty line. Some Canadian editor would immediately assign a writer to uncover the 2 million Canadians living in poverty in the "Other Canada," once again ignoring the realities, such as the fact that U.S. poverty was closely linked to its particular racial dilemmas and that very different welfare systems make comparing incomparables not just a colonial but a misleading exercise.

When the 10 percent solution approach passes from the quantitative to the qualitative, as it inevitably does, you get the great Canadian neurosis: we're only 10 percent as good at anything we try.

As with any psychic disorder, this neurosis creates its own reality and brings with it a smothering fear that the only thing that makes us different is Quebec and that without it, as the Committee for a New Constitution denies, "Canada must break up into weak fragments to be inevitably absorbed into the United States."

It seems to me that the 10 percent solution — the self-destructive America-best syndrome — threatens our survival in English-speaking Canada far more than René Lévesque and all the Quebec nationalists put together. The "enemy within," as Pierre Trudeau calls it, lies in our own fears, not in the ranks of the Parti Québécois.

TWENTY-SIX

The Unquiet American[24]

Saturday Night, November 1984, with Stephen Clarkson

THROUGHOUT THIS politically intense summer and fall — when public issues have been urgently discussed in federal election campaigns in Canada and the United States — Paul Heron Robinson Jr., a normally garrulous man with a vested interest in the politics of both countries, has been forced to sit in his office on Wellington Street in Ottawa, trying hard to keep his mouth shut. Robinson is, of course, the U.S. ambassador to Canada, and in the three-and-a-half years he has held the job he has become the most notorious diplomatic representative his country has ever sent to ours. If Ronald Reagan is defeated on November 6, Robinson, as a Republican appointee, will immediately resign; if he's re-elected, Robinson will probably be assigned elsewhere.

As his tour of duty draws to a close, it's possible to argue that he's been not just the best-known U.S. ambassador we've ever had but quite simply the best. His major contribution to Canadian-American relations in the 1980s has been his aberrant, abrasive, and altogether illuminating style. Unlike conventional diplomats, who are trained to underplay political realities in order to smooth bilateral tensions, Robinson has made it his business to state straightforwardly how his administration views Canada: as a nation Americans can afford to love as long as it accedes to their demands.

Robinson's appointment to his ambassadorial job in the summer of 1981 coincided with the beginning of a serious crisis between Ottawa and Washington. Ensconced in the two capitals — with a new mandate in Ronald Reagan's case and a renewed one in Pierre Trudeau's — were political leaders who in many ways could be seen as the antithesis of one another. Their governments were busy formulating policies (on energy, fisheries, and acid rain) and articulating philosophies (on the economy and the East-West conflict) that were not just different but often antagonistic.

Into this tense situation strode Robinson — and promptly began to exacerbate it. He came to Ottawa fresh from his prosperous insurance brokerage business in Chicago, his chief qualification for the appointment apparently being his ability to raise money for the Republicans in Illinois. Innocent of subtleties, a stranger to guile, he saw himself as a Reaganaut not a diplomat, a man who loved free enterprise, baseball, the U.S. navy, the Scarsdale diet, his horse, who was called Big Red, his wife, who had been his high school sweetheart, and their pre-pubescent daughter, whom he proudly described as a girl who looked on Canada as "one big Idaho."

Within weeks of his appointment he set out to jaw his way up and down the country, speaking to a Canadian Club here and a reporter there, expressing his enthusiasms and excoriating his detractors. He said he would like to take a trip to the North Atlantic because he was convinced the next world war would be fought there. He offered the firm opinion that Canadians should spend more money on defence and less on welfare. He pronounced the metric system "rubbish" and said that the Foreign Investment Review Agency was staffed by "nitpickers." He decided the back-in provision of Canada's National Energy Program — which gave the Canadian government an automatic 25 percent equity share in energy projects on the Canadian frontier regardless of the nationality of the money behind them — violated the U.S. Constitution's fifth amendment and therefore was intolerable. He told a newspaperman who questioned him sharply about his views on the Soviet Union to "shove off." He maintained that things couldn't help but get better between our big, beautiful country and his because "in the crunch" we were one and the same, "two peoples with inter-changeable parts."

And Canadians loved him. Or at least they loved to complain about his outrageous acts and everyday indiscretions. Editorialists suddenly discovered the virtues of Canada's health and welfare systems and howled in derision at his criticisms. Cabinet ministers defiantly asserted that Canada would not let itself be pushed around by a loudmouth Yank. Columnists uncovered the fact that he had fired his chef, an Alsatian of considerable culinary skill, because the chef hated cooking steak and *frites* day after day and dinner after dinner. Hostesses expressed amuse-ment that he had turned up at a dinner party in Rockcliffe wearing a fringed buckskin jacket and radiated disdain when his wife confided that, even though she had hoped Paul would be Reagan's secretary of the navy, she had reconciled to their Ottawa posting when she realized the ambassadorial residence was built on a hill and looked just like a castle. Bureaucrats old enough to remember Hollywood movies from the 1940s and 1950s could hardly contain their guffaws when the ambassador responded to a newspaper report that described him as resembling John Wayne by saying he'd always thought he looked more like Randolph Scott. "By God," they said to each other, "they've sent us Buffalo Bill."

Behind the closed doors where the bargaining between Washing-ton and Ottawa normally goes on, Robinson's Wild West vaudeville act was not all that amusing. He began throwing his weight around at the top-level bilateral meetings of cabinet ministers and senior officials that took place in the fall of 1981, when U.S. reaction against the new nationalism of the last Trudeau government reached a climax. Besides attacking measures in the NEP that offended the American oil companies, Robinson demanded that the Trudeau government publicly disavow its electoral commitments to introduce an interventionist industrial strategy and to expand FIRA's powers. When the Canadian government gave way to these demands and Minister of Finance Allan MacEachen announced in his November 1981 budget that interventionism was out and FIRA was to be curbed, Robinson's was almost the only voice raised in heartfelt praise for MacEachen's political disaster.

That budget probably marked the apogee of Robinson's ambassadorial career; it was certainly the nadir of Canada's compliance with Reaganite demands. Within the next year an extraordinary change in Canadian-American relations began to take place.

Flushed with the victory represented by MacEachen's November budget, the Reagan administration pressed in December for still further concessions, demanding changes that would have effectively gutted both the NEP and FIRA. Realizing that there might be no end to the U.S. demands, the Canadian government abandoned appeasement. Ottawa told Washington that the NEP's back-in clause was not negotiable and that, if the U.S. still objected to FIRA, it could take its complaints to an international jury.

Having dared that much, Ottawa decided to go further and express its own grievances, objecting strenuously in public to the Reagan administration's obvious lack of interest in the problem of acid rain. At the same time, Canadian dissatisfaction with American foreign policy was voiced. Along with most of the major Western powers, Canada decried the Americans' narrowly selfish approach to North-South economic issues and its belligerently intransigent attitudes to East-West military tensions.

Trudeau openly expressed his personal irritation with Reagan's international simplicities after the Versailles summit of June 1982. "Ask Al," he said in derisive response to a reporter's question about Reagan's views, implying that the only way you could figure out what Ronnie thought was to ask his secretary of state, Alexander Haig. (Throughout the early 1980s, the Ottawa mandarinate was abuzz with stories about the incompatibility of Reagan and Trudeau — from Reagan's disturbing fatuities, expressed at the first private meeting in Ottawa in 1981, about uniting all the god-fearing peoples of the Middle East against the Russians to his coarse dismissal of British peace protestors during the 1984 economic summit in London, while standing side by side with Trudeau at a urinal.)

Certainly it was obvious at the Versailles meeting that the Canadian-American relationship had reached an impasse. Ottawa was refusing to be bullied and Washington was refusing to bend. What broke the deadlock were important changes in the people involved at the level immediately below the national leaders. The key shift in Washington was Reagan's replacement of his secretary of state, Alexander Haig, with George Shultz, in the late summer of 1982. Unlike his predecessor, Shultz had both the confidence of the president and a real competence in Canadian affairs — developed first when he conducted a study of continental energy prospects as a member of Richard Nixon's cabinet and expanded later when he served on the board of Bechtel, a multinational engineering firm with important operations in Canada.

In October that year, when the new U.S. secretary of state invited his Canadian counterpart in Washington, he found himself meeting Allan MacEachen, who had been moved back to External Affairs after his debacle in Finance. Some said it was the old acquaintanceship of Shultz and MacEachen that dated back to their days at MIT in the early 1950s, some felt it was their seniority in their respective cabinets, others maintained it was their shared unflappable approach to political problems. Whatever the ingredients of their personal chemistry, that first meeting was a great success. They decided to get together every few months to deal with the bilateral issues that had built up into the logjam and give them continuing cabinet-level attention.

Shultz confirmed his commitment to improving the Canadian-American relationship by strengthening the small State Department office dealing with Canadian affairs and bringing in a political operative from the White House named Jim Medas to coordinate the implementation of decisions taken at the Shultz-MacEachen meetings.

On the Canadian side, the Department of External Affairs finally got itself together after having suffered two debilitating reorganizations in as many years. Derek Burney, an energetic young officer, was promoted to head a reinforced U.S. division. Allan Gotlieb, the former chief mandarin in the department, had already been sent to Washington as ambassador. With his close connections to the Prime Minister's Office and his aggressive self-confidence, he was proving the strongest ambassador we had had in the American capital for many years.

Injecting political energy into the bureaucratic process on a regular basis changed the mood of the Canadian-American relationship and even resulted in some action on the issues. The fact that in late 1983 the two sides began to explore the possibilities of negotiating new free trade deals indicated how far things had come since Paul Heron Robinson first got his act on the road in 1981. Even though it seemed unlikely that these talks would produce any concrete agreements (high levels of unemployment made industries on both sides hostile to the prospect of increased competition), they did indicate "a warming of the relationship's atmospherics," as the diplomatic jargon had it.

By summer's end — with the Trudeau epoch finally over and the Mulroney period about to begin — diplomats on both sides were talking with measured satisfaction about the issues that had been resolved in the previous two years. B.C.'s Skagit Valley had been saved from flooding; the city of Seattle would draw from elsewhere in British Columbia the hydroelectric power that the proposed expansion of the Ross dam would have generated. The continuing complex dispute between Canadian and American fishermen on the West Coast seemed well on the way to a settlement with the veteran negotiator Mitchell Sharp acting as the special Canadian representative. A new tax treaty that had taken years to negotiate and a new agreement on social security were positive achievements that didn't make banner headlines. But they did suggest that Washington had decided to deal pragmatically with Canada as a continental business partner.

This is not to say that all was sweetness and light on the Washington-Ottawa axis. The U.S. secretary of state remained as obsessed by the NEP's back-in clause as the most obdurate American oil company. Canada continued stubbornly to press its case against U.S. toxic emissions. Our ambivalence about testing the cruise missile still nettled the hawks in Washington. The United States' curt refusal last fall to consult over its invasion of Grenada was remembered with anger in Ottawa. Trudeau's peace initiative was widely seen in both capitals as an implicit slap at Reagan's "megaphone diplomacy." But once Trudeau left the scene, "another burr was pulled from under the saddle," as Paul Robinson liked to put it.

While all these changes were taking place, Robinson had been continuing, unchastened, to speak his mind in public, even though his voice was ignored at the private bilateral meetings of the secretaries of state. He went back to his hometown last year to assure a dinner meeting of the Chicago Canadian Club, crowded with his Republican buddies from the business community dressed up in black ties and long cigars, that FIRA was now nothing but a "lap dog," owing in part to the fact that he'd laid their ideas on the line up there in the frozen North. A few months later he pronounced the cruise missile controversy a "non-issue" and the 80,000 Canadians who turned out in one day to protest its testing here "no bigger a crowd than you get at a ball game" and no more relevant to the weapon's role in U.S. defence planning.

Robinson uncorked his last big blurt in May, when he told a reporter from the *Ottawa Citizen* that the U.S. was in a no-lose situation vis-à-vis Canada because — no matter who the new prime minister was, Brian Mulroney or John Turner — things were bound to be better. The Canadian reaction to these remarks was so extreme — radio hotlines buzzed, editorialists protested, politicians thundered — that the U.S. embassy finally decided that the ambassador had to be muzzled for the duration of the Canadian and American election campaigns.

Holed up in uncharacteristic silence behind the heavy doors of his embassy, Robinson was a lonely and peculiarly affecting figure. Some of the Canadians who had laughed at his crudeness and raged at his condescension began to regret the end of the Robinson era. In contrast to the professional diplomatists who had preceded and undoubtedly would succeed him, he'd spent his sojourn in Canada telling us American truths.

TWENTY-SEVEN

De Gaulle's Gaffe Was
a Pivotal Point for Canada[25]

Globe and Mail, July 24, 1987,
with Stephen Clarkson

AT A TIME WHEN the debate about Canadian unity has come down to
such esoterica as arguing over the possible interpretations of the phrase
"distinct society" in the Meech Lake Accord, it is hard to remember
that, just twenty years ago today, a foreign head of state could be seen
as a threat to Canada's very survival.

The occasion was the spectacular arrival of the president of France
at Expo '67 in Montreal on July 24, 1967. General Charles de Gaulle
had been driven in a triumphal cavalcade from Quebec City along the
old Chemin du Roy through towns and villages festooned with bunt-
ing and lined with cheering crowds. When he reached Montreal, and
the huge crowd in front of the municipal centre roared its welcome,
General de Gaulle decided to seize the moment history was offering
him and make an impromptu speech.

After a few grandiloquent sentences evoking the liberation of
France in 1944, he began his fateful litany. First came *"Vive Montréal,"*

which elicited a round of cheering from the crowd. Then came "*Vive le Québec,*" which brought a louder and longer response. General de Gaulle waited a moment, then detonated his bombshell: "*Vive le Québec ... libre.*"

The pandemonium created by his use of the inflammatory slogan of the separatist movement was instantaneous. The crowd, which was generously sprinkled with "*Québec libre*" placards, went berserk. Journalists rushed for the phones. The gaggle of dignitaries waiting inside City Hall to greet General de Gaulle began to buzz. Standing among them, Rene Lévesque, a cabinet minister in the recently defeated Liberal government, remarked to a reporter, "*ça allait accélérer beaucoup de choses.*"

General de Gaulle's "*Vive le Québec libre*" did indeed "accelerate many things," including Mr. Lévesque's own move to separatism. But in dramatizing the cause of independence for Quebec, General de Gaulle's famous four words also helped generate such a reaction in Canadian politics that, in the long run, his celebrated gaffe can be seen as the folly of an aging statesmen who, seeking to redirect history according to his own grandiose design, actually helped stymie what he had hoped to stimulate.

Twenty years later it can be argued that, had General de Gaulle not made the prospect of separatism so palpable for English Canada with his sensational outburst, it is doubtful whether Pierre Elliott Trudeau and his federalist supporters would have been able to win control of the federal government and hold it long enough to contain and roll back the separatist threat to the union.

It wasn't that separatism was a new idea in 1967. It had been brewing in Quebec for a decade. But the feeling about it across Canada was similar to what is thought of western alienation now: the separatists were extremists with little support and even less capacity to achieve their goals. As for Quebec's politicians, they could be assuaged with some placatory concessions at federal-provincial conferences.

Mr. Trudeau himself didn't share this phlegmatic response. He had entered federal politics in 1965 because he felt that even the Jean Lesage Liberals' drive toward special status for Quebec was a threat to Confederation that would also diminish French Canada's potential for development. But his political philosophy — the belief that the legitimate aspirations of French Canadians could best be realized within the existing federation — made him seem as outmoded in Quebec as he was unheralded in English Canada.

General de Gaulle's intervention and subsequent actions unwittingly played into Mr. Trudeau's hands by showing that the notion of autonomy for Quebec was becoming dangerously popular and had the overt backing of substantial world power. Four months later in Paris, General de Gaulle pointedly escalated his defiant approval for what he saw as Quebec's inevitable ascension to independent statehood. In a formal press conference, he clarified his intention that France would support "her children" in "their effort of emancipation" that "will necessarily result in the advent of Quebec to the rank of a sovereign state."

It soon became clear what form of support he had in mind. In a concerted campaign to help Quebec develop legitimate international standing, French ministers were sent on official visits to Quebec without notifying Ottawa, France used its suasion in former colonies such as Gabon to have Quebec invited to international conferences, and Quebec's Paris office was treated as though it were a national embassy.

General de Gaulle's promotion of Quebec's independence so shocked the Canadian public — already troubled by terrorist bombings, pundits' warnings, and the obvious weakness of Lester B. Pearson's government in dealing with Quebec's demands — that the tough, unrepentant federalism espoused by Mr. Trudeau suddenly became widely attractive. When he emerged early in 1968 as a dark-horse candidate to succeed Mr. Pearson, he became an immediate favourite to deal with a poorly understood challenge from Quebec, and the Liberal Party rebounded in the polls to become once again the public's best hope in dangerous times.

Among all the hopes Mr. Trudeau's first election engendered, these were the ones he did not disappoint. No sooner was he elected as prime minister in 1968 than he moved to use the full force of the Canadian state in a campaign to contain France's encouragement of Quebec's autonomy. The foreign-policy review he commissioned led to a new emphasis on a bicultural diplomacy for Canada and a new priority for aid to francophone Africa, where Canadian development dollars could buy off any temptations among the newly decolonized states to grant Quebec diplomatic recognition.

Once the provincial Liberals returned to office in Quebec City in 1970, Ottawa made an agreement with Premier Robert Bourassa that accepted Quebec's activity abroad in areas of provincial jurisdiction, such as education and culture, in exchange for Quebec's acknowledgement of the indivisibility of Canada's sovereignty: Canada would still have only one vote in international organizations in which Quebec wanted to participate.

The Trudeau government's containment strategy was less immediately successful in Paris than it was in Africa. France's efforts on Quebec's behalf had begun to lose their subversive force after General de Gaulle's retirement in 1969, but his successors refused to back down from his formal support for Quebec's autonomy. A stalemate ensued. Quebec had secured a beachhead in Paris for a special relationship with France, but its activities remained within the bounds Ottawa had striven to define. On the economic front, France had made few serious efforts to give Quebec a material alternative to its integration in North America. By the early 1980s, France had become a minor factor in the separatist equation, a mere spectator to the dramatic events — the defeat of the Parti Québécois referendum on sovereignty-association

in May 1980, and Quebec's exclusion from Mr. Trudeau's constitutional settlement in November of the following year — that deflated Mr.
Lévesque's long-term aims.

A complete return to normal in Canada's relationship with France
was denied Mr. Trudeau, who fought for almost two decades to repulse
the French threat to Canada's international integrity. Even two years
after his retirement, at a summit meeting of the francophone countries held in Paris under the aegis of President François Mitterrand,
the Ottawa-Quebec pecking order was the same as Mr. Bourassa had
accepted for Quebec's activity in francophone Africa fifteen years earlier. In return for Ottawa's recognition of Quebec's special cultural
relationship with France, Quebec had confirmed the indivisibility of
Canadian sovereignty while France agreed to keep out of Quebec's
affairs. The standoff of the 1970s had been endorsed as the ground
rules for the future.

Twenty years on, it is apparent that General de Gaulle's "*Vive le
Québec libre*" was a pivotal moment in Canadian history. In stimulating the embryonic independence movement in Quebec without being
able to deliver substantial economic support, he helped set it up for its
eventual political knockout. In exploding anglophone Canada's centennial self-satisfaction, General de Gaulle provoked a response that
has strengthened the country as a bilingual society and made it a more
self-confident player in the world. Had the great man of twentieth-
century France been able to contain his urge to refashion the francophone
world and shouted "*Vive le Canada*" instead, English Canada might
now be struggling with a unilingual Quebec in a novel arrangement
known as sovereignty-association.

TWENTY-EIGHT

Learning French Is No Longer a Courtesy in Ottawa[26]

Saturday Night, October 1968

WALTER GORDON once said to a friend of his and mine, "If you have too highly developed a sense of the ridiculous, you can't get through a day in Ottawa without laughing, and that's not allowed." For those who can't get through half an Ottawa hour, let alone a day, without the relief of laughter, the three months since the election have proved a vintage quarter.

The thing is, almost everybody in the city is convinced Ottawa is undergoing a revolution and it's in the response of the inhabitants of this once proudly old-fashioned town to the idea of change that the fun is found. ("Shall I throw away the vest and buy an Art Nouveau tie?") Some are running scared; some running exhilarated; some claiming they were always yea-sayers to life and agents of reform; some saying they are protectors of tradition and advocates of fair play; all displaying certain symptoms of anxiety and secretly hugging the hope that there is some corner of the Just Society that will be forever theirs.

Nowhere are the anxieties and absurdities more evident than among the English-speaking civil servants who have at last come to grips with the notion that they *must* — indeed can never hope to be assistant deputies unless they can — speak French.

The need for bilingualism in Ottawa was talked about all through the Pearson regime as one of those Good Things, like equality for women, that everybody believes in and hardly anybody does anything about. But now, with a French-speaking prime minister whose office actually conducts business in French, half the cabinet bilingual, and a government whose mandate is based on its pledge to make Ottawa the centre of the country for French as well as English Canadians, the situation is changed.

Learning French is no longer a courteous diversion or a tactical ploy. It's a matter of survival both for the nation as a whole and for the bureaucrats as individuals. With their end-of-June paycheques, civil servants got an institutional green pamphlet telling them in effect to learn French or resign themselves to dead-end jobs. ("By 1970 anyone joining the service in an administrative or executive capacity will be required to be proficient in both languages or be willing to acquire this proficiency at government expense in a reasonable time. This requirement will become part of the promotion process by 1975.")

There's ample evidence that public servants are accepting this reality. In the Ottawa West riding, which has a greater percentage of English-speaking government employees than any other in the country, the voters turned out the incumbent Tory, Dick Bell, who played hard on their secret fears of bilingualism, and elected Lloyd Francis, the Liberal, who campaigned on the straight Trudeau platform of one nation, two languages. There seems to have been in the last few months a stilling of that ugly stream of bigoted tirades against "the bilingual boondoggle" (usually signed "Union Jack" or "Forty Years in Public Works") in the local letters-to-the-editor columns. More positive still, the Public

Service Commission is finding that in recruiting recent college graduates, the bilingualism requirements are an attraction (the young think learning French is an adventure); and among those in the public service now there is considerable jockeying to be included in French classes.

But despite the enthusiasm of the young and the resignation of the middle-aged, the practical process of teaching adults French is a difficult and in many ways ludicrous business. "The trouble is," says one middle-rung bureaucrat, "that you don't dare say you're worried. If somebody happens to remark, 'Look, I'm a statistician, I always had a bad ear for languages, I'm forty-three years old, and I don't know if I can learn,' this is immediately construed as 'The guy's against the French.' Everybody I know finds it just so damned tough to learn another language in middle age. What we're up against is not the revenge of the cradle but the revenge of the rolled r."

Fears of personal inadequacy are fed by the small smatterings of fact that are available and by dozens of apocryphal stories — mostly featuring grey-haired men bursting into tears in language labs and shouting Anglo-Saxonisms at the French voice that keeps repeating and repeating in their ear. Of the facts, the most unsettling is that in the four years it's been in the language-training business, the government has had 5,200 "anglophones" (English-speaking Canadians) in French classes and has managed to bring only ninety (or 1.7 percent) of these to Level III, which means they're capable of understanding most of what is said to them in French but that they can't speak or write the language fluently. Three thousand are still at Level I (they can't communicate or understand sentences above a Dick-and-Jane reader level) and the rest are either at Level II (said with some scorn to be the degree of fluency required to run an elevator bilingually) or have given up.

This low level of achievement is due to a miscalculation made at the time language classes began in January 1964. No one is quicker to admit this than the man in charge. John Carson, the chairman of the Public Service Commission, who was brought to Ottawa from private industry only four years ago, is one of the least stuffy bureaucrats in memory, and is himself struggling hard at Level I. Civil servants previously went to classes two hours a day, five days a week year-round, but it turned out that it would, at that rate, take them seven years to make Level III. Since last fall, everybody starting French courses must go at it full-time for three weeks, three or four times a year. Now, in its Parkinsonian way, the government has created new jargon (involving complete immersion, partial immersion, linguistic level tests, monitors, franco-phones, and mother-tongue input) and a new prestige-rating system. It's almost as easy to tell how important a bureaucrat is by finding out what kind of language classes he attends as it once was by assessing the colour of his carpet or the location of his parking space.

"It doesn't do," explains the director general of the Language Bureau, G.A. Blackburn, "to put a high school graduate in with a professional economist, say. They wouldn't have anything in common to talk about that would prove useful in their jobs." (You have no idea how this remark dashed my hopes; I had a mental picture of a group of formerly sad-faced Calvinists sitting around over Pernod in the Language Training Centre in Hull, laughing, shrugging, and comparing Daniel Cohn-Bendit with the young André Malraux. Now it turns out they're talking about regional disparities in Guysboro County and cadastral surveys of the farmlands.)

The Hull centre, housed in an abandoned college, can take 200 pupils at a time, most of them for what's called partial immersion. This means they stay in school from 8:30 a.m. to 8:30 p.m. and speak French constantly through classes, labs, conversational groups, and cafeteria meals, when French-Canadian students, hired to eat with them, "monitor" their conversations lest there be any mother-tongue input. Even recreation periods are conducted in French; in mid-afternoon, pairs of administrative officers are puffing around a badminton court shouting, "*Sacrebleu!*"

Complete immersion (you sleep in French) can be had at a motel outside Quebec City called Château Bonne Entente. If you qualify as a mandarin you get to be not only bilingual but bicultural. The government has bought twenty houses in Quebec City for a Bicultural Development Program. Senior civil servants can spend up to a year there with their families, at full pay, all of them learning "to go beyond linguistic skills to knowledge and understanding of the second culture." Through these programs, the government hopes to produce 1,000 Level III bilinguals in the 1968–1969 semester and to increase this number gradually, rising to a peak of 5,000 in 1972, after which they will phase out of the language training field and rely on the public school system to send them bilinguals.

By then, the Language Training Division of the Public Service Commission expects to have worked out an elaborate series of tests for measuring English and French Canadians with absolute fairness on a scientific bilingualism scale. (Possible federalist graffiti of the future: *Eric Kierans is more bilingual than René Lévesque. C'est bien vrai!*)

This scale may even solve the delicate problem of what to do about people like the Ottawa functionary who has been immersed three times, has an extensive French vocabulary and a sound grasp of French grammar but no ear at all for language. He talks passionately, rapidly, fluently, and there isn't a French Canadian in the country who can understand him. This wouldn't bother anybody, but he insists he's bilingual and keeps firing his French-Canadian secretaries for inefficiency because they break down under the strain of trying to unscramble his second-language-input dictation.

TWENTY-NINE

Ten Years: From the Quiet Revolution to the Apprehended Insurrection[27]

Chatelaine, January 1971

IT'S JUST A LITTLE over ten years — though it seems more like half a century — since Jean Lesage was first elected premier of Quebec. On the morning after that unexpected victory over the powerful and corrupt Union Nationale in June 1960, a colleague of my husband's in the Parliamentary Press Gallery in Ottawa phoned him in high excitement to discuss its implications. The man was an ardent Liberal as well as a respected pundit, and he ended the conversation by saying, "You'll see — things will soon be back to normal in this country."

What he meant, of course, was that the Liberals would soon be back in office in Ottawa as well as in Quebec City. But the irony of his prediction of "normalcy" for Canada has been very much in my mind during the gloomy weeks since the October tragedy in Montreal.

For that election in the summer of 1960 began both the Quiet (!) Revolution in Quebec and the nervous convulsions in the rest of the country that have marked our desperate attempts, in this far from normal decade, to patch up the century-old imperfect union between the French and the English that is the Canadian Confederation.

It seems to me now — having watched the interaction between French aspirations and English guilt during most of that time from the vantage point of the national capital — that all the efforts made by federalists from both founding races to find out what would make Quebec feel easy within Confederation have come far too late and have been, by their very nature, somehow pathetic. It's almost as though we've been involved for ten years in a holding operation, building flimsy dikes against the tides of history.

It's not that Ottawa's efforts haven't been intense or that reforms haven't been implemented. In that ten years, we have progressed from the stage where we had men in power in Ottawa who regarded the French Canadians as "no different from the other ethnics" ("They just happened to get here first," one Diefenbaker cabinet minister used to confidently say) to the point where we have for the first time in our history, a government controlled at the top entirely by Quebecers. (The two previous French-Canadian prime ministers, Sir Wilfrid Laurier and Louis St. Laurent, shared their power with English proconsuls; Pierre Trudeau doesn't share power with anyone.)

On the torturous road from Diefenbaker to Trudeau, various surefire solutions to the English-French quandary in Canada have been suggested and tried. But somehow each solution has created its own new problems without really having much effect on the basic difficulty — as a recap of the measures that have been taken by Ottawa to satisfy Quebec demands will attest:

1960–1963: During the last three Diefenbaker years, it became increasingly obvious that the prime minister was either out of sympathy with or entirely ignorant of the aspirations of Quebecers. He seemed to think they could be assuaged by such token courtesies as appointing a French-Canadian Governor General, printing bilingual cheques, and keeping in docile bondage in minor cabinet posts a sad sextet of French-speaking ministers, none of whom had any meaningful power base in his home province or any meaning-ful role in federal deliberations. In this period, separatism emerged as a meaningful force in Quebec, and it began to be said in Ottawa, even by non-partisans, that only by turning out Dief's Tories and electing Pearson's Liberals would it be possible to "restore a mean-ingful dialogue between Quebec and the rest of the country," because the Liberals could be counted on to understand Quebec.

1963–1965: Unhappily, the expected entente between Ottawa and Quebec City didn't materialize during Pearson's first term in office. Faced with trying to run a province that had been kept deliberately underdeveloped during Maurice Duplessis's long reign, Lesage began to make grandiose demands on the federal treasury. At the same time, the FLQ hit the news with their first clumsy terrorist efforts, planting bombs in mailboxes and claiming their first vic-tim, the Montreal armouries night watchman Wilfred O'Neill.

The accepted explanation for Pearson's inability to cope with Quebec was that he had been listening to the wrong set of advisers, the so-called Old Guard, led by Lionel Chevrier, Pearson's first Quebec lieutenant, who was said to believe that bilingual signs in airport washrooms would smooth everything over. The cry then arose that Pearson had to put into positions of power the New Guard men like Maurice Lamontagne, Guy Favreau, and René Tremblay — who were still young and enlightened enough to *really* understand Quebec. This group, in turn, was rapidly rendered ineffective by internal jealousies and scandalous allegations. What was needed, everyone now seemed to agree, was a *new* New Guard, who would not only *instinctively* understand Quebec but whose members would come directly out of its reformist elite.

1965–1968: So Jean Marchand, Gérard Pelletier, and Pierre Trudeau were recruited for the 1965 election and, in the second Pearson period in power, especially after Trudeau was appointed Minister of Justice in 1967, the French Canadians had the strongest representation they'd yet commanded in the federal cabinet. In this period, too, the Royal Commission on Bilingualism and Biculturalism, appointed in 1963, finally began to table its reports. Bolstered by its laborious findings, men of goodwill were heard to remark more loudly than ever before, "What we need is to recognize that this is a bicultural country. If we establish a bilingual federal civil service in which French Canadians have equal opportunities and make sure that the language rights of French Canadians outside Quebec are preserved, everything will be all right."

Thousands of middle-aged English Canadians went into language laboratories and total immersion projects in order to learn French, spurred on by the belief that this was the only way they could save their country — and their jobs. But the separatists seemed curiously unimpressed. René Lévesque gave their cause a legitimacy and dynamism it never had before by forming the Parti Québécois; violence was on the increase in Quebec despite the fact that dozens of FLQ adherents were in jail; and Daniel Johnson Sr., who had replaced Jean Lesage as premier, was making demands not just for a fatter share of taxes, but for radical changes in the constitution.

What we need, said the federalists, is not just a strong French-Canadian contingent in cabinet, but a French-Canadian prime minister, who would be able to take a tough line with Johnson without looking like an Anglo-Saxon racist and have an overview on how the constitution could be altered to the satisfaction of both founding races. Miraculously, the man existed — and was elected.

1968–1970: For the next thirty months, it looked as though P.E. Trudeau really was the solution that had been sought all along. Or at least as though he understood Quebec, an impression that was reinforced when Robert Bourassa, said to be cast in the technocratic Trudeau mould, was elected in the Quebec provincial elections last April. (What the federalists were happy to ignore was that René Lévesque's separatists got 23.1 percent of the vote.) Bourassa had promised to find 100,000 new jobs for Quebecers and the Toronto investors were enormously impressed with his practicality — impressed enough to be expansively talking about lending Quebec more money than they'd been willing to gamble for some time.

Then came October's kidnappings and murder, the "apprehended insurrection," the invocation of the War Measures Act, soldiers in the streets — one of the greatest internal crises in Canadian history. In Ottawa these sombre events almost seemed to have washed away ten years of effort — at least, nobody was talking hopefully any longer about understanding Quebec or finding quick cures to Confederation's problems.

One old friend, a federal civil servant who's lived most of this decade on the raw edge of the conflict, summed it up by saying, "Look, we can't give up; we have to keep trying all the things we've painfully worked out. But these days, I feel like a relative standing outside the intensive care unit in a hospital. The patient is Canada and all I can do is pray."

THIRTY

Bridging the Great
Canadian Divide[28]

Saturday Night, September 1978

WE ARE SITTING in the parliamentary restaurant in Ottawa on an early summer evening and the place reverberates with the gossip of politicians at their ease and the scurrying of waitresses in white-laced oxfords, carrying plates of steak and sole and crab croquettes across a crowded room. On the other side of the table, Senator Jean Marchand, his lined face as mobile and attractive as an actor's, is talking about "the English" and how French Canadians have suffered at their hands.

He describes what it was like for him to come to Ottawa as a young union leader in the company of his peers from English Canada and to have the Minister of Labour single him out of the group to tell him, oozing kindness like lemon curd from a pound cake, that he had arranged for Marchand to talk privately with a minor departmental official, because after all, as *confrères* from *la belle province*, they would understand each other, while he, the minister, would talk with the others himself.

Every French Canadian has had such an ignominious experience, he assures me, remembering the slight after more than thirty years, and I nod in sympathy. But what I really want to say to him is, "Look, that was unforgivable, but nearly everybody, French or English, who has ever come to Ottawa has had that kind of experience. This is a place of petty snobberies; they are the currency of the powermonger no matter what his race. Preachers' sons from Nova Scotia put down farmers' sons from Manitoba. Harvard M.B.A.s sneer at B.Sc.s from Queen's. External men feel superior to Trade and Commerce men, and everybody who's anybody treats journalists as though they had just crawled out of a cave."

When I first came to Ottawa as a young magazine writer, I sought and got, after an exchange of many promises, an interview with the Governor General's wife ("Canada's First Lady at Home!"). I was ushered into her sitting room by the press attaché, a French-Canadian ADC who had lingered too long in officers' messes, and he murmured to her in French, as though I were possibly deaf and certainly unilingual, "I'll rescue you from this problem, *Excellence*, in twenty minutes, no more."

I didn't tell the senator that story, though — lest it appear that I was making trivial his own pain — and the conversation moved on impersonally to a discussion of the Quebec wing of the Liberal Party and its role in the Canadian scheme. But that small episode stands out in my memory — that failure to connect — typical of a dozen others that occurred during weeks of interviewing French Canadians in Ottawa and Quebec this past spring and summer. Unorthodox responses, provocative ideas, personal comments were rarely ventured either by the interviewer or the interviewee, although the can-we-English-and-French-continue-together? concern was on all our minds like the ache from an abscessed tooth that has been fed analgesics but won't go away. I asked my questions honestly, and they gave their answers courteously, but — with certain exceptions involving three or four friends — we continued to talk to each other across what I call "The Great Canadian Divide."

This is the linguistic gap, the cultural gap, the gap in understanding between francophones and anglophones that's based on genuinely different historical patterns and social contract as well as ancient fears, irrational angers, and inequities that can't be retroactively redressed. Into this Great Divide, all sorts of debris has been hurled in the last few years by businessmen threatening economic reprisals, politicians predicting cataclysmic crises, and bigots from both sides dumping their hatreds downwind.

The curious thing about the divide is that, although it's publicly more obvious than ever, it hasn't really narrowed in the last fifteen years. Never mind the Royal Commission on Bilingualism and Biculturalism, never mind the Trudeau phenomenon and the federal French ascendancy, never mind the anxious awareness produced in English Canada by the election of the Péquistes, never mind the Robarts–Pepin National Unity Task Force or the constitutional amendments now being proposed — we are still inhabiting two solitudes that meet and greet and part again nearly as bewildered as before.

Just after I dragged my own bewilderment home again after my latest experiences in Quebec, the Toronto *Globe and Mail* published excerpts from a speech by the Catholic philosopher Gregory Baum that contained the most sensible and sensitive public utterance I have read about the Great Divide. It's Baum's contention that the divide can be perceived as a good thing. He feels it defines the dual Canadian reality in a way that all the overheated talk about unity never can. He thinks French-English differences should be respected and, in fact, constitutionally enshrined. He believes we need not unity (which implies homogeneity) but *union*, a contract between two races based on respect, directed toward mutual economic benefit, a common goal of social justice, and independence from the American behemoth.

What Baum is saying may sound simple, but as anybody attempting a "liberated" relationship, based on respect for the partner's "otherness" can attest, it's a bloody difficult idea to attain. Still, the more I observe the Great Divide, the more ardently I believe that kind of respect is the only possible bridge.

THIRTY-ONE

Our Heroes on the Russian Front[29]

Maclean's, August 1971

SHORTLY AFTER MIDNIGHT on a Monday in the middle of May, the Right Honorable Pierre Elliott Trudeau closeted himself with his bride in the forward cabin of a Canadian Armed Forces Boeing 707 jet and flew out of the rainy Ottawa night bound for Moscow and what was billed as "a sparkling foray into international diplomacy," the first state visit to the U.S.S.R. by a Canadian prime minister in office.

In the two airplane cabins behind Trudeau, seated in serried rows and a nearly perfect pecking order were: eighteen prime ministerial aides and civil service bureaucrats who were meant to provide sober advice and were thereafter called the Mandarins; forty members of the press who were meant to transmit descriptions of the sparkling foray to an anxiously waiting electorate and were thereafter called the Media; and three members of parliament who meant to make political hay and were thereafter largely ignored.

In the next twelve days this odd company of Canadians was pushed around a kind of big-time borscht circuit (Moscow to Kiev to Tashkent to Samarkand to Norilsk to Murmansk to Leningrad, boffo all the way) in what was clearly supposed to be a triumphal procession but what seemed, from the inside anyway, like the meanderings of some third-rate road show unaccountably caught up in an international production translated from the theatre of the absurd.

What gave the proceedings their unlikely aura was partly that, on close examination, most of the pronouncements about the Soviet-Canadian protocol, signed in the splendour of the Palace of Receptions on the third day of the tour, made next to no concrete sense; partly that the Canadians were so overexcited by finding themselves in the world limelight that almost everybody from Trudeau on down committed some unholy gaffe (when asked whether he was sure he wasn't being used by the Kremlin, the PM replied quizzically, "I've been asking myself the same question"); and partly that the combination of extreme temperatures (105°F in Samarkand, 32°F in Norilsk), eighteen-hour sightseeing days, straight vodka, long plane flights, breakneck bus rides, sweet champagne, warm mineral water, and the Russians' repressive hospitality produced a maniacal unconcern for the niceties that spread through the group like a contagion.

(On the first day, an eminent columnist, as yet unrecovered from the celebrations of the overnight flight, tottered off the Boeing 707 at the Moscow airport straight into a Soviet honour-guard band who'd been standing with their trombones over their hearts waiting to play "O Canada" and who stared in stony disbelief as two KGB men frog-marched him out of sight of the waiting dignitaries. On the second day, a Canadian-Ukrainian journalist from Niagara Falls swore up and down that he'd seen Margaret Trudeau disappear alone into Lenin's tomb, though the official program claimed that she was at that moment in the company of fourteen ladies in an art museum called the Tretya-kov. On the third day, a Canadian embassy official collapsed under the strain of eight months of preparation and a four-gin lunch and had to be carted off for a rest cure. On the fourth day, an MP drew a small crowd as he sat on the steps of a hotel in downtown Kiev, weeping for his Ukrainian homeland, which he'd never before laid eyes on. On the fifth day, a photographer was stabbed accidentally in the hand by a Russian girl wielding the skewer from a partly consumed kebab. On the seventh day, a mandarin nearly missed his limousine because he'd stayed behind in Tamerlane's tomb to photograph another mandarin who was holding a black umbrella over his head in the heat of the mid-day sun. On the eighth day, the press, angered by the Russians' refusal to allow them into a camel market in Samarkand, decided to stage a rebellion and were told that if they did they would be put out of the country forthwith. On the ninth day, a magazine reporter, flushed with the excitement of being one of the first Western journalists let into the city of Norilsk, which is built on permafrost and has an extensive reha-bilitation program for locals who go stir-crazy in the long dark of the Siberian night, claimed that to him, "it looked just like Paris." And on the eleventh day, the entire group, in a manic fit of bourgeois acquisi-tiveness, stripped the city of Leningrad clean of five-ruble balalaikas. It was enough to make you wonder who was entertaining whom.)

The longer this raggle-taggle company spent on the Russian road, the more it began to look like a Canada in microcosm, displaying in its members' personal idiosyncrasies and group interactions all the conflicts, neuroses, and shibboleths that torture our national psyche.

Outside, the Russian landscape went by like a Chekhovian dream. Inside our buses and limousines — where, on occasion, I began to feel we were sealed like Lenin in his train — all the old Canadian interplays were repeated. The French fought with the English. The mandarin-elite looked down on the press-proletariat. The politicians complained about the unchecked power of the mandarins. The press noisily expressed their disapproval of the prime minister, unless he deigned to notice them, whereon they turned pink from the pleasure of power proximity and fawned on his every word. And everybody displayed the characteristic Canadian ambivalence toward the Americans by wondering aloud continually how Washington was reacting to our daring in taking on the Russians, while at the same time complaining interminably about every single Intourist hotel because none of them was like a Hilton.

The only cool figure in the troupe was, of course, the starring player, Pierre Trudeau, who was referred to throughout the journey by the reverent as "The PM" or "Le Patron," by the irreverent as "Trendy," and by the brassed-off remainder as "Him." Trudeau seemed to have decided before leaving home that he was playing the double role of happy bridegroom/canny statesman.

On balance, he performed rather better as the former, beaming on his treasure at awkward moments, grabbing her hand and running boyishly down ancient stair flights worn smooth by the knees of the faithful in central Asian mosques, giving her little lover-like pushes on the ramps of Siberian icebreakers, looking on with husbandly pride as she chatted shyly with officials in fish factories and state reception lines, and making sure that she was exposed as little as possible to the cruel scrutiny of the press.

From the beginning, the relationship between Mrs. Trudeau and the press — at least a quarter of whom had come along as much out of interest in her as in anything that might emanate from the Kremlin — was made intensely awkward by this protective attitude. On the second day in Moscow, just before Margaret Trudeau was to make her first public appearance, one of the PM's aides gathered together the meek little band of professional voyeurs who were chosen by lot to watch her tour the Palace of Young Pioneers, and told them, "Listen, treat her with delicacy, ya' get what I mean? Don't push or shove and for God's sake on no account try to speak to her. This is not for attribution." (Apparently, the required degree of delicacy was not achieved and on her second public appearance, at the Bolshoi Ballet school, only one reporter was permitted and the photographers were refused the benefit of lights. Thereafter, nobody was allowed to accompany her anywhere.)

Just why this protection was necessary was hard to fathom, since Margaret Trudeau represented in her person a perfection that the press was prepared to embrace with something approaching fervour. She was like all the pretty girls of the 1968 campaign rolled into one entirely acceptable form — young, lovely, and apparently as adoring of her husband and as unharried by internal turmoil as the bride in a baby-oil ad.

What she appeared to need protecting from was not the prying press but the smothering officialdom. Everywhere she went, she was surrounded by at least half a dozen Russian and Canadian women, most of whom were twice her age and thrice her girth. The makeup of this little band of duennas changed from place to place, but the constants were Ludmila Gwishiani, Premier Alexei Kosygin's daughter, who looked comfortable and unaccountably merry; Thereze Ford, the Canadian ambassador's wife, who was incongruously slim, elegant, and foreign in her hard-chic Paris clothes; and Elizabeth Hesketh, a junior officer from External Affairs, who appeared each day Carmen-curled and dressed as though she were going to a garden party at Government House in 1964.

Because Mrs. Trudeau was on no account to be required to speak officially, every quavering commonplace she uttered was strained after. When she tremulously presented the directress of the Palace of Young Pioneers with a gift-wrapped package that contained, I do not joke, an NFB film about bicycling in the Lower St. Lawrence, and said, "Umm, this is a gift from the people of Canada," everybody wrote it down. The next morning at a reception in the garden of the Canadian embassy, a photographer heard her tell a diplomatic wife, "Yesterday at the [official state] luncheon for Kosygin, I felt so out of it, I wanted to die. I just wished I could be off by myself in a corner and watch it all go by." Later in Kiev, the press was made happy for five minutes because she begged her husband audibly to be able to ride in his limousine with him ("Oh, come on, Pierre, *please*," a remark that was translated into the headline, "They're in love!") and another time in Tashkent, while her husband was giving a press conference, she said that she was thirsty and that she thought she'd eat some cherries, two utterances that not even the most resourceful could write very much about.

As a consequence, most of the pre-trip interest in Margie had to be vented on an analysis of her clothes. For the women on the trip, impressions of the U.S.S.R. may well be forever entangled with the memories of distinguished political commentators sidling up to them in places like the Armoury Museum within the Kremlin wall and saying, "Would it be fair to say that what she's wearing is a teal blue midi bound in beige?"

The friction over reporting Mrs. Trudeau subsided after the first two or three days (as a radio reporter remarked, "What can you say about a twenty-two-year-old girl who just got married, anyway?"). But the press had other, more significant difficulties that were to persist to the journey's end.

The chief of these was the journalists' inability to find out the real significance of what was going on in talks between Soviet and Canadian officials. Since he took office, Trudeau has attempted rigorously to curb press activities, but his means of achieving news control on this Russian journey were ingenious in the extreme. He, or more particularly his aides in collaboration with the Russian press office, managed to turn the forty-person press corps into two busloads of croaking tourists who caught glimpses of the official party only on occasion, in between touring museums, consuming gargantuan meals, and going to vodkafests given by various branches of the Soviet Union of Journalists.

The press was housed in different quarters from the official party, transported in different airplanes as the group junketed around the country, and kept away from official talks and social functions (though photographers, who must seem to the Trudeauites less threatening to the PM's image than what they call the "writing press," were allowed five minutes' shooting time at the beginning of the official Kremlin talks and swarmed around him when he laid wreaths and viewed ruins). Official disdain for the press expressed itself openly only occasionally, as when a young External Affairs officer named Sandy Bryce lined up the assembled newsmen on the sidewalk outside the Canadian embassy at 23 Starokonyushenny Pereulok just before a reception was to begin there, and barked: "Now, behave yourselves as you would at a party. Form up and go into the garden; the press is not to be allowed inside." It was as though proximity might result in the transference of some important idea more dangerous than cholera.

Still, every possible token effort was made to keep the press physically comfortable, or at least quiescent, by the three press aides from the PM's office who went along as their keepers. Telex and telephone lines to Canada were readily available and admirably clear; complicated arrangements were made so that film could be transported promptly from the outposts back to Moscow and thence to Canada, and large quantities of liquor were provided in a series of hospitality suites that were kept stocked from a movable bar. (Every Aeroflot takeoff was accompanied by the anxious question, "Did we remember to bring the booze?")

What was in short supply was hard information. And there was something rather poignant about the sight of skilled political analysts who'd come to the Soviet Union prepared to write in-depth pieces about Canada's role in the shifting balance of East-West power wandering around filling their notebooks with scribbles about the sights. (One reporter's leftover notes from Uzbekistan: "Samarkand — cotton, silk, jawbone of a woman. Which was Tamerlane's tomb?")

There were two official-but-not-for-attribution briefings given by mandarins, one full-dress prime ministerial press conference at the end of the three days of talks in Moscow, and two quickie press conferences, one lasting five minutes in the Tashkent airport and one mob scene in a light gale on the deck of the icebreaker *Lenin* in harbour at Murmansk, where only the people in the front row of the ten-deck crowd could hear what Trudeau had to say and radio reporters held up their mikes in hope of catching his pearly words on the downwind.

Canadian officials in public and private seemed curiously nervous about making firm interpretations of events — though some of them, notably Marshall Crowe, Ivan Head, and Marc Lalonde, all of the PM's office, worked hard at being helpful — so the press was left largely to its own imaginative devices and to the sensational reworkings of Trudeau's solipsisms by faraway news desks. The hopeful nationalists in the crowd saw the Soviet-Canadian protocol (which in effect promised only that the two countries would confer with each other regularly in future) as a breaking away from American domination of our economic life, though no one was able to explain how this would come about, since the Russians appeared to have nothing much in the way of manufactured goods that we would want to buy from them and, due to recent mammoth wheat sales, the imbalance of trade was already in our favour.

Trudeau himself seemed at first prone to encourage this anti-American interpretation of his Russian visit by saying that Canada needed to "diversify its channels of communication" because of the "overpowering presence of the United States of America" in our national life. But later he drew back and said that he was "no better than the next man in assessing the effects these talks might have on third parties," and when he was asked by an American correspondent whether he'd been asked to bear any Russian messages to Washington, he said, "I haven't, and if I had I would have told them to go peddle their own papers."

Another interpretation of the entente was that Canada represented in Russian eyes the malcontent in the Atlantic Alliance and that we were to be useful in achieving the Russians' desired reduction in European troop strength by both NATO and Warsaw Pact countries, to become, in effect, Pearsonian honest brokers in disarmament negotiations. But this theory looked less witty ten days later, when the American representative at NATO talks in Europe endorsed wholeheartedly the Russian proposal without any apparent lobbying from Canada.

Much was also made of the fact that Canada and the U.S.S.R. are "polar neighbours," and when asked in Moscow what he thought we could learn about the Arctic from the Russians, the prime minister said, "Lots." But after he'd been to Siberia, he sidestepped left once more and said that he didn't really foresee the building of great cities in our own Arctic, though the Russian achievement was impressive, which left a reporter from a major daily in the position of having to file a story that directly contradicted a piece he'd written the day before.

In brief, the news was disconcertingly vague, and as the days wore on the trip began to look more and more like a gestural exercise akin to a royal tour of Tanzania and meant to bring Trudeau celebrity abroad and popularity at home — until, of course, he did go home and insulted a huge segment of the ethnic vote by comparing the Ukrainian nationalists to the FLQ.

The safest stories turned out to be reports of non-events like "Bolshoi Audience Gives Trudeaus Standing Ovation" or "Trudeaumania in Siberia — Half Population of Norilsk Turns Out to Cheer PM and Bride" or "Street Poll in Kiev Shows Ukrainians Love Canada," pieces that contained lots of "colour," as the dailies call anything real that doesn't fit into the unreal pronouncements made in official communiqués, but that scarcely helped to answer the pertinent questions — Why did he go, really? Why did he stay so long? — that the *Globe and Mail* posed editorially on the day of Trudeau's return.

Just how Trudeau himself would answer these questions was impossible to gauge from his posture during the trip. The prime impression he gave was one of isolation from ordinary human responses. When he was laying wreaths at the tombs of the fallen or posing with Communist bosses on airplane tarmacs or enduring the rigorous sightseeing programs the Russians whirled him through, his face was usually fixed in a mask of undeviating engrossment. He relented very briefly once in the airport at Tashkent when a reporter, joshing him about his barefoot sandals, asked if he realized that he'd been able to keep his feet clean because the Russians had sent a road sweeper to precede his arrival at every dusty historical site and Trudeau muttered in mock astonishment, "You mean there is some evidence of planning in all this?" But most of the time all one could do was speculate on how it must feel for a man who used to set out to see the world with a knapsack to be seeing it now with a cast of hundreds at his back and an interpreter joggling his elbow. Was it lonely, tiring, boring, laughable — who could tell?

This remoteness had an odd effect on the lookers-on, creating what might be called the "I-knew-him-when" syndrome in certain old acquaintances in the crowd. "I knew him when he was still a very minor functionary in Mr. St. Laurent's office and he came to see me to ask diffidently if I thought he'd find a visit to Moscow interesting," said a mandarin nostalgically after watching Trudeau sign the official protocol with Kosygin in Moscow to the sound of thirty cameras whirring and clicking like cicadas. "I knew him when we were both in our twenties," said Roger Lemelin, the Quebec City novelist, who came along to report the tour for La Presse. "He attended a reception that Georges Vanier gave for me in Paris and he had acne in those days and he was thin and shy and the first remark he made to me was, 'How is it that you, a boy from a poor background, have created this marvellous novel [The Town Below] and I have created nothing?'"

The way Trudeau normally bridges this gap between his Powerfulness and other people's Ordinariness is to caper a little and do his swinger turn. He did try this in Russia and left his glum hosts cold at worst and at best profoundly puzzled. In the war museum in Murmansk, in a room devoted to the depiction of Soviet hardships suffered in the Second World War, Trudeau knelt down and squinted through the sights of a submachine gun and started to make ack-ack noises until he caught the stern eye of his waiting guides and hurriedly passed on. In Moscow, at the press conference, he loosened his tie and nuzzled the microphone, which had been placed too close to his nose, in a kind of what-the-hell gesture that the Soviets missed and I thought indicated disapproval. The pretty girls who normally serve as props were simply unavailable, and Trudeau was reduced to expending his Gallic charm on dumpy women with bad dye jobs and small children with round and sombre eyes, neither of whom made the kind of pictures the photographers were after, a situation that created yet another point of friction within the press corps.

What the media's collective frustrations led to, within the confines of their yellow buses, was a lot of loud complaining, some fierce infighting for the right photographic positions and placement in the "pools" of six or seven press representatives who were allowed slightly closer to the official group on certain select occasions, and the kind of intense camaraderie you get at a boys' camp in August after the counsellors have endured a rainy summer and the ministrations of an inadequate cook.

One morning in the middle of Siberia, a photographer from *Life* stood up in the front of the bus, tightened the belt on his trench coat and said through tight-closed teeth, "I just wonder if our editors are going to think it was worth spending all this money to send us here so we could send back b—all." The rough cost per journalist was $1,200, plus transmission charges, but some media managements seemed to think it was worth investing a whole lot more. A Toronto daily staked its reporter to a crash course in Russian and several sessions with a hypnotist to cure her of a long-time fear of flying so she could endure the thirty-five hours spent in the air. A Windsor television outlet was represented by a three-man crew who mysteriously functioned without any camera equipment (they used CBC videotape), and an ethnic radio station in Toronto ventured boldly into the foreign-corresponding field by dispatching a station announcer who was linguistically gifted (she spoke Italian) and had been named Miss Byline by the Toronto Men's Press Club a month or so before. Seven people from the CBC English network and three from the French conducted a bicultural competition for news that left the French wounded, the English unwittingly triumphant, and the onlookers amazed. (When the English network won the pool to Norilsk, in a rigorously fair draw from a brown jug that contained everybody's names, a French Canadian remarked darkly, "You see, it is because they are Anglos — we will never forget this, never.")

It would all have been well worth it, of course, if the trip had turned into what a Canadian embassy official hopefully forecast at the start: "An exercise in Soviet-Canadian friendship, an educative experience on both sides."

Some Canadian misconceptions about Russia were righted (on the second-last day, a radio reporter who'd come to the Soviet Union holding hard to the old Cold War notion that the Soviet masses were just waiting to be released from their bonds, said in wonderment as he viewed his thousandth flower-decked portrait of Lenin, "Listen, I think the Russkies really believe this stuff") and some small ignorances were dispelled (the cameraman who asked, as he watched the patient crowds lining up in front of Lenin's tomb, "You mean, they got the guy's body in there?" now realizes that indeed they have, and the radio reporter, who looked at a wall portrait of a bearded man in a museum in Murmansk and wondered if it was Stalin, now knows what Trotsky looked like). But for the most part, close Canadian contact with Russian life was limited to conversations with Intourist guides; shoving matches with KGB men, who were everywhere, almost indistinguishable from one another, hard of eye, dark of baggy-panted suit and impervious to any kind of blandishment; quick exchanges with kids on sidewalks who wanted to trade lapel badges or cadge Western goods (boy outside the Kremlin wall, holding a tiny lapel badge of the Communist messiah, "Hey, lady, a little Lenin for some chewing gum?"); and glimpses through streaky bus windows of hordes of heavyset men and women moving hurriedly through the streets or standing patiently in shop lineups or being led in abject docility out of buses to serve as flag-waving crowds at airports when the Trudeaus arrived. (The exception was Norilsk, where the eight-man press pool said afterward the inhabitants' response was warm, spontaneous, and real.)

Just what the Russians learned about us was impossible to fathom. A Russian reporter said to me indiscreetly in Moscow when he heard a group of Canadians complaining about the slowness of the elevators and the condition of the bathrooms, "You are a spoiled people. You have the American disease — if everything is not perfect, your nervous systems are destroyed." Later in Leningrad, at the end of the tour, some of the Canadian correspondents got together and made a presentation to an Intourist guide who'd endured the whole tour with the group and was immensely popular because of his youth, his knowledgeability about the West (he could discuss in detail possible candidates for the 1972 Democratic presidential nomination), and the warmth of his responses. What they chose to give this sterling young man as an expression of undying friendship was a copy of *Playboy* magazine. After he opened it, flushed, made a highly charged speech rejecting it, and rushed out of the room intensely insulted, the Canadians stood around weakly trying to explain that the whole thing was a joke. For the ten hours that remained of the trip, the whole Intourist-KGB-Russian-press group stopped feigning international conviviality and turned stony-eyed and careful in the presence of the bourgeois mob.

It was a bruising incident to end on, but it prompted from one of the rueful Canadians a remark that somehow seemed to sum up the whole crazy, infuriating, incomprehensible tour: "Trudeau can talk all he likes about our relationship to the Americans being like a mouse lying down with an elephant. But what we've seen in the last twelve days is what happens when the mouse gets into bed with a bear."

THIRTY-TWO

The Exotic Mindscape of Pierre Trudeau[30]

Saturday Night, January–February 1977

LATE THIS LAST bleak autumn, not long after the Quebec election, I went to a small dinner party given by a political scientist of some distinction at his house in the heart of Toronto. Most of the guests he and his wife had invited were also academics, and the talk at table, over the *boeuf bourguignon* and the Beaujolais, naturally turned to the country's future.

Everybody contributed according to his ability and/or his discipline's needs. The historian drew parallels with the great national crises of the past. The law professor made donnish jokes about the ways in which René Lévesque might twist the wording of the upcoming referendum to suit his party's purposes. The economist compared the financial viability of Quebec with that of the Scandinavian nations. And so it went until the moment, midway through the meal, when the host said in a voice that seemed oddly discordant because it was touched with passion, "Dammit, this is a time for big men, a time when Trudeau will have to show his mettle, a time —" The entire company turned to stare and somebody interrupted to say soothingly, "Come, come, let's not argue ad hominem."

I wanted to shout, "Listen, we have to argue ad hominem. We need to have a feel for the personal dynamics of the struggle that lies ahead. We should discuss how we think Trudeau will react when he's up against Lévesque in the fight of his life — and maybe the fight of ours, if we want to continue as Canadians." But the moment passed, and I didn't shout, and the conversation went back, in a peculiarly Canadian way, to the safety of impersonal civilities.

In the weeks since then — while the Quebec/Canada drama has begun to unfold — I've continued to think, as Trevor-Roper contends so cleverly, that individuals as much as ideologies determine the course of history. Like him or not, much of what happens to Canada in the next few years will depend on Pierre Trudeau. He is the champion of the federalist cause, and we are the uneasy bystanders. We'll have to wait to find out whether reason will overcome passion, whether Trudeau, the man of grey matter, will outdo Lévesque, the man of heart.

In the face of that reality, it's unsettling to realize that although he's been a centre of public attention for nearly a decade now, Trudeau is in many ways a curiously unfathomable figure. In that time he's been cast in several guises — intellectual dandy, cabinet dictator, incautious reformer, arch conservative, political pragmatist, economic bungler, and national saviour, to name a few. He's been called cold, arrogant, courageous, brilliant, rigid, uncaring, feckless, and fanatic. But despite all the images laid on him, all the questions hurled at him, all the praise that's been heaped on him and all the rage that's been vented, nobody — to my mind, anyway — has ever caught his essence or been able to predict his fate.

When I first met Trudeau, ten years ago this month, he was standing alone in the hall of my house in Ottawa, holding a glass of sherry that a harried bartender had filled too full. He had come late to a reception in honour of the publisher of a powerful newspaper who was in the capital to take a preliminary look at the candidates for the leadership of the Liberal Party. (The position was not actually vacant, but Lester Pearson had said it would be declared so once centennial year was over.)

The probable contenders had turned out in force — Martin, Hellyer, Winters, Turner, MacEachen, and the rest — and they were crowded into the living room with a number of lesser beings, talking, laughing, and gesticulating in their attempts to capture the publisher's attention and his editorial favour. After exchanging a few pleasantries, Trudeau glanced briefly at this scene, sipped his sherry carefully, remarked that the guest of honour seemed to be fully occupied, and as for himself, he thought he would leave now, thank you very much.

Because he was, as an MP, still "a nobody" (by his own later definition), the powermongers didn't notice when he slipped away. In fact, nobody at the party — besides me and the barman — seemed to realize he had even been there at all. I was left trying to decipher the emotion reflected in his glittering blue eyes when he took in the antics of the office-seekers. Was it amusement, disdain, boredom, shyness? I opted for shyness because it was a feeling I understood readily and he was a man whose work as a writer and activist-intellectual I had heard about and admired.

But after all these years of observing him in a hundred different situations and talking about him with scores of people who have tried to know him well, I have come to suspect that what his eyes were reflecting was not emotion at all. Probably he was being "coldly intelligent," an attitude, as he wrote in *Federalism and the French Canadians*, he assumes as often as is humanly possible. Reason would tell him there was nothing to be gained at that party, and reason would soon prove right.

Trudeau's predilection for denying feelings in favour of reason is the one constant in the descriptions of him given by people of various temperaments who've observed him from various vantage points before, during, and particularly since his rise to prime ministerial power. Few of them are foolish enough to claim he doesn't have feelings — he's displayed his quick anger too often in public for that — but all of them claim he consistently suppresses them.

One of his friends, a man who knew him well in the 1950s and 1960s in Montreal, says with the special wisdom of the novelist that his lack of rapport with people on an individual level, and "the people" on a national level, is due in part to his "consistent denial of the importance of intuition. To be intuitive you have to be vulnerable, and Pierre didn't want to be open to hurts. He puts on reason like a suit of armour, little realizing that although it might protect him, it isolates him too."

Certainly if you examine the statements of his colleagues — and the positions he's taken during his three terms in office, from his sweeping changes in the civil service to his handling of the economy to the making of his cabinets — the picture that emerges is of a Cartesian man, applying logic rigorously to the problems of governing and to the management of people.

A very wise woman, the wife of a well-known French Canadian, was trying recently to comfort a dazed ex–cabinet minister who found himself relieved of his portfolio after several years of faithful service and a few hours of illogical, exhaustion-fostered tantrums. "You have to realize," she said, "that Pierre was seduced very early by logic; and as a mistress she served him well for most of his life. It's only now in his fifties that it's become apparent that logic doesn't always work."

Certainly logic doesn't work when it's used to explain the compounded blunders the Trudeau government has made since 1974. Any one of the prime minister's close advisers — and he's surrounded by intelligent, decent, and above all reasonable men — can argue persuasively that when he was electioneering in the late spring of 1974, making cruel fun of Robert Stanfield by denying the need for wage-and-price controls, the PM's position was absolutely sound in the economic context of the time. It was only later, they say, quoting complicated economic formulas and international scholarly opinions, that the need for controls became imperative. If you answer, well, okay, but doesn't he realize that it makes ordinary voters feel as though he deliberately misled them, they react with incomprehension. They will run through the same exercise defending the "new society" musings on television; or the reinstatement of André Ouellet to the cabinet after his contempt of court conviction; or the Polymer — now Polysar — kickbacks, which they describe as "normal business rebates"; or any one of half a dozen other political errors that lend themselves to reasonable explanations, but that a leader with an intuitive understanding of the electorate — Mackenzie King, say — would have been unlikely to perpetrate.

If syllogistic reasoning isn't workable in defence of policies that have gone wildly awry, when it's applied to relationships with people it can prove tragic.

There is a belief abroad that Trudeau has a close circle of friends, a cabal of people drawn mainly from the Prime Minister's Office and the Privy Council Office who run the country. But if you seek out the supposed members of this cabal, they deny to a man any special rapport with the prime minister, saying that during periods when they aren't "in play" — i.e., called on to perform their jobs — he doesn't communicate with them.

Any team sense that exists among the important job holders in the PCO and the PMO tends to spring from old friendships formed before the Trudeau era. Much was made of the fact that Marc Lalonde and Michael Pitfield were close friends of each other's and of the prime minister's in the years from 1968 to 1972, when Lalonde was principal secretary and Pitfield was a deputy clerk of the Privy Council.

Pitfield and Lalonde had known each other for a decade (they started out in Ottawa in 1959 as assistants to Davie Fulton when he was Minister of Justice), much longer than they had known Trudeau, whom they both met in Montreal in the 1960s. Their friendship was based on similar reformist ideas about government and federalism. Once Lalonde became an MP and cabinet minister and Pitfield left the PCO to spend twenty-one months as a deputy minister before being appointed clerk of the Privy Council after the 1974 election, they ceased to meet as a trio on either a professional or personal basis. Lalonde saw the prime minister in cabinet; Pitfield saw him only at large functions, such as the Governor General's garden party. As pragmatic, not to mention phlegmatic, Trudeauites, this was in their eyes and phraseology "entirely appropriate."

The three men who currently form the most important non-elected advisory group to the prime minister — Senator Keith Davey, his chief political organizer; Jim Coutts, his principal secretary; and Richard O'Hagan, his special adviser on communications — are also old friends of one another's but not of Trudeau's. They are "splendid retreads," as Gordon Fairweather wittily described them in the House of Commons, their connections with one another having been formed during the Pearson era, and their camaraderie based on old times and old jokes. ("Remember J. Watson MacNaught?" they'll say to one another. "Remember Roger Teillet?" And if you don't remember those illustrious privy councillors, you'll never know what holds this trio together and what breaks them up.)

Davey says he is the only person in Ottawa who doesn't "relate to Mr. Trudeau on a cerebral basis." (The senator is a very able and intelligent man who has gone far on the fiction that he's "just an ordinary guy.") Certainly Davey is one of the few people in the capital who doesn't live in fear of the prime minister — as an entertaining, if telling, incident during November proved.

The prime minister had not been pleased with the text for the November 24 television address to the nation provided by the speech writers in his office and retreated to 24 Sussex to write his own speech, having alerted Davey, Coutts, O'Hagan, and three or four other people that he would read it to them in his office for their assessment on the day before the telecast. The company duly assembled, and there was no doubt in their minds, as the prime minister read his words with fire, that he thought it a brilliant speech. But for the anglophones listening, it was an agony to know what to say since the rendering was in French and none of them was sufficiently fluent to get more than its gist. "We all sat there gripping the edge of our seats until our knuckles turned white," one of them recalled afterward. Finally, the PM said, "Do you want to hear it in English, too?" "Yes, sir, prime minister," said Davey blandly. "I'd like to hear how it reads in the other official language."

Still, despite his easygoing ways, Keith Davey sees the prime minister mainly on party business and usually in official settings. Trudeau rarely asks colleagues to his house on a casual basis. One cabinet minister from Quebec who might be considered a familiar said recently that in four years only one invitation to 24 Sussex had been forthcoming and that was to a formal dinner.

Furthermore, Trudeau won't lend himself to requests for the usual small courtesies a prime minister dispenses as a matter of form — such as a note to an official's wife who was ill in hospital with cancer, which he refused on the basis that it would be phoney and an intrusion on her privacy because he hardly knew her. He doesn't need psychic stroking, and he doesn't comprehend why other people might.

Outside the circle of his family he seems to function as a loner — as he had all his life until his marriage — his temperamental isolation compounded by the fact that he holds the loneliest job in any democracy. An old friend from his radical days, now working in the Department of Finance, who used to be invited occasionally to 24 Sussex for drinks and conversation, was foolish enough to tell a few people a story Trudeau had confided about his mother-in-law's dislike of bilingual labels. The story got into print in Douglas Fisher's column in the *Toronto Sun*, and the friend now finds that messages left with the PM's secretary go unanswered. He was indiscreet and he was dispensable.

A senior bureaucrat describes Trudeau's relationships with people by comparing him with Lester Pearson. "Mike always made you feel you were needed even if this was far from the case. Pierre makes you feel he doesn't give a shit even though he may need you badly. He just can't bring himself to say 'Help me,' though if the phrase passed his lips a hundred people would rush to his aid."

Probably the most important formal function a prime minister performs at a personal level is as cabinet leader. When he sits down with his ministers as the first among equals, he must deal with the abstract problems of running the country and the human problems of managing people. He must knit together factions, drawing out uncertain ministers, directing the energies of the bombastic, and soothing the fears of the dissatisfied, all the while seeking the consensus that will best serve the federation.

If you move among Trudeau's past and present privy councillors, asking them about his abilities as cabinet maker and cabinet leader, they usually display three attitudes:

1. They respect his patience in trying to reach a consensus and his intellectual grasp of an amazing variety of policy problems. PCO officials produce for every Thursday meeting of the whole cabinet about six inches of documentation to go with policies coming up on the agenda. Trudeau invariably is familiar with the contents of these briefs, and he expects his ministers to display similar diligence. He is courteous to those who are prepared to argue a position

backed up by facts, savage to those who are "feelies" — as in, "I've got a feeling this won't wash in Wetaskiwin," a legitimate remark among most ordinary pols who operate on three-parts hunch to one-part fact, but anathema to the fastidious Trudeau.

2. They fear his wrath if they are seen to be self-seeking or to have revealed cabinet secrets. One minister, in response to an innocuous question about which ministers the PM relies on and admires, answered: "Macdonald, Lang, and in a funny way MacEachen." Then he whispered nervously, "If you print that I told you that, I'll never speak to you again."

Trudeau respects ministers who show loyal devotion to duty and icily disposes of those he considers malingerers. When he was Minister of Consumer and Corporate Affairs, Herb Gray was asked by the prime minister — on a day when ministers with major economic portfolios all happened to be out of town or otherwise engaged — to answer questions in the House about newly released figures on unemployment and inflation. Gray turned back the request with the remark that the prime minister himself was better equipped to take on this unpleasant duty, and from that moment, as a former Privy Council Office official says, "we knew his days as a minister were numbered." Gray's misfortune was not only to be shown up as overly concerned with his own skin but to be recognized as unable to "deliver" anything to the PM. He didn't have "coattails" in his region, and he had no special knowledge that added anything to the PM's perspective. Trudeau likes Eugene Whelan, for instance, because he is "a whole man" in his eyes and he is thought to understand the farmers. James Richardson, on the other hand, was not considered "whole" and, despite his famous family name, was perceived in 1974 not to have "coattails." (The Liberal vote in Manitoba, already low, went down by 5 percent in that election.)

3. They dislike the collegial system of cabinet government, which was described variously as alienating, exhausting, and erosive of ministerial authority. This system of running cabinet business through one of several committees before introducing it to cabinet as a whole was instituted under Pearson and has been continually refined under Trudeau. Its workings are complex and of interest mainly to political scientists and other familiars of Ivor Jennings, Richard Crossman, and Michael Pitfield. What is most important about it in terms of understanding Pierre Trudeau as cabinet leader is that it is a concerted attempt to impose technocratic order on what is essentially a human, fluid, and messy interchange as ministers clash with one another and with their bureaucrats over competing policies. On paper, it's an important, forward-looking development in cabinet government. In practice, many ministers complain bitterly that it saps their energies and prevents the emergence of strong figures in cabinet.

The only way John Turner managed to enhance his reputation as a political star under this system, according to his friends, is that he chose to ignore it. He rarely went to cabinet committee meetings, sending instead his deputy ministers, a move that left him free to be present regularly in the House and to travel the country frequently, making speeches, polishing contacts, getting feedback. His detractors say that this is too simplistic by half, that Turner flourished because Trudeau was large-spirited enough to give him free rein in the important portfolios of justice and finance.

Both friends and enemies agree that the loss of Turner from his cabinet is one of the most important failures Trudeau has sustained. In reasonable terms, it made sense. Turner was tired of being crown prince, and he went into private practice as a corporate lawyer. In human terms, it was a disaster. By losing Turner, Trudeau was seen to be unable to get along with strong men and to have lost control of the economy.

Trudeau's reputation for haughty indifference increased when Bryce Mackasey resigned from the cabinet in open chagrin just one year after Turner's departure, at the moment when a cabinet reshuffle was supposed to show a revitalized ministry. Turner and Mackasey are very different men in temperament and ideology, with Mackasey occupying the left of the Liberal spectrum and Turner the right. Furthermore, their relationships with Trudeau were essentially different. Turner had always been seen as a rival power and probable successor. Mackasey was always an open supporter, the only cabinet member who was unabashedly sentimental about the PM. (When Margaret Trudeau fell ill in the autumn of 1975, Mackasey, in his inimitable way, passed a note to the prime minister during a cabinet meeting that quoted Tennyson's line, "More things are wrought by prayer than this world dreams of." "He didn't say a word," Mackasey related later, "but I knew he was touched — I could feel it.")

Despite the differences between Turner and Mackasey, the manner of their resignations was curiously similar. They both went to Trudeau threatening to resign, and they both emerged from his office traumatized by his acceptance of their threats at word value. They had expected him to beg them to stay and to offer them blandishments. Turner wanted some kind of reassurance that Trudeau didn't intend to stay in the PM's office forever (the kind of reassurance that Liberal prime ministers have traditionally offered to eager heirs apparent) and that his labours in finance were appreciated. Mackasey wanted another portfolio and a place on the all-important Priorities and Plans Committee of the cabinet. They both ended up stonewalled and disbelieving.

"You can't threaten Pierre Trudeau," says one of his advisers. "He won't stand for it, and anyway both of them were expendable. It was

Turner as much as anyone who was responsible for the state of the econ-omy, and nobody would ever say that Mackasey was a good minister — he was all heart and no work."

However reasonable the explanation for the departures of Mack-asey, Turner, and their several other colleagues, the plain fact is that this winter, with the biggest national crisis in our history burgeoning, there are no "star" ministers in Trudeau's cabinet, men or women with large public followings of their own who can come to the aid of the federalist cause.

The list of those who have jumped ship or been thrown headlong overboard is long: besides Turner and Mackasey, it includes Paul Hellyer, Eric Kierans, Gérard Pelletier, Jean Marchand, Mitchell Sharp, Bud Drury, and James Richardson, to name the big names.

The list of those left is made up of exhausted loyalists (Donald Macdonald and Allan MacEachen, both of whom are doing yeoman service in difficult, engrossing jobs they didn't want and don't like); discredited rationalists (Marc Lalonde, Otto Lang, and André Ouellet, all three of whom have shown a lack of political judgement that dam-ages their well-deserved reputations for ministerial capability); a few men with ready identification within specialized groups but no magic on the national scene (Eugene Whelan among farmers, Barney Danson in the Jewish community, Don Jamieson in Newfoundland, Romeo LeBlanc among fishermen, and Daniel MacDonald with war veterans); and a slew of lesser figures most Canadians couldn't tab with a name, much less a portfolio.

His solitude is yet another way in which Trudeau's position is in direct contrast to Lévesque's. The Quebec premier, newly ensconced in office with all the energy and optimism his unexpected victory generated, is buoyed up by strong colleagues (Parizeau, the two Morins, Payette) with separatist fervour equal to or surpassing his own.

It will be a long time before Lévesque suffers the isolation and dis-
enchantment that elevation to high office almost invariably brings.
Thousands of French Canadians will remember for years the way he
was on the hustings last fall, exuding not charisma (which in Max
Weber's original definition places the leader far above the crowd that
worships him) but understanding of their aspirations. I saw him at
a speech in the Msgr. Parent high school auditorium in Longueuil, a
working-class suburb of Montreal located in his own riding, a week
before his victory, talking to a crowd so packed together there was no
air. With Lise Payette sitting behind him, and his posters pinned on
the auditorium's curtains, Lévesque was Chaplinesque, "the little man"
personified, his feet turned out, his ill-fitting suit looking like something a factory foreman would wear on Sunday, smoking constantly,
telling jokes ("Trudeau sent us Mackasey — *C'est un cadeau des Grecs*;
Trudeau sent us Marchand — he's supposed to drive the government
of Quebec, but he can't even drive his own car"), making promises,
lifting hopes, speaking, as he kept saying, "*au fond de mon cœur.*" I
haven't been in a crowd that was so loving since 1968, and when the
musicians played the Gilles Vigneault song "*Gens du pays c'est votre
tour,*" the people went into a kind of ecstasy.

On many levels, the Trudeau-Lévesque confrontation has about it
a mythic aura. Each man represents a tradition rooted in Quebec's
history. Lévesque comes out of the nationalist tradition of Papineau,
Bourassa, Taschereau, and Duplessis, based on tribalism and emotion;
Trudeau comes from the pragmatic, federalist-constitutionalist tradition of Lafontaine, Cartier, Laurier, Lapointe, and St. Laurent, focused
on the accommodation of the French Canadians to the finality of the
conquest and based on reason and a more abstract concept of brother-
hood beyond blood ties.

On the surface, Trudeau — burdened by the fatigue of his ministry
and myriad difficulties beyond the Quebec situation, and alienated

from his fellow French Canadians by long absence and a reputation for being remote and aristocratic — would seem the probable loser in a separatist-versus-federalist referendum. Still, he has seemed like a loser and come up a winner before. Earlier in the fall, when the Quebec results weren't known yet and every indicator pointed to his downfall, I kept thinking of a remark made a few months before he died by Grattan O'Leary, the Conservative senator who had been observing prime ministers for sixty years.

"You can't weigh Trudeau on ordinary scales," he said. "It isn't just that he's brilliant — Arthur Meighen was easily his equal in brains — but that there clings to him something mysterious, which for want of a better word I'll call 'luck.' Fortune has a way of turning in his favour. For him the centre holds."

Those of us who want Canada to hold will have to hope that in this assessment of O'Leary's there was more moxie than Irish mysticism, or — to put it another way — more reason than emotion.

THIRTY-THREE

Bowing Out:
John Turner's Resignation[31]

Globe and Mail, May 6, 1989,
with Stephen Clarkson

JOHN TURNER'S resignation this week — amid pious pronouncements of regret from people who have been trying to bludgeon him to death for years — signalled the end of something far more significant than the Turner years in the Liberal Party. It marked the demise of the old Liberalism and, some might say, the old Canada.

When he became his party's leader in 1984, John Turner was virtually the last man standing who still believed in the Liberal alliance that Mackenzie King put together, Louis St. Laurent refined, Lester Pearson extended, and Pierre Trudeau ostensibly destroyed. That Liberal alliance defined the old Canada and governed it for fifty years. It was based on a proven formula: the party could maintain itself in power if it held onto the fortress that Wilfrid Laurier built in Quebec; cultivated its connections in the West through regional elites; drew on the nation-building ideas of a progressive federal bureaucracy; and straddled the political middle ground by impressing the business community with its managerial competence while leaning slightly to the left on social issues in order to hold the voters' support.

Mr. Turner was, in many ways, the living embodiment of that formula, the perfect Liberal man of his time, when he joined the party in 1962. An athlete and a Rhodes scholar, he was the son of an Ottawa bureaucrat, the stepson of one prominent western business-man and soon-to-be son-in-law of another, an adequately bilingual lawyer practising in Quebec who expressed a noblesse-oblige belief in social justice in the manner of John F. Kennedy, with whom he was compared.

These attributes served him well for the next dozen years as he moved in a kind of princely progression from glamorous backbencher to Minister of Finance. When he quarrelled spectacularly with Pierre Trudeau in 1975 and withdrew to a tower on Bay Street, he continued to espouse the old Liberal formula for success. It was Mr. Trudeau, with his abrasive disdain for business and the West, who was destroy-ing Liberalism, Mr. Turner maintained in private for the benefit of his peers. If only he were in charge, then the party and the country could be put back on the proper course.

When Mr. Turner's hopes for a return to glory were fulfilled after nine years in exile and he was elected leader by Liberals who were motivated in equal parts by fear of a bewildering future and by nostal-gia for a simpler past, he didn't seem to realize at first that the old formula was an anachronism. It wasn't just that Mr. Trudeau had dis-turbed the cosy Liberal alliance of elites. The world had altered and Canada, the Liberal Party included, had to adjust.

Nothing Mr. Turner tried in the next few years could put the old alliance back together again. Not running in Vancouver-Quadra in order to attract support in the West. Not trying to persuade other business leaders to stand with him. Not agreeing to the decentralizing principles of the Meech Lake Accord in order to please Quebec. Not opening up the party to the new ethnic elites. Not looking for fresh ideas by turning to a new generation of Grits.

Western rage against Liberalism — and its centralizing interventionism — had become irreversible. Quebec had a new native-son champion in the leader of the Progressive Conservative Party. Keynesianism, on which the old bureaucratic elite had constructed its nation-building policies, had failed. Neo-conservatism had the governments of the United Kingdom and the United States in its grip and the Canadian business community in its thrall. It didn't matter that Mr. Turner had so lately been that community's darling; it now had a better front man in the boy from Baie Comeau.

This was a Hobbesian world where transnational capital was becoming insolent and Canadian business increasingly continental. Where huge deficits meant that social policies and national institutions were in jeopardy. Where the press was surly and cynical and regional leaders dismissive of calls for solidarity. Where women didn't know their place any more and all the policy innovators were making big bucks in slick consulting firms rather than contacts in the backrooms of the Liberal Party.

The horrors that befell John Turner as he struggled with these new political and economic realities are imprinted on our collective consciousness like some awful upside-down morality tale in which the good-man would-be hero is destroyed rather than vindicated by his valour and his toil. Party uprisings, caucus divisions, financial travails, staff betrayals, private humiliations, and the assorted other woes Mr. Turner suffered in his five years as leader laid to rest forever the notion that Liberalism meant competence and loyalty.

It was enough to make even John Turner question the premises of the past. And in October 1987, he began to do just that. That month, the outline of what became the Canada–United States Free Trade Agreement was published. A close reading of the text convinced Mr.

Turner that the Canadian state was in jeopardy and the Canada he had been brought up to serve was unlikely to survive. As he saw it, integration with the United States in one continental economy would mean Canada's inevitable cultural and political decline. That the deal had been dictated by his former clients and friends in the business community, and was espoused by his former political allies in Quebec and the West, added to the shock. From his point of view, the Canadian elites were no longer combining benignly to run the country. They were conniving to sell it out.

Over the next year and a half he turned himself into the champion of the anti–free trade movement, which he took to calling, in a tone nobody had ever heard him use before, "the cause of my life." For the first time as leader, he began to display the smarts he had been famous for twenty years ago. He used the Liberals' majority in the Senate to prevent the passage of the FTA before an election could give the public a chance to vote on this momentous question. During the 1988 campaign his action precipitated, he broke through the mystification surrounding free trade to communicate his outrage directly to voters. For a few intense weeks he gave daily voice to the anxiety felt by a broad coalition of Canadians in the regions: the churches, farm organizations, trade unions, the women's movement, and ethnic, cultural, environmental, and Native people's groups.

But his passionate pleas on behalf of the Canada he believed in were drowned out. His sorry leadership record weighed too heavily for him to rouse his own party and to prevail against the propaganda counterattack mounted by the Conservatives and their big business mentors and friends. He lost the election and with it any hope of future political success.

This last-stand effort to reaffirm and recast the beliefs of his past — an effort that redeemed him as a man if not as a politician — left the Liberal Party largely unmoved. Untouched by Mr. Turner's vision of

Canada, exhausted by the struggle to supplant him, it is now apparently without any real consensus about where it stands.

In a politics polarized along regional and class lines by neo-conservatism, it is no longer obvious to Liberals that there's still a place for an umbrella party straddling the ideological middle. Nor is it clear that a party that defends a strong federal state with effective nation-building institutions can expect support from a business community that looks to the continental market for its salvation. Nobody's sure any more that the Quebec question can be resolved, that the West can be assuaged, that social programs can still be universal. In the new Canada there seems to be no centre, and old ideas and ideals cannot hold.

One night in April 1988, in the middle of the last, worst caucus revolt that Mr. Turner suffered, an old friend called him in Ottawa to find out how he was. He discovered Mr. Turner, with his family away and his aides gone home, all alone at Stornaway, working on his speech for the annual press gallery dinner. When the friend expressed commiseration on the latest round of betrayals, Mr. Turner responded with the mixture of gentlemanly fortitude and manic optimism that buoyed his last years in politics. "Don't worry, fella," he said. "Everything's gonna be fine."

Nothing ever was fine, of course, in Mr. Turner's years as leader. But in his response to his vicissitudes, he displayed a grace under pressure that did the old Liberalism proud.

THIRTY-FOUR

Jim Coutts and the Politics of Manipulation[32]

Saturday Night, September 1980

THE TWENTY-SIXTH of March, 1979, that miserable Monday when
Pierre Trudeau finally called the federal election he had been post-
poning for more than a year, was not the kind of day James Coutts, his
principal secretary, enjoyed. Coutts had been working for weeks acti-
vating the battle plan for his campaign to come, and the last-minute
details he had to attend to on Monday were dispatched with his usual
efficiency but not his usual zest. Coutts loved to conduct every aspect
of his life with what he thought of as style. He didn't like sandwiches
at his desk, whiners on the telephone, pessimistic forecasts, or criticisms of Liberalism; and he had been forced to put up with all of these
annoyances on the twenty-sixth of March.

What he really liked was having his secretary summon important
Liberals to eat lunch with him on Sundays in the pink and grey mock
splendour of the Park Plaza dining room not far from his clever little
house in downtown Toronto where he usually spent his weekends. Or
ordering a mineral water with a twist of lime from room service at the

Inn of the Provinces, where he stayed in Ottawa during the week, before settling down in his suite to gossip the late-night hours away with a Liberal crony from out of town. Or sauntering over to enjoy a long lunch at the Château Laurier across the road from his office in the Langevin Block after a morning spent on agreeable tasks, such as advising the PM on an important appointment or consulting with the clerk of the Privy Council on the cabinet agenda.

Ever since he had become Trudeau's right-hand man in August 1975, Coutts had made the Château Grill his personal lunching club. Such was his importance in the city in the late 1970s that his presence there had turned the restaurant into a more fashionable place to eat at noon than the Rideau Club or Le Cercle Universitaire. He was seen in the Grill as often as three or four times a week, always in the fourth alcove on the east side of the room, his fair head clearly visible in the gloom beneath the green flocked hangings that gave the place the aura of a bordello in a story by de Maupassant. He would sit on the velvet banquette like an Irish landowner on rent day, bestowing his benign interest on the waiters ("How's your wife, Pasquale?"), ordering the same food and drink (martini straight up, minced steak medium-rare, sliced tomatoes, black coffee, and then, oh sin, oh sweet sublimity, a fat chocolate cream from the silver bonbon dish that was brought only to the tables of the favoured), dropping his pearly perceptions for the benefit of his guests, waving in acknowledgement as privy councillors and deputy ministers respectfully passed by, his cool eyes surveying, his small presence commanding, the room that lay before him. It had taken Coutts a quarter of a century to propel himself to that table and he was shrewd enough to savour its significance.

He knew that within a few months of his second coming to the capital — he had been Lester Pearson's appointment secretary from 1963 to 1966 — people had begun to say he was a political wizard, capable of concocting strategies that would have taxed the ingenuity of Jack Pickersgill in his prime. In a way, Coutts's devotion to Liberalism was very much like Pickersgill's. He was a party man, first, last, and always. He served Liberal prime ministers because he believed in Liberalism. It was almost as though he had encompassed the party's past, sponged up its primordial lessons, and turned them into personal truths.

Outside the concentric circles of the Canadian elite, he was very little known before he came to Trudeau's office, though the second year he was in town, journalists filing background reports from Ottawa who were accustomed previously to attributing rumours of intra-party deals to "the prime minister's chief honcho, Senator Keith Davey," took to writing sentences that began, "The prime minister's closest political advisers, Keith Davey and Jim Coutts, are known to have urged him..." Inside the party itself, Coutts's name began to be mentioned more often than Davey's as the arch expediter, the man operating in the vortex of power and operating surpassingly well. Some scenes were telegraphed along the Liberal information exchange: Coutts conducting the search for Margaret Trudeau the weekend she ran away from home with the Rolling Stones and gave her Mountie escort the slip; Coutts meeting secretly with Jack Horner, the Alberta MP, when he was skittish as a broodmare about leaving the Conservative Party for a seat on the Liberal front bench, promising a Senate seat if all went wrong at the next election and a cabinet portfolio in the meantime.

Coutts, Coutts, Coutts. How did he get to that banquette in the Château? What did his success mean?

Coutts was in his late thirties when he came to work for Trudeau, but his looks remained remarkably boyish so that it was possible to imagine him easily as an undersized, clear-eyed, rosy-cheeked fourteen-year-old, riding his bicycle down a side street in his hometown of Nanton, Alberta (population 1,100), on that idle summer Sunday in 1952 when the direction of his life was set. He had stopped to gaze over a hedge at the guests enjoying a backyard breakfast in honour of the Alberta Liberal leader, Harper Prowse. The hostess told him to "get off that bike and come on in, you hear, Jimmy! Harper's going to speak." Harper did speak, eloquently, about the miracles of eternal progress, the importance of "little people," and similar sacred touchstones of postwar Liberalism, and young Coutts was hooked for life by the romance of the moment and the force of the Liberal myth.

Politics for him was a ticket to the world outside Nanton, where the goings-on were even more fascinating, where he could stretch his mind and perfect his talents, where a face like that of a kid in a toothpaste commercial and a mind like Niccolò Machiavelli's were both formidable assets — especially when you knew instinctively the advantages to be wrung from one and the importance of concealing the other.

When he was in his teens and twenties, Coutts loved politicians and politicians loved him. He was adorable in those days, with his red-blonde hair and his china-blue peepers, getting up at riding association meetings to cut short the ramblings of his elders with his surefire jim-dandy ideas; volunteering to work for Joe McIntyre, a mine manager and riding boss, when he ran for the Liberals in the 1953 federal campaign and reaping publicity out of the fact that there he was, a campaign manager, at the tender age of fifteen; fetching up at the University of Alberta a few years later as Liberal prime minister in the model parliament, along with another boy from southern Alberta named Joe Clark, who was a member of the Tory Opposition. A few years after that, when Coutts was in law school, he got himself elected national president of the Canadian University Liberal Federation and began to form the cross-country network of friends who were to prove so important later in his life.

By the time the federal campaign rolled around in 1962, when the Liberals were all set to save the country from John Diefenbaker, Coutts had a law degree and the nomination to run as the candidate in his home riding of Macleod. He lost resoundingly but cheerfully. (In fair times and foul, good Liberals are supposed to be cheerful, and Coutts learned early on how to be a good Liberal above all else.) The next year Keith Davey, who liked Coutts's sunny style and reputed left-Liberal leanings, named him campaign chairman for Alberta, the job no one else wanted, mainly because the province had been hostile to Liberalism since 1921, when the United Farmers of Alberta had swept the Liberal Party out of power provincially — apparently forever. Again Coutts performed optimistically and well, helping elect Harry Hays, the former mayor of Calgary, who had been cajoled into running by Keith Davey almost against his will and certainly against his better judgement.

Later that spring, when Coutts was invited to work in Ottawa by Lester Pearson, he already had a reputation in Liberal circles as a wit, "a natural," "a great little guy." Few people realized how circumspect he had been at checking out what he was getting into and how determined he was to learn from every experience that came his way. He was twenty-five years old and he already knew the basic lessons about how to climb the ladder of success — "the greasy pole," as he was given to describing it — who you needed to know, how you ought to dress, the ways in which to ally yourself with other men on the move. He had asked his friend Tony Abbott, an easterner who had been working in Calgary when Coutts was articling in a law firm there, to introduce him to his father, Mr. Justice Douglas Abbott, one-time Minister of Finance in Louis St. Laurent's cabinet, long since gone to his reward on the Supreme Court's bench.

Before beginning his job in Pearson's office, Coutts had trotted along to consult the senior Abbott in his august, red-carpeted chambers about what to expect from political Ottawa. Abbott told him that a political assistant's job could be an invaluable training, but to keep his mouth shut and his eyes open and on no account to stay at that level in Ottawa too long. Two years preferably and certainly no more than three. After that, Abbott warned him, you're liable to turn into an Old Faithful, to get hooked on the trappings of power, and to be of diminishing use to the party and no use at all to yourself. Best to get out and make a stake in the business world and run for office when you had an established reputation of your own.

Coutts stayed three years in Pearson's office, and afterward he remembered them as the most valuable learning experience of his life. From the beginning he loved Pearson with his wonderful anecdotes about international affairs and cataclysmic events, his self-disparaging wit, his seemingly casual attitude to the power of his office, his liberalism. Pearson made Coutts feel like an instant insider and Coutts was able to watch the government system from the centre and to figure out how it worked. Weekdays, he sat in Pearson's outer office on the second floor of the east block, keeping the leader's appointment calendar, making friends with the powerful and the has-beens and the would-bes who waited there before passing to the ancient green baize doors on their way to talk to "good old Mike." Evenings he went to big cocktail parties and to little dinners and to have drinks in hotel bars, soaking up news of what was happening from middle-echelon civil servants, minor diplomats, press gallery reporters, Liberals from the outlands. He was friendly to everybody, from the political assistants in ministers' offices to the wives of his associates in the PMO, who found Coutts cosy, funny, and altogether — well, adorable was the word. He watched monetary crises and cabinet scandals and the rise and fall of the reputations of many men. He came to understand who did well at politics and who did badly and why. And he accomplished all this without making his elders uneasy or his contemporaries jealous. He was so popular, in fact, that when a television documentary called *Mr. Pearson* was made by Richard Ballentine at the urging of Pearson's press secretary, Richard O'Hagan, in 1964, nobody minded that Coutts seemed to figure prominently in frame after frame, though Pearson joked that it "looks as though my grandson is running the country."

By the spring of 1966, when the Pearson regime began to fall apart after the disappointment of the previous fall's election, Coutts had served his apprenticeship. He announced to his friends that he was not going to go back to Calgary to practise law since he had met the tough admission standards of the Harvard Business School and meant to amble down to Boston, Massachusetts, to get his M.B.A..

During the next two years at Harvard, Coutts made friends with other young and ambitious managerial men from all over the United States and Canada, went to seminars on corporate management and political power given by famous American academics — Henry Kissinger and Richard Neustadt among them — and finished his degree with creditable standing.

He then went to work briefly in New York City with the management consultancy firm of McKinsey & Company and, among other duties, took part in a study of the organization of John Lindsay's mayoralty office. In 1969, McKinsey sent him to Toronto. But functioning as a factotum in a U.S. branch plant office was not to Coutts's taste and he soon struck out on his own with half a dozen other young men, some of whom had also been to Harvard. They formed the Canada Consulting Group, which was described in its handsome brochure as a firm of "management consultants to the Private and Public Sectors."

The Canada Consulting Group had a "business philosophy" that was formed on Harvard principles. It set out to meet the needs of "top managers," to provide them with "strategies...to keep [their] organizations effective in a changing environment." In brief, they were hiring themselves out as troubleshooters to the men in the executive suites, advising a vice-president here and a deputy minister there, instigating analytical studies, proposing "concepts" that would help Canadian businessmen "turn a profit corner" and Canadian bureaucrats "actualize" their political masters' plans, using Harvard Business School jargon and Harvard Business School techniques to dazzle their clients a couple of decades after these notions had begun to wow them in New York and Washington.

He had a talent for other kinds of friendships, too. He loved the arts world and the media world and the glitter that went with both. His old friend Martin Goodman, who had been in the Ottawa press gallery in the 1960s, became the editor-in-chief of the *Toronto Star* in the 1970s and Goodman's wife, Janice, an interior designer, helped Coutts decorate his house. His old friend John Roberts, who had been an executive assistant to Maurice Sauvé during the Pearson years, had become MP for York-Simcoe and married Beverley Rockett, a Toronto fashion photographer, and Coutts did his Paul Martin Sr. and Mitchell Sharp imitations at their parties. Coutts went to the ballet and to the commercial art galleries downtown and filled his house with Canadian paintings.

And Coutts kept away from politics "like an addict keeping away from his drug," as he himself described it. Keith Davey was still his closest friend and he saw other Liberals, particularly John Aird, George Eliot, the party's advertising man, and John Nichol, John Roberts, and Tony Abbott, almost as often as he had of old. But essentially in the first Trudeau regime, Coutts's most important party connections — the self-described Pearsononian Liberals — "were out of the play," to use their euphemism. For four years the prime minister ignored them and they were lying low.

Within hours of absorbing the first shock of the Liberals' poor showing in the 1972 election, two Toronto lawyers, Jerry Grafstein and Gordon Dryden, were on the phone to each other urgently discussing what could be done "to save the party." Though neither of them had ever run for office, both were devoted to the Cause. Grafstein was thirty-seven, a successful communications lawyer, the kinetically energetic, chronically enthusiastic son of a poor immigrant Polish Jew who had owned a catering business in London, Ontario; Dryden was forty-eight, a dutiful tax expert working for the Unity Bank, known for his loquacity, his loyalty, and his horse sense. What they shared was a kind of mystical approach to Liberalism. They were not just true Grits but true believers. For them, the party was a vehicle for progress, a marvellously adaptable institution that was able to renew itself generation after generation for the greater good of Canadians. They were given to reminding their confreres in bad electoral times like these of Mackenzie King's rule of thumb that if you straddle the centre and lean to the left in Canada you will triumph. They believed implicitly that whenever the Liberal Party turned right — as they thought it had in the first Trudeau regime — it lost its way and its natural constituency. Grafstein and Dryden decided during that post-election conversation that something had to be done to save the party from the forces of reaction, and they set about convening a meeting of Liberal friends in Grafstein's office on Richmond Street West to decide just what that "something" should be.

Coutts once told Grafstein that it was his belief that there were 200 good men in Canada, something like the Twelve Just Men of Judaism expanded into a great big Liberal team, who would come together instinctively when Liberalism was in trouble in order to put it right. But they all thought of themselves as progressive and ultra-loyal Liberals, and they were all intensely pragmatic in their approach to politics.

They quickly came to a conclusion — worthy of Canada Consulting — that as a group they had three priorities: first, to re-establish their political presence in the party by devising a winning plan for the next campaign; second, to convince the prime minister that he needed the group; and third, to get Keith Davey named co-chairman of the National Campaign Committee. They were tough goals because of Trudeau's known disdain for professional politicians and because of Davey's deflated reputation as an organizer.

The senator was dragging with him, nearly a decade after the fact, the blame for Lester Pearson's failure to win a clear majority in three elections in the early 1960s. It was an article of the modern Liberal faith that the leader was never blamed for disasters; the leader had to be beyond reproach. St. Laurent was not blamed for 1957; it was C.D. Howe's fault for being so arrogant. Pearson was never faulted for the failures of 1962, 1963, and 1965; it was Keith Davey's fault or Walter Gordon's fault for not getting him a majority; they gave him the wrong advice, they let him down. This same attitude was put to work for Trudeau after the near-defeat of 1972. It was his advisers, Ivan Head, Jim Davey, and the rest of the technocrats in the PMO, who were blamed for having "isolated the PM from the political process," as if he were some passive object without free will.

Despite the drawbacks his reputation as a three-time near-loser represented, Keith Davey was still the best-known and best-liked member of the Toronto group, both inside and outside the party. He possessed what the American Senator Eugene McCarthy once described as "the perfect political mentality — that of a football coach, combining the will to win with the belief that the game is important." Even after eight years on the sidelines, Davey had maintained his network across the country among Liberals in the party's English-Canadian progressive wing.

As part of the same campaign to get Davey appointed, John Roberts, who had a temporary job in the PMO as a policy adviser, arranged a dinner for the Toronto group at 24 Sussex Drive. The Torontonians made their pitch, summing up what had gone wrong with the campaign just past ("no juice, no guts, no fight"), and pledging that they would work their fingers to the bone and their brains to the nub in the campaign to come ("lotsa juice, lotsa guts, lotsa fight") if the leader saw fit to use their talents and heed their advice.

After a few minutes of this rhetoric, Pierre Trudeau cast upon the assembled company his cold, cold eye and said in quizzical tones, "Look, when my friends and I came into politics in 1965, we had a fire in our bellies — we wanted certain things for Quebec. But I don't understand what motivates you guys. What's in it for you anyway?"

The Torontonians were furious: they felt they were being insulted, treated as though they were nothing but ward pols on the make. Abbott wanted to say, "Well, we had a fire in our bellies in the Second World War when you were riding around like a goddamn fool on a motorcycle wearing a Nazi helmet," and Grafstein felt like hollering, "Listen, I was a Liberal — and a *real* Liberal, when you are attacking Mr. Pearson in *Cité libre*." But they contained their anger, having promised themselves that they weren't there to score debating points, they were there to "save the party." Instead, they patiently explained to Trudeau what the party meant in their lives — the whole "vehicle for progress, circle of friends" number they did so well.

Trudeau was sceptical but he was also desperate. Having first succumbed to the deep shock that lasted for several weeks after the election, he had roused himself to go over the 1972 results riding by riding. He and his French-Canadian colleagues, particularly Marc Lalonde, were convinced they were the victims of an English backlash against French power. At the same time, Trudeau knew he needed expert political advice on how to win back the allegiance of English Canada. After many consultations and much thought, he finally decided in April 1973 that the Toronto group was the best vehicle available to provide that help, and he telephoned Keith Davey to ask him to be co-chairman with Jean Marchand of the campaign committee for the next election.

In the year following Davey's appointment, Trudeau and the Toronto group were fused into an electoral team under the senator's prodding, with Coutts figuratively hovering at his elbow, providing expert managerial advice. In the end, Trudeau learned their tricks and they learned his.

In May 1974, the minority Liberal government engineered its own defeat and was released, at last, from the grip of the NDP, which as a condition for its support in the Commons had forced the Trudeau cabinet into more progressive legislation in eighteen months than had been passed in the previous four years. The Toronto group let it be known to the press that the prime minister had not wanted an election at this time (which was partly true, since Trudeau disliked campaigns and never wanted an election) and pretended the party apparatus was in disarray.

In fact, the party was so geared up for the election that in the next eight weeks the Toronto Liberals were able to conduct the campaign of their dreams, the campaign that rivalled in their fevered minds the Kennedy campaign of 1960 for sheer professional style. Davey operated from his Senate office in Ottawa, directing and coordinating the national and provincial campaigns by telephone, with particular attention paid to Ontario, the crucial province, where Dorothy Petrie was in charge of the campaign committee. (Davey and Petrie functioned so well as a team that six months after the campaign was over, the senator left Isobel Davey, his wife of more than twenty years, and Mrs. Petrie left her husband, an accountant named Bill Petrie, and both sought divorces. They were married in December of 1978.)

To fill what he regarded as the campaign's other key appointment, the party's man travelling with the prime minister, Davey had told Trudeau that the best person would be Coutts. Coutts pleaded reluctance on the grounds that the job would take too much time away from his business, until Davey arranged to have Trudeau himself telephone to convince Coutts that his presence was crucially important.

"When I heard about that phone call I practically choked," another member of the Toronto group said later. "It was so much a Davey-Coutts caper. Deals within deals. Everything Coutts had observed over the months we had been negotiating with Trudeau convinced him that to have purchase with this guy you had to be bringing him something, not just asking him for something; you had to have your own base. Coutts didn't want to look eager, and he figured his return to a public role in politics could come later, when he had built up his financial stake, unless the conditions were absolutely right. At the same time, Davey knew that Trudeau was worried about having Coutts in such a key advisory position in case his own staff was disturbed. Finally, everybody was finagled out of their fears. Davey got what he wanted. Coutts got what he wanted. And it was seen as an all-around triumph."

Coutts had known Trudeau when he was Lester Pearson's parliamentary secretary and Coutts was still in the PMO as appointments secretary. But they were a long way from cronies, and, like most of his Liberal friends, Coutts was wary of Trudeau. But unlike most of them, Coutts knew how to make a personal connection with the prime minister. He spoke the language of technocrats, he had read the requisite American journals and the touchstone books, he had been to Harvard, he had travelled widely in Europe and Africa, he spoke some French. He was tough, he was witty, he was smooth. He was able to bring twenty years of political experience in English Canada to the job. And if Trudeau wanted to be cold-eyed, well, what the hell, Coutts would be cold-eyed too.

What Trudeau wanted was to win, and Coutts knew how to help him do it. He accompanied Trudeau by train, plane, limousine, and cable car for eight weeks, and he talked all day long. He talked to Trudeau's staff, smoothing over their feelings. Weekends, Coutts talked non-stop to Davey in the suite where they holed up in the Carleton Towers Hotel in Ottawa. Weekdays, Coutts talked to Davey back in Ottawa by telephone, as often as four times a day, describing what was going on, fitting in the "tactics" with the "strategy," i.e., what do we do today that will fit in with our overall game plan. Coutts talked to Liberals out in the country, that vast network of strivers and achievers who were giving their all lest the party lose and they lose with it. Most of all, Coutts talked to Trudeau, cajoling, persuading, informing, entertaining, reminding him at every stop who was important locally, what kind of one-line joke the crowd might respond to, which policy might attract notice from the press.

They made an odd pair, sitting at the front of the Liberals' chartered DC-9 campaign plane: Coutts with his fair hair over his coat collar, his face still rosy, his eyes as lively as a twenty-year-old's; Trudeau with his angular cheekbones, his expression opaque as a Chinese mandarin's, his mouth an austere line. Under Coutts's influence, Trudeau not only bounded onto platforms and made crassly political speeches every day, it got so that he actually enjoyed them. It seemed as though Coutts had made another friend, or at least an admirer of his considerable talents.

Looking back, Coutts decided that a crucial moment in their relationship came in the railroad station in Rimouski, Quebec. Very early in the campaign, after the Trudeau entourage had just finished an old-fashioned campaign-train swing through the Maritimes, Jean Marchand and Gérard Pelletier, Trudeau's old friends, climbed aboard the train to report to the prime minister, like barons reporting to their prince on how things were going in this part of his fiefdom. Coutts immediately rose to move into the next train car. Trudeau called out that he should stay, and turning to his confreres remarked that Jim spoke French and he needed his advice. Coutts knew that the Liberal French never talked to the Liberal English about strategy: to be in on the inside talk about Rimouski as well as Red Deer was a feeling of acceptance beyond his expectations. He also knew better than to give the slightest sign that he thought this was unusual. So he snapped his red galluses for good luck and casually sauntered back to sit down.

None of the other members of Davey's campaign team had roles quite as visible or as delicate as Coutts's, but they all ran full out, their collective enthusiasm fuelled in equal parts by their lust for victory, their fear of failure, and the fun they were having together. Grafstein conducted a lively ad campaign from Toronto through a newly formed organization called Red Leaf Communications. Dryden, as party treasurer, managed the flow of money. Policies were made by an ad hoc committee that included Jack Austin, a lawyer from Vancouver who was now Trudeau's principal secretary, and Eddie Rubin, Trudeau's former executive assistant from the justice department who had come back from practising law in Hong Kong to help the cause for a few months, as well as Martin O'Connell, Davey, and Coutts. The policies concocted were highly political in content, coordinated closely with what Keith Davey was hearing from his professional pollster, Martin Goldfarb of Toronto, who had been talking to the electorate for months, trying to gauge their concerns. During the course of the campaign, Trudeau promised easier home ownership for the aspiring middle class, more equality for women, fairer freight rates for the West, an industrial development strategy, and a broadened social security system for the aged — all "progressive" legislation that was designed to attract the left-wing vote from the NDP. When he was attacked in Calgary over oil prices, in Metro Toronto over the planned Pickering Airport, and almost everywhere on inflation, Trudeau responded brilliantly, turning aside his hecklers with strength, charm, and some elegantly elliptical evasions of his past record. The party's most popular English-Canadian cabinet ministers, John Turner, Eugene Whelan, and Bryce Mackasey, were persuaded to stump the country tirelessly on Trudeau's behalf and the French-Canadian cabinet ministers were persuaded to stay home. When a party worker mistakenly booked Jean

Chrétien to give a speech at a riding meeting in Ontario, she was repri-
manded: French power was being downplayed, though it was the raison
d'être of the leader's political life.

In brief, the Toronto group scripted a role for Trudeau that he, the
consummate actor, was able to play to perfection. They turned him
into something that they themselves could love: a fighting leader, a
gentle father, adoring husband, and all around "beautiful guy" — as his
bride of three years, Margaret Sinclair Trudeau, described him in a
speech in Vancouver. This was no arrogant intellectual, the Liberal
strategists told the Liberal troops and the bug-eyed press. This was a
misunderstood man, running as an underdog, a supporter of the little
man, fighting against the heinous wage-and-price-control policies of
Robert Stanfield, the Progressive Conservative leader, that awkward,
not-so-beautiful guy who was forecasting economic doom and who
wanted to freeze wages to forestall it. Tory times are bad times, remember! Liberal times are boom times! Trudeau cares!

The whole campaign drove home this theme. The standard Trudeau
speech, contrived to make him seem if not folksy at least accessible,
ridiculed Stanfield mercilessly for his honestly considered solutions to
the country's economic problems.

Since Trudeau's marriage in 1971 to the daughter of Jimmy Sinclair,
the Minister of Fisheries in St. Laurent's cabinet, he had been obsessively concerned that his wife not be exposed to press scrutiny. On a
state visit to Russia in May 1971, shortly after their wedding, his press
secretary, Peter Roberts, had instructed the accompanying journalists
on their first morning in Moscow that they were on no account to
speak to the bride, and this directive had held, with a couple of exceptions, ever since. But now Mrs. Trudeau, dressed as an artless young
mother in simple blouses, skirts, and earth shoes, was seen on the
television news almost nightly, speaking out on her husband's behalf,
shaking voters' hands, or publicly hugging her nursing baby, her sec-

ond son, Sacha, who was only six months old. Her presence inspired some of the most favourable prose ever printed about a Canadian public figure — prose that when read later, particularly in juxtaposition with Margaret Trudeau's own book about the period, *Beyond Reason*, sounded as much like Liberal propaganda as the party's own effusions. June Callwood, one of the country's best-known journalists, wrote in *Maclean's* that Margaret was "a perfectly preserved flower child" who listened at rallies "with an ethereal smile and rapt eyes full on her husband while he delivered his speeches," a woman whose "truthfulness and trust are like the artistry of a high-wire act, all guts and beauty." (This was written just six weeks before Mrs. Trudeau went to a celebrity tennis match in the U.S. and fell in love with a prominent politician she referred to as "my American," her attempted suicide with a kitchen knife at the prime minister's weekend retreat at Harrington Lake, and her subsequent admittance for severe depression to a hospital in Montreal.) "She was so flaky, even then, we were scared as hell every time she spoke during that campaign," one of the Liberals from Toronto said later, "but we were counting on her being mostly seen and not heard."

The Liberals drew on nearly every political axiom in their considerable repertoire, and their concerted effort worked. On July 8, the party won a majority, a victory far more telling than even the most optimistic among the original Toronto group had ever dared hope. For the first time in twenty years and eight campaigns, the Liberals ended a campaign with a higher percentage of the electorate's support than the polls had given them at the start.

A few days later, a triumphant dinner was staged at 24 Sussex Drive in honour of the "key players" in the campaign, the kind of celebration Trudeau had never held in his life but that Coutts and Davey believed in as crucial for maintaining morale. A group photograph was taken on the lawn behind the house, to be mounted later on the office walls of several of the English-Canadian Liberals, their hour of glory frozen in an eight-by-ten glossy and framed in aluminum, with Pierre and Margaret standing in the middle of the group, hands clasped in front of them, smiling demurely into the camera like a Presbyterian minister and his sweet young wife at a church elders' picnic.

After dinner, toasts were proposed and speeches made, contrived of inside jokes and fulsome flattery for all concerned, and finally Trudeau got to his feet amid loud applause. He paid tribute with becoming if unaccustomed modesty to the party that had just rescued him from the ignominy of a defeat that had seemed almost certain since 1972, and then told a story that proved to the assembled company that he had indeed been "humanized" by the campaign.

Trudeau said that his first experience of politics had been with his father, an ardent Conservative (Charlie Trudeau had been a supporter of the Union Nationale, as well, and had raised money for Maurice Duplessis, one of his classmates at law school, and for Camillien Houde, the mayor of Montreal). What he remembered best from the election nights of his childhood was his parents' friends damning the all-too-often-successful "Liberal machine" with righteous fury. These outbursts had so impressed him that until he was well into his teens, he had visualized the machine as a huge Rube Goldbergian device that whirred, clicked, and threw off sparks that had a diabolical influence on the electorate.

Above the loud laughter the story inspired, Jean Marchand called out, "But Pierre, haven't they showed it to you yet?" The Anglos in the room greeted that sally with even louder laughter. For them a "machine" was what had existed during the bad old days of C.D. Howe and Jimmy Gardiner, and what existed still in Quebec, though they would never have been so indiscreet as to say this in front of French Canadians. But *they* weren't a machine. *They* were a company of stout-hearted friends with admirably liberal ideas, and they left Sussex Drive that night on a wave of euphoria.

They felt that a new Liberal alliance between French and English had been forged. They thought they had taught Trudeau what Liberalism was all about and delivered him from the technocrats who held him captive in the PMO. They were certain he would henceforth run a government that would be consistently more "political" and therefore more "progressive," reflective of his real nature and of their lifelong beliefs in Liberalism.

What they did not realize was that Trudeau had never been the captive of anyone, that he had run his government from 1968 to 1972 in the way that he himself thought best, that his approach to people would remain elitist, and that, in fact, he did think of them as "a machine." They did not know either that the next five years would turn into a bad dream for the Liberal Party, that before those years were over they *would* behave like machine pols, and would argue desperately among themselves about whether the leader should be told that, for God's sake and the party's, he really must step down. But all that was far in the future. On that victorious July night in 1974, they all went happily home bathed in self-satisfaction, bilingual bonhomie, and the afterglow of the *vin mousseux*.

In their own triumph in post-election discussions, Coutts and Davey agreed that Trudeau now knew the importance of keeping in touch with the party and congratulated themselves on having set up a series of "structural interfaces" to make sure he would continue to consult Liberals on a regular basis. They also realized that Trudeau was never going to be what they called a "gut politician" in the way John Turner was, the kind of guy who just rings you up to shoot the breeze, nice and easy and how ya' doin' boy? Still vivid in their minds was the attitude Trudeau displayed in the early meetings they convened for him with party members in 1973, behaviour that had caused their old friend Gordon Edick — the man who sometimes functioned as their ambulatory "grassroots opinion" — to say Trudeau was "the most perverse s.o.b. I've seen in my life. As soon as you give one sign you don't agree with all his actions and ideas, he chews you up and spits you out."

To counteract Trudeau's tendency to treat party affairs and party members at best mechanically, at worst contemptuously, Davey and Coutts decided Trudeau should be persuaded to rely on the senator to be his "nose" in English Canada between elections as well as during them.

Trudeau made a number of decisions that left Davey uneasy: the appointment to the important position of clerk of the Privy Council of Michael Pitfield, whose friendship with Trudeau had already caused unfavourable comment in the press and grave mutterings in the bureaucracy; plans for a $200,000 swimming pool at 24 Sussex; an order for a new $83,500 Cadillac; permission for Margaret Trudeau to accept an invitation to visit Japan on a trip the press estimated would cost $20,000, to be paid for by a Hong Kong businessman trading with Canada; the gloomy statement in his traditional New Year's interview with the CTV television network to the effect that 1975 was going to be a bad year economically and Canadians would have to lower their expectations, remarks that didn't fit in with the extravagances of his own life. Trudeau had no feel for the English-Canadian outlook, Davey realized, and it couldn't be instilled in him during one or two conversations a week.

When the job of principal secretary in the Prime Minister's Office fell open in the summer of 1975, Davey was relieved. He advised Trudeau to hire Jim Coutts so he could benefit from hard-headed political advice on a daily basis. Davey felt Coutts would be able to affect the prime minister in a way he himself could not; after all, Davey said to their mutual friends, Coutts was bilingual, Coutts was an intellectual, Coutts knew what all those charts they had in the PMO were supposed to mean, and Coutts as a bachelor could be on the job sixteen hours a day.

Coutts himself was both apprehensive and intrigued. His plan had been to withdraw from politics entirely after the 1974 campaign while he built up a personal fortune that would be useful later on if he decided to launch a personal political career. He was earning close to $200,000 a year from his Canada Consulting partnership and his investment income, and his political activity was proving a financial disadvantage. Not only did it cut into his working time, but he was beginning to believe it hampered his firm. As much work as he and his partners could handle was available from the private sector, and he was sick of the carping he heard that government contracts came to Canada Consulting because of Coutts's political connections. After all, the firm had contracts with the Conservative government in Ontario and with the NDP in Saskatchewan, and recognition of his partners' competence went far beyond the Liberal Party.

On the other hand, nothing gave Coutts the heady feeling he had experienced during the 1974 campaign; after that, even the biggest business deal seemed oddly flat. He weighed the decision carefully, as he had been taught to at Harvard. "Do I want to commit the next time block of my life to this job?" he asked himself, and the answer came out Yes.

The list of men who had served as chief aide to Liberal prime ministers before Coutts took the job on in August 1975 was long and distinguished. But probably no one else ever came to the job with so clearly defined an idea of how it should be done.

What Coutts wanted above all was to run "a professional shop." He was not an intellectual, as his best friend, Senator Davey, fondly imagined. He was a Harvard M.B.A. What he was versed in was technique. Any task, however formidable, was "doable" (a favourite word) in Coutts's view, if only you could find the right technique. What he loved was not policy or principle, not causes or issues, but management. At this stage of his life, Coutts was no longer asking — as Davey still occasionally did —"Is this right?" He was asking, "Is this smart politics?"

Smart politics in 1975 was to bring to Pierre Trudeau's attention, in as proficient a manner as possible, the viewpoint of much of Canada, so another electoral victory would be "doable" once more. In taking on the principal secretary's job, Coutts didn't expect to be the prime minister's creature, but he didn't expect to be his friend either. The years in Pearson's office had taught him that if you're "worrying about where you fit into the PM's scheme of things, you're no good to yourself or anybody else." In the Pearson years there was what he called "a gashouse gang" quality to the PMO, everybody scrambling in undefined jobs with seemingly informal attitudes, waiting for Pearson to tell them how dependent he was on them to make his life bearable. "Help me, I need you," was the sentiment Pearson expressed countless times in countless ways, confident of the effect of his charm.

Coutts observed from conversations he had with Pearson's contemporaries that the prime minister had displayed this same attitude to the External Affairs crowd when he was undersecretary and then secretary in that department, and that now these same old buddies were of minor importance to him. Before he went to Trudeau's office he cannily decided, as he told an interviewer, that "You can't feed on your relationship with your boss; it puts you in bad shape as a person. People all over Ottawa — secretaries, executive assistants, policy advisers, feed on the great man, basking in his fame, making endless sacrifices for him, and getting their jollies from the little words of praise. As a consequence, they become defensive of the great man, protective of him, and they don't tell him the bad news. I'm never going to be like that."

The second thing he determined — and, in fact, a condition of his acceptance of the job — was that under his aegis the prime minister's office would be highly political, in fact as well as in theory. To make it so, he swiftly cut the staffs of the PMO's policy unit and regional desks, which he thought were impractical as concepts. Marc Lalonde had been concerned mainly with policy and with process when he was principal secretary from 1968 to 1972, and these remnants of his high-minded, theoretical approach to party politics had hung on during the disjointed 1972–1975 period.

The other formal change Coutts made as principal secretary was to set up a political planning committee to meet every Tuesday without fail from nine to ten o'clock in the morning with the inner cabinet (the same group of ministers who belonged to the all-important Planning and Priorities Committee of the Cabinet, which met Tuesdays at ten), plus officials from party headquarters and Keith Davey in attendance. The business of the political planning committee was to discuss from a tight agenda devised by Coutts the factors, large and small, that could affect the Liberals' chances of winning the next election.

The next election was primary in Coutts's mind the minute he arrived in Ottawa, even though in all likelihood it was probably three years away. News of fresh disasters left him unmoved in his dedication to this goal of a big electoral victory, despite the fact that the next eighteen months brought one crisis after another to the Liberal government.

In February of 1976, the Conservatives held a leadership convention and won a round of favourable publicity, a boost in the public opinion polls, and a new leader in the person of Joe Clark, Coutts's old antagonist from the University of Alberta, who was presented as a sterling young man with a sterling young wife, a law student named Maureen McTeer. To make matters worse for the Liberals, their own leader's wife, Margaret, was in the news again after a brief period of calm while she had borne her third son, Michel. This time, the response was not nearly as favourable to her unorthodoxies as it had been before. During a parliamentary winter recess in January 1976, Margaret accompanied Trudeau on a trip to Latin America, impulsively sang a ditty she had composed at a state dinner in Venezuela, to the amazement of the assembled dignitaries, flirted outrageously with Fidel Castro in Cuba, appeared at official functions brassiere-less in a cotton T-shirt and jeans, and, when she returned to Ottawa, telephoned a hotline radio show to defend her actions between the show's commercials and crank callers.

As the winter and spring months passed, Mrs. Trudeau openly defied her husband's obsession with privacy, appearing one night at the Press Club on Wellington Street in Ottawa to order a drink and began a now-familiar "let's-be-soulmates-and-chat" act with the men at the bar. When the prime minister appeared to take her home, she exhorted the bartender to "Give the man a soda pop — that's about his speed." Stories about her bizarre behaviour surfaced all over the country. Old friends from her university days at Simon Fraser in Vancouver talked openly about her taste in hallucinogens. Party regulars began to whisper to one another that she was a manic depressive who would not take the drugs prescribed for her illness.

As if the worsening economic situation and the disastrous state of the leader's marriage were not enough trouble for the Liberals, other serious problems quickly arose. The summer of 1976 brought a bitter air strike by the country's anglophone air controllers when their French-Canadian colleagues' demands for bilingualism in the skies set off open English-Canadian hostility toward the government's whole bilingual program. Then Jean Marchand quit the cabinet and so did Bryce Mackasey, Bud Drury, Mitchell Sharp, and James Richardson, resignations made for varied reasons but that, together with Turner's departure of the year before, fed the public belief that Trudeau could not get along with people, particularly strong-minded English-speaking people. What's more, it appeared that he didn't care, either about the country's economic difficulties or the views of his colleagues. Instead of showing the restraint he had called for from Canadians, he set off on a trip to Yugoslavia, Jordan, Israel, and Italy with Margaret, which infuriated all those who had listened conscientiously to his adjurations to tighten their belts. It seemed to Liberals in those years that the Trudeaus were always travelling, to the sun, to the ski slopes, to the yachts of the international rich. Coutts kept saying that for a man of his wealth, sophistication, and onerous responsibilities, Trudeau travelled very little. But nobody bought the line. "Who does he think he is," English Canadians were asking one another, "some kind of maharajah?"

Finally, in September 1976, the cumulative result of the Liberals' problems hit home. The party's popularity fell to an alarming low in the Gallup Poll; only 29 percent of decided voters said they would vote Liberal if an election were held then, as against 47 percent who said they would vote Progressive Conservative. (At the same time, 40 percent could not name the new Progressive Conservative leader, confirming what every shrewd Grit thought he knew anyway: that the hostility was not to the party but to Trudeau.) In the wake of that poll, the prime minister set out on a fence-mending tour of Atlantic Canada to explain his economic measures and encountered crowds unprecedented in the ugliness of their hostility to him. At a service-club lunch, the audience refused to stand when he finished speaking; in one crowd there was a placard with a swastika on it, in another a homemade sign reading, "We need Trudeau like we need VD." Days later, the Liberals were trounced in two by-elections: in Newfoundland, a former Liberal turned Conservative named John Crosbie won the riding of St. John's West; and in Ontario, Jean Pigott, a woman who managed a large bakery business, won John Turner's old seat, Ottawa-Carleton. After these results were announced, Jerry Grafstein got on the phone to Keith Davey to say hotly, "We're going down the tubes, man. What's the matter with Coutts?"

Coutts felt there was nothing the matter with Coutts. He refused to lose his composure. If we just do our best, keep our cool, and wait it out, Coutts told Davey, Grafstein, and whoever else asked, our luck will change.

When the Liberals' luck did change, with a surprise election of the separatist Parti Québécois in Quebec in November 1976, Coutts didn't flicker an eyelid or murmur an "I told you so." He simply proceeded to advise Trudeau to press the Liberals' advantage as the party of national unity. Within the next several months, Trudeau made a series of major speeches on Canadian federalism, including one before the U.S. Congress in Washington that caused an infusion of praise from President Jimmy Carter, Vice-President Walter Mondale, senators Edward Kennedy and George McGovern, and several important American political columnists and newspaper editorialists. Canadians basked in this praise as though it were the Florida sun. The Americans said he was a great man; it must be so. Even in the previously hostile press, Trudeau was described as a champion of confederation.

With this flurry of positive action, the opinion polls began to rise. Everything seemed to be going in the Liberals' favour in 1977, even the final "freedom trip" of Margaret Trudeau, who ran away from home in March to Toronto and New York to be with the Rolling Stones at concerts and other kinds of capers. After the Trudeaus were formally separated in May, Trudeau was the beneficiary of waves of sympathy from the electorate for his dignity in handling the situation; his emotional pain in the spring of 1977 altered his face and turned him into a romantic figure once more. He was no longer the arrogant s.o.b. He was the wronged husband, the faithful father, the hero felled by domestic sorrow of the kind that could be readily understood.

Coutts and Davey began to make plans for an early election. They paid Martin Goldfarb to do an extensive survey of the electorate in June and assess attitudes toward issues. They discussed a western strategy (in which the recruitment in March of Jack Horner was only the first step); they worked hard at attracting new candidates in

Ontario to replace the anglophone ministers who had departed. They even discussed what would be the best seat for Coutts to contest when he made his first bid for elected office since his hopeless try in 1962. Alberta beckoned him home; visions of Jimmy Gardiner, the Minister of Agriculture who had held the West for Mackenzie King, danced in his head. But in the end reason prevailed and Parkdale, a solidly Liberal seat in Toronto, was provisionally chosen.

Despite all these favourable indicators, Trudeau refused to go to the country in a September election as Davey and Coutts urged. At a press conference he said calling an election would look like opportunism, and his caucus backed him up in this opinion. In the quiet of his office he told Davey and Coutts he had not yet been able to come to terms with the failure of his marriage. He wanted time to think and to be with his children; he couldn't face the demands of the campaign.

Coutts and Davey were daunted, since Goldfarb had warned them that the Liberals' high standing in the polls was possibly temporary. But their chagrin was soon swallowed. They went back to politics as usual, figuring with their usual optimism that this was one good moment for the party; another would come to them in time. Davey set out to make greater efforts in readying his campaign team and his campaign strategy. Coutts agreed that he would stay on in the PMO and forget about winning a nomination, that he would work at his contacts inside and outside the government with constant energy and subtle strokings. He knew that he had become the ne plus ultra of principal secretaries, the PM's man beyond compare.

He did not know that by the time the long-awaited election was finally called in 1979, what he had persisted in thinking of as "sound management of ongoing problems" would be seen by reporters in the press gallery as plain trickery. That his politics would be described as the politics of manipulation. That he would be called cynical, Machiavellian, and worse. That he would be so intensely disliked within Liberal

Party ranks that some people who had been his friends for fifteen years, who had admired his managerial skills enormously when he first displayed them in the PMO, would start to say that he had been altered alarmingly by the power of his position. That Liberals by the hundreds would believe he had become the captive of all those remote, snobbish, apolitical elitists who had surrounded Pierre Trudeau from the beginning — people who, in the collective party mind, were not really Grits at all.

Endpiece

WHAT GLENN GOULD could do with the keys of his piano, Christina did with the keys of her typewriter: leave you gasping at her inventiveness and the mastery of her medium. "What Won't Appear in My Next Paradise" introduced me to her as a writer five years before our first marriages disintegrated. I had asked her to write one of the essays for *Visions 2020*, the volume I was editing to celebrate the 50th anniversary of the *Canadian Forum*. Our contributors were invited to offer their vision of Canada fifty years in the future — 2020. In this brief essay, you have one last sample of Christina's flair and feminism, her wit and her wisdom. It was written at the zenith of her career as a journalist, but it also marked its end. I read it aloud to the friends who joined our daughters at her wake, and *Maclean's*, the magazine that had run her first piece of journalism in 1957, appropriately published it as her last in 2005.

It's the kind of writing that made her father, with whom she had a difficult relationship, give her the only compliment she remembered ever receiving from him. Responding to a profile she had done on a fellow Irish-Canadian, the Liberal Minister of Labour, Bryce Mackasey, he said, "I wished it would never end." For the many of her generation who also wished she would never stop writing her original, entertaining, acute, engrossing, provocative, even devastating critiques, this tour de force provides the end to this celebration of the writing of Christina McCall.

— SC

THIRTY-FIVE

What Won't Appear in
My Next Paradise[32]

**From *Visions 2020: Fifty Canadians in Search of
Their Future*, Stephen Clarkson, ed. (Hurtig, 1970)**

WHEN YOU GET right down to it — staring at the blank paper, plumbing
the depths of the even blanker imagination, reviving forgotten fantasies left over from world-beating yapfests in college common rooms — it
soon becomes obvious that the postulation of a paradise for women of
my age and general persuasion is pretty bloody difficult, if not to say
impossible.

For I belong to that nameless generation of the 1950s, that uncom-
mitted company of the cool who were born in the years just before the
Second World War: educated in the expectation of equality, confronted
by the realities of domesticity and the double standard, too young to
have been gulled into believing in the feminine mystique (as was the
generation of the 1940s, for whom happiness was supposedly a man,
four children on three levels, Birks sterling, real pearls and a grand
slam at the Victoria College Alumnae annual bridge tournament) but
too old and —oh! shameful admission — too liberal to be affected

by the Sisters, Unite-Against-the-Capitalist-Imperialist-Phallic-Society! militancy of the new women's liberation movements.

If you add to the uncertainties of my whole generation my own specific experience — too many dues paid to feminism in the form of five years spent on a women's magazine writing such mind-blowers as "Why Can't We Treat Married Women Like People?" and "Working Wives Are Here to Stay!" — you realize that it would be paradise enough for me if by A.D. 2020 people had simply stopped talking about women as though we were a national problem like the Indians and the surplus of wheat.

In brief, it's far easier to describe what my utopia won't be like than what it will, and to say that everything will be groovy half a century from now if:

- All women's organizations, including women's institutes, women's press clubs, associations of women electors, women's Christian temperance unions, and all Old Girls' associations everywhere (as well as all schools that produce Old Girls) either have ceased to exist or have amalgamated with similar men's groups so that the Elks and the Eastern Stars, the Shriners and the Daughters of Empire will lie down together like the lion and the lamb, donning their fezzes and reciting their creeds in blissful asexual community.

- Betty Friedan and her ladies of NOW are all sleeping securely underground in some corner of Westchester County, happy in the knowledge they were lowered there by female gravediggers earning union scale; New Feminist Abigail Rockefeller is clipping coupons in the First National City Bank of New York, having long since abandoned the karate chop, test-tube babies, and Freedom Now!; Pierre Elliott Trudeau and Julia Verlyn LaMarsh belong to the same branch of Swingles International; the quintessential New

Woman, Baby Jane Holzer, has married the quintessential New Man, Andy Warhol, and Lionel Tiger is spending his declining days in a leatherbound chair in the McGill Faculty Club, cackling occasionally and murmuring constantly, "Males bond . . . males bond . . . males bond."

- No one ever says, "She thinks like a man," "She's a person in her own right," or "A toast to the ladies, God bless 'em," or talks about penis envy, castration complexes, momism, and a confusion of roles, or uses such phrases as "my better half" or such words as poetess, sculptress, authoress, and housewife. (It's a funny thing about the word "housewife." I've seen it turn sweet and reasonable women into sullen shrews. A famous Canadian writer-editor not very long ago interrupted a dinner-table conversation about inflation he was having with my husband to say kindly to me, "Aren't you complaining about the price of chops like every other housewife in the country?" I wanted to shout, "Listen, I'm no housewife. I'll admit to being a hundred other things: schemer, dreamer, sloth, wife, lover, mother, sometime journalist, one-time correspondent, part-time char, lapsed Presbyterian, disenchanted humanist. But not a housewife. Never!" I didn't do it, though. I figured it would show a confusion of roles.)

- No dear friend of mine — and no dear enemy either — will ever be found in my living room complaining that she isn't getting ahead in journalism/academe/television/politics "Just because I don't have b—s." (Come to think of it, in a well-ordered paradise it will not be necessary to print "balls" as "b—s.") Instead, women will be able and willing to admit that in this best of all possible meritocracies, they aren't getting ahead because they're chronically lazy, hopelessly ill-educated, secretly disinterested, or victims of a widespread prejudice against people over five foot eight.

- Publishers have abandoned forever magazines devoted exclusively to fashion, food, royalty, and your child, and no serious newspaper editor thinks that in publishing a whole section of cooking and marketing trivia he's taken care of the interests of his female readers. This will mean that I'll have to give up collecting dimwitted headlines like "Whom Will Prince Charles Marry?" "Don't Be Fooled about Italian Onions" and "Spend the Summer under a Big Black Sailor," a line that appeared once years ago in a fashion spread about hats and is still one of the four sentences I mutter to myself when I'm in total despair. (The other three sentences come out of *Paradise Lost,* madam, so hold your snotty remarks.)

Lest this appear entirely negative, I'll finish in solemnity by stating that I do have a few positive and not entirely improbable ideas about what the next fifty years ideally will bring to women. I hope that by A.D. 2020 women will not have to consider choosing *between* being wives/mothers and career women; that it will be possible and seem natural for them to be both (or one or the other) without feeling guilty or unfeminine; that employers and educators will provide courses and jobs so that girls can get married early, work or learn part-time while their children are young, without the worry and hardship such arrangements now impose, and return full-time to work later if they want to ; that we will have a society that, as Bruno Bettelheim said, "can afford to accommodate itself to the real intellectual and emotional needs of people, not just to the demands of economy and efficiency or of ancient prejudices"; a society in which women aren't and don't even feel like an oppressed minority, a society in which they are truly equal to men. But not, of course, the same.

After Words

PART ONE: THE JOURNALIST'S JOURNEY

1   In the late 1950s, talented young women often were hired to do research for established writers on magazines such as *Time*, *Newsweek*, and *Maclean's*. Rarely did they graduate and become feature writers, who were almost all male.

   Christina McCall must have shown exceptional promise to be given this *Maclean's* feature on Viola MacMillan, the extraordinary president of the all-male Prospectors and Developers Association in Canada. Published when she was only twenty-two, the profile demonstrates her ability to master the subject and in graceful, incisive prose touched with a sense of humour, entice the reader.

   Soon after this, she applied for a job at *Chatelaine*, where I hired her as our staff writer. She proved herself a skilled writer on a wide variety of subjects and developed the distinctive voice and style for which she became famous.

   — Doris Anderson, former editor, *Chatelaine*

2   Reading this article reminded me of a story Christina loved to tell about Ken Whyte, who, recently arrived from Alberta to edit *Saturday Night*, queried a line in a profile she was writing about a woman who "probably has a Balenciaga somewhere in her closet." Deep in his own brand of Prairie guyness, Ken asked whether this was some kind of Italian assault rifle.

Christina's wry reflections on manliness from a quarter-century ago display her usual blend of gimlet-eyed observation and deft reference — from the sociologists Max Weber and Margaret Mead to hockey star Derek Sanderson and gay biker clones. But there is also a warmth and humour that few writers today could hope to bring to the subject. Here, presciently, on the cusp of our present gender confusion, she celebrates the allure of virility while puncturing its pretensions. It's a crooked tribute, maybe, but the piece even manages to make the old CBC-TV star Bruno Gerussi seem plausible as a sex symbol.

— Mark Kingwell, writer on politics and culture
and professor of philosophy

3 This light column contains two heavy insights about our obsession with cultural fads. First, trend-spotting is always a form of disguised status competition. Second, it perverts the realm of the political by presenting the consequences of this competition (namely, the constant turnover in consumer products) as a form of political activism.

Christina McCall notes that mag-cult is aimed primarily at women, preying on their insecurities, a phenomenon that has only worsened in recent years, being amplified by such televisual heirs as *Sex and the City* and *Desperate Housewives*. It is small consolation to note a growing gender equality in this domain: the mag-cultists have taken over the men's side of the magazine racks as well.

— Andrew Potter, commentator on social trends
for *Maclean's* magazine

4 When I came from the West to be editor of *Saturday Night* in 1994, one of my objectives was to engineer the return to its pages of Christina McCall, whose political reportage had been an inspiration to me early in my career. Christina eventually did accept a commission, but I wasn't thrilled about her choice — basically a book review. Worse, she had chosen a political book by Ron Graham, another former *Saturday Night* writer, a stalwart of the Toronto liberal media elite. Journalists, I knew, are seldom forthright about members of their own club.

My worries were misplaced. Christina wasted little space on Graham's book, and where she treated it directly her language was so uncompromising that the old *Saturday Night* crowd was left gasping. In the end, the piece wasn't a review so much as this essay on the practice of insider journalism, a craft to which Christina had devoted much of her career and for which she had developed the highest professional standards. She demanded these of herself and expected them of her peers.

— Ken Whyte, editor, *Maclean's* magazine

PART II: CANADIAN SOCIETY: THE LOW AND THE HIGH

5 The Nova Scotia mine disaster of 1958 captured headlines, as urgent efforts finally rescued forty-six miners while seventy-five died — trapped over two miles underground.

Eight months later, Christina McCall took her readers back to Springhill to visit the "people who endured that soul-tearing time." With her unique empathy, she got inside their lives and their sense of community, recording the anguish of both the survivors and the families of those who did not make it out alive. The miners she talked to were brutally frank about their limited choices in providing for their families and maintaining their Maritime way of life.

Christina's prose is like a symphony of which she was both composer and conductor. To appreciate its beauty and power, her writing needs to be read carefully as she takes us on a timeless visit to an indomitable Nova Scotia community that refused to give up.

— Libby Burnham, Maritimer, lawyer, and
PC adviser to premiers and party leaders

6 Premier Peter Lougheed presided over a secretive, self-contained, business-oriented government, which defended its rights against real and perceived challenges from the federal government — a political ethos Christina McCall memorably defined as Aggressive Conservatism.

We can see how many of the psychological continuities of the contemporary Alberta experience — deep pride laced with the lingering sense of insecurity that the new oil wealth produced — had instilled a state of mind among the province's population and in its political and business elite, as they attempt to transcend the boom and bust cycle of their petroleum-based economic expansion.

— Toby Zanin, political researcher

7 Amidst the energy crisis of the late 1970s, Canadians were mystified that an international consortium of multibillion-dollar companies was floundering in

its bid to gain Ottawa's approval for a pipeline up the Mackenzie Valley that would tap the oil and gas riches of the Far North.

Telling her story as the personal tragedy of Bay Street boy wonder William Wilder, Christina McCall foresees the demise not only of his megaproject but of the business establishment, which was being eclipsed by rival stakeholder groups representing Native peoples, environmentalists, and institutional investors at odds with corporate Canada.

Through her pen we observe the twilight hour of a system in which decisions shaping the economy were made by Upper Canada College Old Boys over a discreet lunch at the Toronto Club. Wilder confided he had led a "sheltered" existence — one of many surprising revelations from a leading member of a business caste unaccustomed to speaking candidly about its inner torments.

McCall's account is strikingly relevant — when a pipeline is again being projected for the Mackenzie — in explaining how even today's powerful CEOs can be brought down by their own arrogance or insularity.

— David Olive, business and political affairs writer, *Toronto Star*

8   Some interviews date quickly, but the best begin by asking important questions and follow with careful writing so that the exchange remains fresh and relevant in its recounting. Christina McCall's reflections on meeting Jane Jacobs fits this model.

Jane's voice, which became so clear in Toronto in the thirty years following the publication of this profile, rings true today. Her warnings of what could damage the city — the levelling of old buildings and the proliferation of suburbs — have proved prophetic. Recommending that we rely on "Canadian common sense" may not feel entirely reassuring, but the need to provide local economic opportunities for immigrants is on the money, as is her call for neighbourhood action. And think how widespread today is the sentiment that returning home to Canada after travelling abroad is something of an escape from the insane asylum.

— John Sewell, civic activist, former mayor of Toronto

9   This sensitive and witty examination of the mid-1970s campaign to rid Toronto's Yonge Street strip of porn and stripped-down massage parlours has striking resonance today — with some characters in the drama actually still active in local politics.

Christina McCall's article portrays a Conservative government that, wanting to strengthen its electoral chances, was suddenly willing to give Toronto's leaders, and their apparently impotent police, the capacity to save the city from its "moral turpitude." If this doesn't remind us of more recent campaigns that play on fears about law, order, and moral decline — and of the police's concomitant demands for greater powers — it should.

— David Rayside, University of Toronto
political scientist and gay activist

10   I have just read this "Requiem" for the first time. The piece is of course brilliant — and so like Christina! It vividly brought back to me her amazing capacity to look and understand so much. See how, from one hilarious vignette, she encapsulates the passing of an era. Stylish and intelligent herself, she lays bare the tyranny of Good Taste and the revolt of the new order.

In September 1971, in my thirties, I was working full tilt in the Paris fashion world. I was travelling back and forth to New York, never quite understanding the organized look of those "slick" American ladies — so rigidly, perfectly "pulled together." In Europe we spoke of "having style," not "being slick." Here, Christina puts her finger on it: a "marriage of American insouciance with European insolence."

And now, in my sixties — a "ghost of slick"? — I still listen to Cole Porter, sip champagne from a tulip glass, wear spike heels, go to the "flicks," eat an occasional œuf en gelée, but you'll be happy to know, dear Christina, that I also "let it be!" Good taste is boring — style is not. You had it.

— Krystyne Griffin, jewellery designer

11   What a luxury it is to slip into the prose of one of Canada's finest journalists. Christina McCall's stylish writing and crisp insights are as timeless and classic as, well, one of the smart suits from Creeds, whose opulent spirit still haunts Canada's richest retail strip, Bloor Street, from Yonge west to Avenue Road. McCall's opening scene is animated by the chatter of the women — married, kept, or salaried — who went there to drop a secretary's weekly wage on designer dresses, and her theme is familiar: the tension between rigid tradition and passion. Here, the passion is for spending money, and at the story's centre is Eddie Creed, a Jew, the Toronto-born son of a Ukrainian immigrant, who

both served and epitomized those new Torontonians who were unafraid to spend big time on flash and style.

McCall's lovely writing is as sensual and exuberant as her subjects. But because she is, as she confesses, "cursed with a reflective turn of mind," she also understands that the social changes she writes about mean "the loss of the work-scrimp-save syndrome that gave the city and the country its underlying principle." In the end, rather than giving us a report on a store, she has composed a sociological opera, one that ends on a deeply thoughtful note.

— Val Ross, *Globe and Mail* arts reporter, former managing editor of the *Globe's Toronto Magazine*

PART III: FEMINIST IN ARMS

12 Meeting Christina McCall in the 1960s, when I was a young French professor at Ottawa's Carleton University, was one of the happiest moments of my life. Already a brilliant journalist, Christina was also beautiful and elegant. She had a marvellous face with a white complexion, lively eyes full of curiosity, and a genuine interest in people. I loved her voice, both soft and profound. She was witty and at times ironical, hating mediocrity.

Our understanding was immediate. We spoke about everything: our lives, feminism, our country, federal politics, of which Christina was a wise connoisseur, and Pierre Trudeau.

We shared an enduring passion for literature and in Ottawa, Toronto, and later in the hills near Florence, we discussed the writings of those she admired: Northrop Frye and Robertson Davies, Mavis Gallant and Alice Munro, Marie-Claire Blais and Réjean Ducharme. She was curious about my deep friendship with Simone de Beauvoir and Jean-Paul Sartre, and we often compared the situation of women in Canada and Europe.

Normally discreet about herself in public, here she describes a young girl confronting a path full of obstacles and reveals the resilient woman she was to become. This fidelity to herself and to those she loved radiated through her writings as through her life. She was my truest friend.

— Madeleine Gobeil-Noël, former Director of Art and Cultural Life, UNESCO in Paris

13 As a young woman in the 1960s, I remember gobbling up Christina McCall's magazine articles, because she wrote with such authority. Here was a fresh voice broadening the way we thought about politics and speaking so perceptively to our own concerns. I had no idea she was just my age: she had the capacity to see through received ideas and the brilliance to take them further. With clear but sympathetic eyes, she nailed women's self-subversions and deep fears, while suggesting through her humour and verve that we could overcome.

She regretted that the official Report of the Royal Commission on the Status of Women did not give voice to the dramatic testimony heard from women all over the country during the Commission's hearings. Whereas the report subverted its own impact by speaking in bureaucratic generalities, Christina's vivid prose, eloquence, and passion helped convince lawmakers to take seriously such issues as child care and maternity leave.

— Wendy Blair, National Public Radio producer,
based in Washington, D.C.

14 The key point in this gutsy argument is that women need to change the way they think about work. They need to recognize that the only training that will guarantee their future is their own. This is not a counsel against supporting a spouse; it is a warning against the dangers of sacrificing one's own capacity for financial independence to the expectations of marriage. Dignity comes not from refusing alimony but from not needing it.

— Kim Campbell, former
prime minister of Canada

15 "This new pervasive grief": with one devastating phrase, Christina not only captures the agony of her marital split, but also the fact that divorce was indeed becoming commonplace. Still, that did not lessen its trauma, including "a sense of awful loss, a questioning of self."

Who could say it better today? Great personal journalism must deftly tack between the universal and the particular. Christina succeeded here, allowing us a glimpse of her own pain (with not a shred of self-pity), a rueful look at divorce as a social phenomenon, and, finally, a hopeful declaration of her new independent spirit — and her proudly reclaimed name.

— Judith Timson, author, magazine journalist,
and columnist with the *Globe and Mail*

16   When Pierre Elliott Trudeau referred to women as "babes" in a 1970 quip, Christina McCall refused to smile along with a nation enthralled by a playboy prime minister famed for his "love" of women. Instead, she deftly delineated, example by example, how the throwaway line was symptomatic of the calcified categorization of women in Ottawa, a code of subtle put-downs that forestalled female advancement — noble Royal Commissions on the Status of Women notwithstanding.

Decades later, McCall's incisive column remains relevant, disconcertingly so. The fossilized attitudes and double standards she exposed persist, and her voice resonates still, a wake-up call from the past to the present.

— Anne Kingston, senior writer with *Maclean's* magazine

17   Almost twenty-five years have passed since Christina McCall wrote this article, and on the surface much has changed. Women have held positions from prime minister to clerk of the Privy Council. Indeed, women playing senior roles in elected office, in the public service, and as political staff has begun to seem normal.

She claimed that women don't band together to achieve political power by creating and sustaining loyalty groups that offer them mutual support in the long haul to power. Even if we did so, this is still a world in which a group composed entirely of women would be dismissed as marginal. Large numbers of women have now been elected or worked as senior political staff in all major political parties. Most belong to mixed-gender loyalty groups from which will likely come the next female prime minister and the one after her.

However, one cannot assume much about our political values. Women politicians are not necessarily concerned about the condition of women as a group. Women's interests are just as divided by class, social position, race, and sexual identity as are men's.

— Chaviva Hošek, former minister in the government of Ontario
and policy adviser to Jean Chrétien

PART IV: THE DRAMA OF POLITICS

18   There could hardly be a better example than this of Christina McCall's acute perceptions of politics, her feminism, her brilliant observations about social change, her humour, and her thoughts about the nature of Canada.

This personal analysis of the fraught political tensions during what is referred to by some historians as Canada's forgotten decade — from 1957 to 1968 — eloquently captures one of its great paradoxes. John Diefenbaker and Lester Pearson were profoundly different prime ministers in temperament, upbringing, and political perspective, but together they made indispensable contributions to the significant social progress achieved in that period.

— Adam Chapnick, historian of postwar
Canadian diplomacy

19   Reading this deft piece, one is struck by how little has changed since 1945, never mind since 1985. The issues that George Ignatieff — Michael's ambassador father — grappled with postwar still dominate the headlines today: India and Pakistan, the Koreas, the Middle East, and, hovering over all, the baleful genie of nuclear proliferation.

More than two decades after this piece was published, Canadians continue to pine for a mythical past when the country was seen as a "middle power." Christina McCall presents this as an age of naivety, admirable if unavailing.

The salad days of the "Ottawa men" and of the United Nations — roughly, from VE day to Suez — coincided for a reason. The UN many now recall so fondly was not unlike the old Department of External Affairs: the "right sorts" were in charge, principally eastern seaboard Americans who were WASPy if not actual WASPs.

Nostalgia for the anglophile elite of the old Canada is the common, if unstated, element in such elegies, but Christina's prose punctures some of its pretensions.

— Andrew Coyne, columnist for *Maclean's*

20   The first time I encountered Christina McCall was during several long sessions in the editorial offices of the *Globe and Mail*, which had asked her to interview a number of Canadians about the future of our country for a series of feature articles she then wrote.

I was quickly struck by how well prepared she was, how perceptive and witty, how quick to get to the point when others would have been pontificating or meandering. It was only later that I realized what a truly special person she was, what a brilliant researcher and talented writer.

Walter Gordon was a good friend, and in some ways my mentor. He was also one of the bravest and most principled men I've ever met, defying his peer group, standing up for what he believed, regardless of the political or social costs. Christina's *Saturday Night* article captured him perfectly.

— Mel Hurtig, publisher of the *Canadian Encyclopedia*

21 Today the Waffle is a fading memory, its legacy more problematic than Christina thought. Pierre Trudeau's begrudging economic nationalism of the 1970s was followed by the exuberant continentalism of Brian Mulroney.

I prefer to think of the Waffle as part of a fiercely patriotic milieu that included the budding writer Margaret Atwood, the artist Greg Curnoe, the CBC television producer Mark Starowicz, the novelist Margaret Laurence, the *Chatelaine* editor Doris Anderson, Gar Mahood (the anti-smoking crusader who persuaded me to quit), and, in due course, labour union leader Bob White and our current national champions, Maude Barlow and Jack Layton. Which explains why the young today take the existence of Canada for granted. So do I.

— Mel Watkins, subject of this profile

22 Canadian nationalism was, Christina tells us, a "countervailing force against the neo-colonial pragmatism." That said it all.

Some thirty years later, her article reads as an Epistle to the Canucks. It is a vivid recollection of the time when we were all young and everything seemed possible, a time when "Sleepers Awake" had become our second anthem. From somewhere on high, we had acquired a mandate to challenge the grey Canadian alter ego — the Liberal Party and the mandarins of the civil service.

The article remains evocative of time, place, and person, poignant in all its detail: Lo, the winter is gone and new voices are heard in the land — heard at least for a while.

— Abraham Rotstein, political economist and editor of the *Canadian Forum* in the 1970s

23 This brilliant essay could have been written today, not in 1977, which says a great deal about both Christina McCall and Canada. Lamenting a general preference for all things American among the Canadian progressive elite, McCall notes the "great Canadian neurosis"—that, since we make up only 10 percent of the population of North America, we are only 10 percent as good at anything we try. She asserts that this complex, not Quebec nationalism, is the real threat to the Canadian state.

Christina McCall hugged to herself the notion of Canada as an independent (and interdependent) nation taking its rightful place in the world. Lucky us for her life and her work.

— Maude Barlow, Chair, Council of Canadians

24 In this profile of onetime U.S. ambassador to Canada Paul Robinson, Christina McCall and Stephen Clarkson provide us with an entertaining, absorbing account of one man's attempt to export the Reagan revolution to Canada. This piece foreshadowed the collaboration that led to the artistic triumph of McCall and Clarkson's award-winning biography of Pierre Trudeau.

An outstanding writer, McCall not only absorbed knowledge as an academic would, she wanted to know the players and be there when the action occurred. As a stylist and a storyteller, she created an interest in the Canadian political world, while her readers got to listen in on the goings-on behind the scenes in Ottawa. A wonderful conversationalist herself, she had an ear for dialogue, so that her subjects revealed themselves between quotation marks. Christina made herself a complete student of Canadian politics, and we became much the wiser for it.

— Duncan Cameron, former editor, *Canadian Forum*

25 The tectonic plates of power have shifted over the last forty years with the development of global trading blocs, the rise of ancient powers in Asia, and the bursting of fundamentalist Islam onto the world stage. With France no longer bestriding the international landscape, the issue of separate sports teams for Quebec and Canada at international competition has more traction than representation in the Francophonie, now taken for granted. Quebec has adjusted domestically as well. Its premier has enfolded his province within the new Council of the Federation, whilst the once pure laine Parti Québécois is appealing to the allophone communities.

Christina McCall's "reflection" with Stephen Clarkson on the shock wave caused by General Charles de Gaulle's provocative *"Vive le Québec libre!"* in 1967 is an important marker showing how much separatism has changed as the universe continues to unfold.

— Aidan McQuillan, professor of historical geography,
University of Toronto

26 Christina McCall brought a wry, teasing tone, a sharp eye, and an acute ear to Ottawa, and many of her best observations involved spotting small details: how Paul Martin Sr.'s socks slipped down around his ankles, how Ottawa bureaucrats drove more modest cars and wore more boring ties than their Toronto equivalents.

What is astonishing about this piece is not only her insight into how language policy unnerved public servants and how the government's approach to language teaching was subtly hierarchical — but how little has changed in the four decades since she wrote it. Reading it now brings both a smile and a sigh.

— Graham Fraser, author of *Sorry I Don't Speak French*

27 Christina's column is a masterly summary of federal-Quebec relations from the Quiet Revolution of 1960 to the FLQ crisis. She observed that, despite the excellent recruitment of Quebecers to the federal government culminating in Pierre Elliott Trudeau, the nationalist situation remained volatile. Bilingualism did not resolve the problem of rising separatist sentiment. There was little constitutional discussion of substance. And the invocation of the War Measures Act in the fall of 1970 was an overreaction to the FLQ's violence that, as Minister of Justice at the time, I tolerated only because I insisted on a six-month termination clause.

— John Turner, former prime minister and
minister in Liberal cabinets from 1967 to 1975

28 This column reminds me of how very different Christina was from the person I thought I was meeting when I was a cub reporter in Toronto, stringing for *Le Devoir*, and she was a sophisticated national political writer and commentator living in Rosedale. I couldn't imagine there would be much ground for communications, let alone friendship: I could only see the "Great Divide."

But I was soon to experience how the breadth of her intelligence was matched by a depth of emotions and understanding, along with the curiosity and the power of observation of a great artist. She understood — and she cared.

— Patricia Dumas, freelance journalist and translator

29 When *Maclean's* published "Our Heroes of the Russian Front," it was seen as the
    first puncturing of the Margaret-as-flower-child balloon, largely because the art-
    work poked so much fun at the recent bride being whisked around the Soviet
    Union with her prime minister husband under relentless Secret Service control.

    This is a late addition to the anthology because the actual text is something
    quite else — an interrogation about whether Trudeau knew what he was doing
    for Canada by playing footsie with the Soviets. Displaying her usual balanced
    point of view, the piece is neither Trudeauphobic nor Trudeaumanic. But Chris-
    tina cuts Canadian pretensions down to size and reports on the embarrassing
    buffoonery displayed by the accompanying gaggle of reporters.

    — Stephen Clarkson

30 Unlike so many of her fellow journalists, Christina McCall was unmoved by
    Trudeaumania when first in full force. Instead, she anticipated the characteris-
    tics of Pierre Trudeau's political persona that would cause him grief in the years
    ahead. She shrewdly conveys the combination of naivety and arrogance that so
    often intoxicates a new government in the heady period following an election
    victory and plants the seeds of political hubris.

    Immediate in its portrayal of a political moment and timeless in its observa-
    tions, McCall's text exposes the dynamic tension between government and the
    media, each vying to set the agenda, each suspecting the other's motives, and
    each jealous of its own prerogatives. Since politicians and the press depend on
    each other, this relationship is at once symbiotic and antagonistic, a situation
    that is even truer today in this age of twenty-four-hour news and the Internet.

    — Peter Donolo, communications director
    for Jean Chrétien from 1990 to 1997

31 John Turner truly was, in McCall and Clarkson's words, a leader of "gentle-
    manly fortitude and manic optimism." He was also — as those of us who
    covered him at the time knew — strangely out of date. Not until the free trade
    debate of 1988 did Turner find himself once again in sync with the mood of
    what was then mainstream English Canada. Ironically, the man who tried to

resurrect the continentalist business party of Louis St. Laurent ended up fighting both continentalism and business.

In 1989, when this article was written, it did indeed seem the end of an era. Who could have anticipated that, fourteen years on, the Liberals would choose another leader focused firmly on the past? In many ways, Paul Martin was John Turner redux. I wish I could have read Christina's political obituary of him.

— Thomas Walkom, political columnist for the *Toronto Star*

32 This essay's continuing significance lies less in showing how the government's "back room" worked three decades ago than in the consequences for Canadian politics of Jim Coutts's unusual skills. Twice, in 1972 and 1979, the Liberal government lost its majority. Twice, in the subsequent election campaigns of 1974 and 1980, Coutts was the guiding genius who rescued Trudeau from political failure.

Coutts had Liberal hopes for the policies to follow. But when the votes had been won, Trudeau went mostly his own way, little influenced by colleagues or associates. Coutts's unintended achievement was therefore to make possible a major change in the governance of Canada. It moved away from the genuine cabinets of King, St-Laurent, Pearson, to the prime ministerial autocracy that Trudeau established and his successors have entrenched.

— Tom Kent, principal assistant to Lester B. Pearson
and a deputy minister in the early Trudeau years

ENDPIECE

33 In *Maclean's, Chatelaine,* and *Saturday Night,* Christina McCall was a brilliant provocateur. Her insightful magazine articles on politics and society helped start a revolution — leading the way as women writers broke out of the journalistic ghetto that had long confined their subject matter to kitchens and gardens. But hers was a tricky balancing act as both a star player in the feminist movement and one of its most perceptive analysts.

As this wickedly witty essay shows, McCall's passionate convictions did not stop her from chronicling the absurdities and contradictions she encountered in an era of change and confusion. Unlike her more serious political writing, this piece reveals the edgy sense of humour McCall usually reserved for private conversations with friends.

— Martin Knelman, *Toronto Star* arts columnist

Index

Abbott, Douglas, 317–18
Abbott, Tony, 317, 320, 323
access journalism, 68–74
Aird, John, 106, 320
Alberta as the "New West",
    89–100
    FIGA (Federal and Inter-
        governmental Affairs
        Department), 94, 95
    Heritage Trust Fund, 90, 96
    oil wealth of, 77–78, 90,
        94, 95–96
    Syncrude, 94
    United Farmers of Alberta,
        317
Allen, Ralph, 6, 43
Anderson, Doris, 6, 77, 153,
    349n1, 358n21
Atkinson, Joseph, 125
Atwood, Margaret, 358n21
Austin, Jack, 327
Ayre, John, 21–22

Ballentine, Richard, 318
Bannerman, Duncan, 202–3
Barlow, Maude, 358n21,
    359n23
Baum, Gregory, 278–79

the Beatles, 59
Beauvoir, Simone de, 29, 41,
    153, 354n12
Beckett, Dick, 120, 127
Bégin, Monique, 192
Bell, Dick, 267
Benjamin, Richard, 58
Beny, Roloff, 133, 172
Berger, Thomas, 112
Bernstein, Leonard, 134
Berton, Pierre, 43, 234
Bettelheim, Bruno, 348
Bickle, Edward, 106
Bickle, Judith Ryrie, 105–6
Bissell, Claude, 218
Blackburn, G. A., 269
Black Panthers, 134
Blair, Robert, 109–10
Blair, Wendy, 355n13
Blais, Marie-Claire, 156,
    354n12
Blake, William, 35
Bodsworth, Fred, 43
Bogart, Humphrey, 58
Bolt, Carol, 251
Bourassa, Henri, 306
Bourassa, Robert, 264, 265,
    275

Bourjailhy, Vance, 32, 34
Bowles, Paul, 34
Brando, Marlon, 58
Brecher, Irving, 225
Broadbent, Ed, 233
Bryce, Sandy, 286
Bunche, Ralph, 132
Burgess, Guy, 219
Burney, Derek, 258
Burnham, Libby, 7, 351n5
Burns, John Horne, 32

Callaghan, Morley, 23, 24–27,
    79, 241
Callwood, June, 43, 143, 153,
    329
Cameron, Duncan, 359n24
Cameron, Stevie, 69
Camp, Dalton, 70, 234
Campbell, Kim, 72, 355n14
Canadian–American relations,
    196–97, 212
    brain drain, 207
    Canadian inferiority
        complex, 249–52,
        359n23
    economic relations
        between, 225–26, 228–37,

238–48, 310–11
Free Trade Agreement, 74,
   199, 310–11, 361–62n31
Paul Heron Robinson Jr.,
   253–60, 359n24
Vietnam War, 212, 217,
   232, 244
Canadian Institute of
   International Affairs, 224
Canadian nationalism, 195
   and Canadian unity, 261–
   65, 278, 359–60n25
   Committee for an
   Independent Canada,
   109, 245
   vs. foreign ownership and
   continentalism, 229–32,
   238–48, 310–11, 358n22
   French–English
   relationship, 211, 212,
   276–79, 360–61n28
   Gordon Commission on
   foreign investment, 222–
   27, 231–32, 243–44
   official bilingualism, 197,
   266–70, 360n26
   separatism and
   sovereignty-association,
   199, 261–65, 271–75,
   294–95, 305–7, 338, 359–
   60n25, 360n27
   socialism, and the Waffle,
   228–37, 358n21
Caplan, Gerry, 232
Capote, Truman, 32, 134
Carlyle, Thomas, 22
Carmichael, Stokely, 57
Carpenter, Edmund, 29
Carr, Emily, 43
Carrington, John, 49, 52
Carson, John, 269
Carter, Jimmy, 338
Cartier, George-Étienne, 306
Castro, Fidel, 336
Chapnick, Adam, 357n18
Chevrier, Lionel, 273
Chiang Kai-shek, Madame,
   178
Chrétien, Jean, 70, 189,

327–28
   Free Trade Agreement
   and, 74
   Straight from the Heart, 71,
   73
Churchill, Winston, 218
Clark, Gwen, 180
Clark, Joe, 99, 189, 221, 316,
   335
Clark, Peter, 121, 123, 124, 127
Clarkson, Stephen, 361n29
   Trudeau and Our Times, 197
Cleaver, Eldridge, 57
Clement, Wallace, 140
Coburn, Kathleen, 20, 28–29,
   39
Cohn-Bendit, Daniel, 269
Committee for an
   Independent Canada, 109,
   245
Counsell, Elizabeth, 223
Country Joe & the Fish, 59
Coutts, James, 189, 199, 299–
   300, 313–40, 362n32
   1974 election campaign,
   324–29, 331
   1979 election campaign,
   313–15
   Canada Consulting Group,
   319–20, 333
   fall from favour, 338–40
   as Pearson's appointment
   secretary, 314, 317–19,
   325
   as Trudeau's principal
   secretary, 332–35, 337–
   38, 339
Coyne, Andrew, 357n19
Coyne, James, 205
Creed, Edmond Martin, 136–
   50, 353–54n11
Creed, Jack (father of
   Edmond), 142–43, 145, 147
the Creeds Woman, 147–49
Creighton, Donald, 218
Crombie, David, Yonge Street
   cleanup, 78–79, 120–28
Crosbie, John, 337
Crossman, Richard, 303

Crowe, Marshall, 111, 287
cultural fads, 62–65, 350n3
Curnoe, Greg, 358n21

Dafoe, John, 69
Dalholt, Lisa, 148
Danson, Barney, 305
Davey, Isobel, 324
Davey, Jim, 322
Davey, Keith, 188, 189, 299–
   300, 317, 332, 333, 335, 337–
   38, 339
   1974 election campaign,
   320, 321–23, 324–25, 327,
   331
   1979 election campaign,
   315
Davidson, Joyce, 133
Davies, Robertson, 354n12
Davis, Bill (William), 78–79,
   120–28, 352–53n9
Deacon, William Arthur, 27
Debray, Régis, 57
de Gaulle, Charles, 97, 197,
   218, 261–62, 263, 265, 359–
   60n25
Desmarais, Paul, 139, 140
Diefenbaker, John, 55, 195,
   243, 316
   comparison with Pearson,
   201–14, 357n18
   French–English
   relationship, 272–73
   "Pearsonalities", 220
   on Walter Gordon, 226
Diefenbaker, Olive, 207–8,
   209–10
Dietrich, Marlene, 25
diplomacy, golden age of, 215–
   21, 357n19
Dirstein, Robert, 145
Donolo, Peter, 361n30
Don Quixote, 59
Doriot, Georges, 105
Dowling, Colette, 191
Doyle, Dic, 6
Draper, Ruth, 29
Drea, Frank, 126
Drew, Fiorenza, 133

Drew, George, 202, 219
Drury, Bud, 248, 305, 336
Dryden, Gordon, 320–23, 327
Ducharme, Réjean, 354n12
Dumas, Patricia, 360–61n28
Duplessis, Maurice, 208, 273, 306, 330

Eayrs, James, 217, 245
Edick, Gordon, 331–32
Eliot, George, 320
Elizabeth, Princess, 142
Elizabeth, Queen, 43
Endicott, Giles, 233
English, John, 197
Evans, John, 106

Fairweather, Gordon, 299
Farrell, James T., 57
Favreau, Guy, 212, 273
feminism
    alimony, 167–71, 355n14
    Canadian women's
        movement, roots of, 213
    Christina McCall and, 153–
        54, 345–48
    divorce law reform, 170–
        71, 172–75, 206, 355–
        56n15
    International Women's
        Year, 155
    mag cult, 64
    and the new machismo,
        57–58, 60–61
    societal evolution of in
        English Canada, 155–61
    women and political
        power, 180–81, 182–92,
        356n17
    women as "babes", 179
    see also Royal
        Commission on the
        Status of Women;
        women, status of
Fisher, Douglas, 301
Fitzgerald, F. Scott, 31
FLQ, 273, 275
Ford, Thereze, 284
Francis, Lloyd, 267

Fraser, Blair, 43, 69, 70, 207
Fraser, Graham, 360n26
Friedan, Betty, 56, 346
Fry, Christopher, 27
Frye, Northrop, 13, 19, 27, 29–
    30, 354n12
    as lecturer, 20–22, 27–28,
        35
Fulford, Robert, 5, 6, 245
Fullerton, Douglas, 225
Fulton, Davie, 299

Gable, Clark, 58
Galbraith, John Kenneth, 121,
    196, 225
Galbraith, Ken, 92
Gallant, Mavis, 354n12
Gardiner, Jimmy, 330, 339
Gardner, Ava, 25
Gay Liberation, and the new
    machismo, 60
Gerussi, Bruno, 13, 54, 350n2
Getty, Don, 92, 93, 94–95, 96
Gillespie, Alastair, 103, 106
Gilroy, Ralph, 86
Glasso, J. Grant, 225
Gobeil, Madeleine, 153, 155–
    61, 354n12
Godfrey, Dave, 234
Godfrey, Paul, 126
Goldfarb, Martin, 327, 338,
    339
Goodman, Janice, 320
Goodman, Martin, 320
Good Taste vs. slick, 129–35,
    353n10
Gopnik, Adam, 68
Gordon, Elizabeth, 213
Gordon, Walter, 188, 212, 223–
    26, 231–32, 236, 242–45,
    246, 266, 322, 357–58n20
Gordon Commission, 196,
    222–27, 231–32, 243–44
Gotlieb, Allan, 258
Gould, Glenn, 43, 343
Grable, Betty, 158
Grafstein, Jerahmiel S. (Jerry),
    7, 320–23, 327, 337–38
Graham, Ron, 350n4

All the King's Horses, 70,
    71–74
One-Eyed Kings, 70, 72
Granatstein, Jack, 201, 217
Grant, Alison. see Ignatieff,
    Alison (née Grant)
Grant, George, 72
Grateful Dead, 59
Gray, Herb, 230, 238, 241, 302
Greene, Joe, 229
Grierson, Jeanne, 148
Griffin, Krystyne, 353n10
Griffin, Marvin, 85–86
Guare, John, 202
Guevara, Che, 57
Gundy, Reginald, 104
Guthro family (Springhill,
    N.S.), 82–84
Gwishiani, Ludmila, 284
Gwyn, Richard, 70

Haig, Alexander, 257
Hammarskjöld, Dag, 241
Harding, Malim, 246
Harper, Stephen, 198
Harries, Hu, 93
Harris, Lawren, 208
Harris, Walter, 224
Hastings, Earl, 93
Hays, Harry, 93, 317
Head, Ivan, 93, 287, 322
Heeney, Arnold, 217
Hellyer, Paul, 296, 305
Hemingway, Ernest, 25, 31, 33,
    57
Hendrix, Jimi, 59
Hepburn, Audrey, 133
Hepburn, Katharine, 158
Hertzberg, Hendrik, 5
Hesketh, Elizabeth, 284
Hoffman, Abbie, 57, 131
Hoffman, Dustin, 58
Holmes, John, 217
Holzer, Baby Jane, 347
Honderich, Beland, 244
Hood, William, 225
Hopalong Cassidy, 59
Horner, Hugh, 93
Horner, Jack, 315, 338

Horte, Vern, 112
Hošek, Chaviva, 7, 356n17
Houde, Camillien, 330
Howe, C. D., 107, 224, 243, 247, 248, 322, 330
Huggard,Thomas, 47
Humphrey, John, 164
Hungarian uprising, 42
Hurtig, Mel, 98, 358n20
Hutchison, Bruce, 69, 70, 182–83
Hyndman, Lou, 93, 96

Ignatieff, Alison (née Grant), 213, 216, 219
Ignatieff, George, 196, 215–21, 357n19
  The Making of a Peacemonger, 216–17, 221
Ignatieff, Michael, 196
Innis, Harold, 218
insider journalism, 68–74
International Women's Year, 155
Irwin, Arthur, 43

Jacobs, Jane, 114–19, 352n8
  Dark Age Ahead, 78
Jacobs, Robert Hyde, 115
Jamieson, Don, 248, 305
Jennings, Ivor, 303
Jewett, Pauline, 177–78
Johnson, Daniel, Sr., 274
Johnson, Harry, 244, 245
Johnson, Lyndon, 217

Kelly, Grace, 133
Kempt, Gorley, 86
Kempt, Marguerite, 87
Kennedy, Edward, 338
Kennedy, Jackie, 132, 133
Kennedy, John F., 59, 149, 205, 309, 324
Kent, Tom, 212, 362n32
Khrushchev, Nikita, 219
Kierans, Eric, 109, 270, 305
King, William Lyon Mackenzie, 43, 69, 202, 204, 216, 298, 308, 321

Kingsley, Charles, 166
Kingston, Anne, 7, 356n16
Kingwell, Mark, 349–50n2
Kinnear, David, 246
Kissinger, Henry, 319
Klein, Naomi, No Logo, 14
Klein, Ralph, 78
Knelman, Martin, 7, 362n33
Koffler, Murray, 143–44
Kosygin, Alexei, 284, 289
Krock, Arthur, 68
Kronby, Malcolm, Divorce Practice Manual, 170

Laberge-Colas, Réjane, 180
Lafontaine, Louis-Hippolyte, 306
Lalonde, Marc, 59, 183, 188, 212, 287, 298–99, 305, 323, 334–35
LaMarsh, Judy (Julia Verlyn), 163, 177, 188, 213, 346
Lamontage, Maurice, 212, 273
Landsberg, Michele, 153
Lang, Otto, 302, 305
Lapointe, Ernest, 306
Lasch, Christopher, Culture of Narcissism, 80
Laskin, Bora, 111
Laurence, Margaret, 358n21
Laurier, Wilfrid, 69, 272, 306, 308
Lawrence, D. H., 31
Laxer, James, 233, 246
Layton, Jack, 358n21
LeBlanc, Romeo, 305
Lebowitz, Fran, 63
Leigh, Dorian, 133
Leitch, Merv, 93, 96
Lemelin, Roger, 289
LePan, Douglas, 225, 227
Lesage, Jean, 205, 263, 271, 273, 274
Lévesque, René, 199, 262, 264–65, 270, 274, 275, 294–95, 305–7
Lewis, David, 236
Lewis, Stephen, 236
Liberal Party

  1968 leadership campaign, 295–96
  Cell Thirteen, 188
  continentalist views of, 247–48, 361–62n31
  popularity of post 1974 election, 337
Liddy, Gordon, 69
Lightfoot, Gordon, 59
Limbaugh, Rush, 69
Lindsay, John, 319
Linetsky, Arnold, 121–22, 125, 128
Lippman, Walter, 68, 69
Lougheed, Peter, 77–78, 351n6
  aggressive conservatism of, 78, 89, 91–93, 96–99
  European mission, 95–96, 97, 99–100
Lovelace, Richard, 60

MacDonald, Daniel, 305
Macdonald, Donald, 92, 189, 302, 305
MacDonald, Flora, 192
Macdonald, Mary, 213
MacEachen, Allan, 212, 256, 257–58, 296, 302, 305
Machiavelli, Niccolò, 316
machismo, reflections on manliness, 54–61
  macho-measuring guidelines, 58–60
MacInnis, Grace, 177
Mackasey, Bryce, 304, 306, 327, 336, 343
Mackenzie Valley pipeline, 78, 101–13, 351–52n7
  competing pipeline proposals, 109–10, 112
Maclean, David, 219
MacLennan, Hugh, 25
MacMillan, "Black Jack", 48
MacMillan, George, 46, 47, 48–51
MacMillan, Viola Rita, 13, 44–53, 349n1
MacNaught, J. Watson, 299
Macpherson, C. B., 98

mag cult, 62–65, 350n3
Mahood, Gar, 358n21
Mailer, Norman, 32, 57
Malone, Richard, 182–83
Malraux, André, 241, 269
Mansfield, Harvey, 13–14
Mansfield, Katherine, 208
Marchand, Jean, 188, 212, 248,
    274, 276–77, 305, 306, 336
    1974 election campaign,
    323, 326, 330
Martin, Claire, 156
Martin, Lawrence, 69–70
Martin, Paul, 361–62n31
Martin, Paul, Sr., 296, 320
Masaryk, Jan, 219
Massey, Alice, 218
Massey, Vincent, 216, 218–19
Mathews, Robin, 246
Matthews, Bruce, 139, 140
Maugham, Somerset, 133
McCall, Christina
    academic influences, 20–
    22, 27–30, 203
    as editorial secretary
    (Maclean's), 37–43
    feminist evolution of, 153–
    54
    Grits, 199
    parental influences, 16,
    157, 166, 202–3, 343
    "The New Novelists and
    the Era of the Naked
    Zero", 30, 31–34
    Trudeau and Our Times, 197
    "What's the Matter with
    Callaghan?", 24–27, 30
McCarthy, Eugene, 322
McCarthy, Joe, 203
McCarthy, Mary, 42
McCulley, Joe, 47
McGovern, George, 338
McIntyre, Joe, 316
McKeough, Darcy, 127
McLeod family (Springhill,
    N.S.), 86–88
McLuhan, Marshall, 116
McNaught, Kenneth, 221
McNaughton, A. G. L., 219

McQuaig, Linda, 69
McQuillan, Aidan, 359–
    60n25
McTeer, Maureen, 335
Mead, Margaret, 58, 350n2
Medas, Jim, 258
Meech Lake Accord, 261, 309
Meighen, Arthur, 307
Mill, John Stuart, 212
Millett, Kate, 168
Millican, Harold, 97
Milne, David, 208
Mitchell, W. O., 43
Mitchum, Robert, 58
Mitterrand, François, 265
Mondale, Walter, 338
Moore, Jake, 246
Morin, Claude, 305
Morin, Jacques-Yvan, 305
Mulroney, Brian, 220, 260
    continentalism, 358n21
    Free Trade Agreement and,
    199, 310–11
Munro, Alice, 197, 354n12
Murray, Anne, 77

National Energy Board, and
    Mackenzie Valley pipeline,
    109–10, 111
Native peoples
    land claims, 78
    and Mackenzie Valley
    pipeline, 102, 103, 112
NATO, 220, 288
NDP, 74, 248
    socialism, and the Waffle,
    228–37, 358n21
Nemni, Max and Monique,
    197
Neustadt, Richard, 319
Newman, Peter, 70, 198,
    244–45
Nichol, John, 320
Nicholson, Jack, 58
Nickle, Carl, 94
Nixon, Richard, 68, 240, 247,
    248
Nixon, Tricia, 135
NORAD, 220

Notley, Grant, 98

O'Connell, Martin, 327
O'Hagan, Richard, 299–300,
    318
O'Leary, Grattan, 307
Olive, David, 351–52n7
Olivier, Laurence, 160
O'Neill, Wilfred, 273
Ostry, Sylvia, 180–81
Ouellet, André, 298, 305

Pacey, Desmond, 27
Papineau, Joseph, 306
Parizeau, Jacques, 305
Parti Québécois, 264–65, 274
Payette, Lise, 305, 306
Pearson, Lester B., 43, 188,
    195, 215, 217, 218, 225, 226,
    241, 243, 296, 303, 308, 322
    comparison to Trudeau,
    301
    comparison with
    Diefenbaker, 201–14,
    357n18
    as opposition leader, 204–
    6, 211
    as peacemonger, 219, 220
    Quebec separatism, 263,
    273–74
    Suez crisis, 42, 204, 219
Pearson, Maryon, 208–10
Peck, Gregory, 133
Pelletier, Gérard, 188, 241,
    248, 274, 305, 326
Pépin, Jean-Luc, 239, 248, 278
Peterson, Kevin, 91
Petrie, Bill, 324
Petrie, Dorothy, 324
Philby, Kim, 219
Pickersgill, Jack, 196, 217, 315
Pigott, Jean, 337
Pirie, Margaret, 29–30
Pitfield, Michael, 188, 298–99,
    303, 332
Plaskett, Joe, 208
Porter, Cole, 133
Porter, John, 207, 209
Potter, Andrew, 350n3

Powe, Bruce, 197
power politics, 184–92
  golden age of diplomacy,
    215–21, 357n19
Pratt, Larry, 98
Proctor, John S., 45, 50
Prospectors and Developers
  Association, 44–53
Prowse, Harper, 316
Public Petroleum Association
  of Canada, 109

Quebec, 195, 248
  FLQ, 273, 275
  French–English
    relationship, 211, 212,
    276–79, 360–61n28
  Parti Québécois, 264–65,
    274, 338
  Quiet Revolution, 211, 271–
    72
  separatism and
    sovereignty-association,
    199, 261–65, 271–75,
    359–60n25
  War Measures Act, 197,
    275, 360n27

Radwanski, George, 198
Rae, Saul, 218
Rankin, Joe, 50
Rayside, David, 352–53n9
Reagan, Ronald, 196, 199,
  359n24
  Canadian–American
    relations, 253, 254, 256,
    257–58, 259
Redford, Robert, 58
Reid, Escott, 217
Reisman, Simon, 225
Renoir, Claude, 148
Richardson, James, 302, 305,
  336
Riese, Laura, 28
Ritchie, Charles, 217
Robarts, John, 278
Roberts, John, 188, 189,
  320, 322
Roberts, Peter, 328

Robichaud, Louis, 205, 212
Robinson, Paul Heron, Jr., 197,
  253–60, 359n24
Rockefeller, Abigail, 346
Rockett, Beverley, 320
Rodgers, Richard, 131
Rolling Stones, 59, 315, 338
Ross, Val, 353–54n11
Rotstein, Abraham, 231–32,
  236, 242, 244, 358n22
Royal Commission into
  Canada's Economic
  Prospects. see Gordon
  Commission
Royal Commission on
  Bilingualism and
  Biculturalism, 274, 278
Royal Commission on the
  Status of Women, 154, 162–
  66, 179, 213, 355n13, 356n16
Rubin, Eddie, 327
Ruddick, Maurice, 84–86
Russell, Bertrand, 160
Russell, Rosalind, 158
Rykiel, Sonia, 137

Sagan, Françoise, 41
Salinger, J. D., 32
Sancho Panza, 59
Sanderson, Derek, 56, 350n2
Sartre, Jean-Paul, 64, 354n12
Sauvé, Jeanne, 178, 186
Sauvé, Maurice, 178, 320
Schlesinger, Arthur, Jr., 132
Schreyer, Edward, 216
Scott, Frank, 70, 71
Scott, Randolph, 255
Scott, Reid, 126, 127
Servan-Schreiber, J. J., 234
Sewell, John, 352n8
Sharp, Edie, 143
Sharp, Isadore, 143–44
Sharp, Mitchell, 106, 196, 248,
  259, 305, 320, 336
Shaw, Irwin, 32
Shultz, George, 257–58
Silver, Harry, 137
Sinatra, Frank, 132
Sinclair, Ian, 107

Sinclair, Jimmy, 328
Sinclair, Margaret. see
  Trudeau, Margaret (née
  Sinclair)
Sinclair, Sonja, 216
Skelton, O. D., 196
slick vs. Good Taste, 129–35,
  353n10
Smith, David, 125
Snow, C. P., 140
Solanis, Valerie, 56
Sontag, Susan, 79
Sorensen, Ted, 59
Spark, Muriel, 208
Sparrow, Allan, 126, 127
Springhill mine disaster, 81–
  88, 351n5
Stanfield, Robert, 229, 248,
  298, 328
Starowicz, Mark, 358n21
Steele, James, 246
Steinbeck, John, 32
Steinem, Gloria, 60, 167
Stewart, Walter, 198
St. Laurent, Louis, 52, 204,
  224, 272, 306, 308, 317, 322,
  328
St. Vincent Millay, Edna, 208
Suez crisis, 42, 204, 219

Taschereau, Louis-Alexandre,
  306
Taylor, Ken, 224
Teillet, Roger, 299
Thomson, Lord, 97
Tiger, Lionel, 59, 347
  Men in Groups, 187
Timson, Judith, 355–56n15
Tito, Marshall Josip, 219
Travolta, John, 63
Tremblay, René, 273
Trevor-Roper, Hugh, 295
Trudeau, Charles, 330
Trudeau, Margaret (née
  Sinclair), 198, 280–93, 304,
  315, 332, 335–36
  1974 election campaign,
    328–29
  Beyond Reason, 329

"freedom trip", 338
Trudeau, Michel, 335
Trudeau, Pierre Elliot, 59, 183,
185, 187, 195, 212, 216, 308,
346, 361n30
    1974 election campaign,
        320–23, 324–29
    1979 election campaign,
        66–67, 313–15
    as cabinet leader, 301–3
    Canadian–American
        relations, 254, 257–58,
        259
    economic nationalism,
        230, 247–48, 358n21
    intuition, denial of, 297–
        98
    Just Society, 214, 266
    as loner, 188–89, 300–301
    media coverage of, 197–99
    as Minister of Justice, 274
    National Energy Program,
        255, 256
    official bilingualism, 197,
        266–70, 360n26
    Quebec separatism, 261–
        65, 272, 275, 294–95,
        305–7, 338
    and Ron Graham, 71
    separation from Margaret,
        338, 339
    state visit to Latin
        America, 335–36
    state visit to southern
        Europe/Middle East,
        336–37
    state visit to U.S.S.R.,
        280–93, 328, 361n29
    style and, 163
    War Measures Act, 197,
        275, 360n27
    Western feelings about,
        96–97
    women as "babes", 176,
        356n16
Trudeau, Sacha, 329
Tuchman, Barbara, 213
Tupper, Rev. Douglas, 84
Turner, John, 183, 189, 199,

220, 296, 337, 361–62n31
    1974 election campaign,
        327
    Canadian–American
        relations, 260
    Free Trade Agreement and,
        74, 310–11
    as party leader, 308–12
    and Ron Graham, 71
    separatism and
        sovereignty-association,
        360n27
    in Trudeau government,
        303–5, 309, 336
Turner, Lana, 158
Twaits, W. O., 107
Tweedsmuir, Lady, 142

Underhill, Frank, 234–35
University League for Social
    Reform, 231
University of Toronto, as
    reflection of 1950s Ontario,
    15–20

Van Horne, William, 102
Vanier, Georges, 289
Veblen, Thorstein, 146
Vidal, Gore, 32
Vigneault, Gilles, 306
Vreeland, Diana, 132

Wahn, Ian, 229
Walkom, Thomas, 361–62n31
Ward, Barbara, 213
Warhol, Andy, 63, 347
Watkins, Mel, 7, 196, 244,
    358n21
    "Canadian Economic
        Policy: A Proposal", 231
    socialism, and the Waffle,
        228–37, 246
Waugh, Evelyn, 121
Wayne, John, 255
Weber, Max, 55, 306, 350n2
Western alienation, 94–95,
    96–97, 203, 310
Whelan, Eugene, 302, 305, 327
White, Bob, 358n21

White, Katharine, 42
Whyte, Ken, 5, 349n2, 350–
    51n4
Wilde, Oscar, 41
Wilder, William Price,
    Mackenzie Valley pipeline,
    78, 101–13, 351–52n7
Wilder, William, Sr., 104
Wilhelmina, 133
Williams, Tennessee, 32, 33
Wilson, Ethel, 25
Winston, Jack, 145
Winters, Robert, 296
Wolf, Naomi, *The Beauty Myth*,
    14
Wolfe, Tom, 79–80
Wolfit, Donald, 160
women, status of, 182–92,
    356n17
    alimony, 167–71, 355n14
    as feature writers, 43, 183–
        84, 206–7, 349n1,
        362n33
    impact of Pearson era on,
        212–13
    and mag cult, 64, 348
    "old maids", 158–59
    in Ottawa, 176–81, 356n16
    and political power, 180–
        81, 182–92, 347
    see also feminism; Royal
        Commission on the
        Status of Women
Worthington, Peter, 198
Wright, Robert, 197

Yonge Street cleanup, 120–28,
    352–53n9

Zanin, Toby, 351n6

CHRISTINA McCALL (1935–2005) was a writer of literary non-fiction who worked as a socio-political analyst for *Maclean's, Saturday Night, Chatelaine,* and the *Globe and Mail. Grits,* her portrait of the Liberal Party, was acclaimed as "one of the most important Canadian books." With her husband, Stephen Clarkson, she co-authored *Trudeau and Our Times,* the classic two-volume study of Pierre Elliott Trudeau and his impact on Canadian society and politics, the first volume of which won the Governor General's Literary Award in 1990.

STEPHEN CLARKSON is a professor of political economy at the University of Toronto. A frequent commentator on Canadian affairs in both French and English media, he is the author of several books on national and international politics, including the prize-winning *Canada and the Reagan Challenge.* He lives in Toronto.